IMAGES
of America

LARCHMONT

On the Cover: **Seasons Greetings from Larchmont Merchants, 1955.** This picturesque view of Larchmont Boulevard looks north, with Hollywood and the Santa Monica Mountains in the distance. Holiday decorations hang from the railway lines of the Los Angeles Railway. LARY 3 Line cars operated along Third Street and Larchmont Boulevard. Starting in 1948, rail service was gradually phased out in the neighborhoods around Larchmont. A new 3 Line trolley coach replaced rail service west of Larchmont Boulevard, operating as the S Line shown in this photograph. (Courtesy of the *Larchmont Chronicle*.)

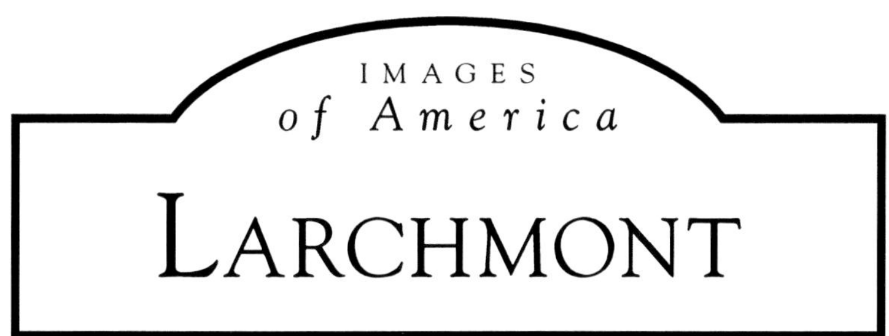

Patricia Lombard

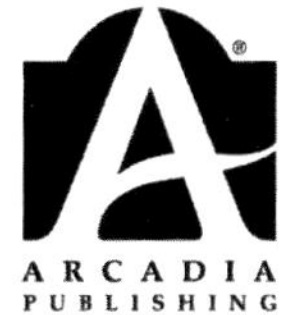

ISBN 978-1-4671-3411-8

Published by Arcadia Publishing
Charleston, South Carolina

Printed in the United States of America

Library of Congress Control Number: 2015945755

For all general information, please contact Arcadia Publishing:
Telephone 843-853-2070
Fax 843-853-0044
E-mail sales@arcadiapublishing.com
For customer service and orders:
Toll-Free 1-888-313-2665

Visit us on the Internet at www.arcadiapublishing.com

For everyone who loves Larchmont and seeks to preserve this charming, neighborhood-serving village

Contents

ACKNOWLEDGMENTS

Thank you to Jane Gilman, founding publisher of the *Larchmont Chronicle*, for her invaluable assistance in providing photographs for this book. Unless otherwise noted, all the images in this book are from the *Larchmont Chronicle*. Thanks to John Welborne, current publisher of the *Larchmont Chronicle*. Thanks to Mark Wanamaker at Bison Archives. Thanks to Jason Lavitt, Keith Nelson, and Carolyn Ramsay, who also donated photographs.

INTRODUCTION

This is the story of Larchmont Boulevard, a quaint neighborhood street located in the middle of the city of Los Angeles between Melrose Avenue and Third Street. Surrounded by historic neighborhoods that grew up around it, Larchmont has been described as an island of small town in an ocean of urban sprawl. Known as the "village" by locals, Larchmont has easy-angle parking and charming, tree-lined sidewalks that offer the opportunity to shop and stroll and meet and greet as much today as 95 years ago. The result is an enduring sense of neighborhood and community, provoking profound affection for this historic district among newcomers and old-timers alike.

Larchmont was originally named Glenwood according to Los Angeles city archives. The name was changed to Larchmont in 1912, most likely after the residential village on Long Island Sound. Los Angelenos were mostly transplants from the East Coast and imported much of that ethos to their new home, creating a better, sunnier version of where they left. Los Angeles city records show improvements to the street, including sewers and street curbs constructed around that time. Between 1900 and 1920, the population of Los Angeles exploded. In 1900, the Los Angeles city population was 102,479; by 1910, it had tripled to 310,198; and by 1920, it swelled to 576,673. That five-fold increase is central to understanding the nature of Los Angeles and the neighborhoods built by these newcomers that would create the city of today.

Julius J. La Bonte and his business associate Charles Ramson were among those newcomers. They were successful businessmen who came to Los Angeles with their families to retire and enjoy the Southern California climate.

Born in Traverse City, Michigan, in 1879, La Bonte married the former Pauline Leitelt of Grand Rapids, Michigan, in 1910. He sold his general store in Traverse City to manage the Leitelt Iron Works and Foundry in Grand Rapids for his wife's family. La Bonte was ready when World War I increased the demand for metal. The family business was so successful, he sold it to his employees in 1919 and retired to Los Angeles in 1920. The La Bonte family wintered in Los Angeles and knew it well. They bought a house at 340 South Arden Boulevard. "It was a huge house, built by the Stanton Lumber heirs," recalled their only daughter, Charlotte La Bonte Lipson, in an interview with the *Larchmont Chronicle* in November 1991. "When he arrived in Los Angeles, my father wanted something to do. He walked all around this area and met with a number of city planners and decided that commercial real estate was the way to go," explains Lipson. La Bonte bought lots along the boulevard when the streetcar line was extended to run north on Larchmont from Third Street up Melrose Avenue to the Hollywood Mineral Hot Springs.

In September 1921, The *Los Angeles Times* reported that Julius La Bonte and Charles Ramson purchased seven lots on Larchmont Boulevard to create a business district of 30 stores between First Street and Beverly Boulevard. He was credited with building 70 percent of the structures on the street as well as having the vision to create the first neighborhood shopping street in the city of Los Angeles that catered to the adjacent new neighborhoods of Larchmont Heights (now known as Larchmont Village), New Windsor Square (now known as Windsor Square), and Hancock Park. According to the *Times*, every store was leased before the buildings were finished. Streetlights fitted to railway power poles makes this "one of the best illuminated sections of the city."

"My father always had a very clear idea of what Larchmont Boulevard should be," Charlotte Lipson recalls. "He always saw it as a service street for the carriage trade of Windsor Square and Hancock Park. It was the first neighborhood shopping center in Los Angeles."

La Bonte's original buildings were Mission Revival–style architecture with clay tile roofs. Early shops and businesses included the Windsor Square Pharmacy, Larchmont Cafe, Larchmont Electric Company, AA Carpet Company, and Larchmont Motor Service Station, which sold ARCO gasoline at the corner of First Street and Larchmont Boulevard.

"J.J. La Bonte was the one who put the money together with the dream," says Lipson. "Except for one building at 124 North Larchmont, which he built as an investment for his family. He financed the other buildings by selling their mortgages to his contacts in Michigan. His main contractor was Clarence Bean."

She further recalls, "My father stipulated that his buildings be constructed of brick, because that was the material he was familiar with in the Midwest. He planned for a theater, bank, grocery store, drugstore, bakery, dry cleaners, and candy store and always looked for continuity in the business of his tenants. He knew customers would come back to the same locations."

Fortunately, La Bonte got out of the stock market six months before it crashed, but when the government closed all the savings and loans during the Depression, the real estate bubble burst. La Bonte sold all his properties except for the one he owned outright and the one his daughter (who married Jack Lipson, a plumber who rented office space from her father) still holds today. In 1982, Lipson chose to save the building, renovate it, and bring it up to seismic code at great expense rather than tear it down. "I didn't have the heart to demolish it," she told the *Larchmont Chronicle* in November 1991. "I owed it to Larchmont not to."

After the Depression, life changed for the well-healed residents surrounding Larchmont; however, the next generation, no longer able to afford their own houses, returned to their family homes to raise their children. This brought life back to Larchmont. By 1940, there were over 40,000 people employed in the film industry, many at the movie studios located next door to Larchmont. The population of Los Angeles was 1.5 million.

Despite the tumult surrounding Larchmont, La Bonte's legacy of continuity among businesses remained. While stores would come and go, they were generally operated by the same kind of owner, usually a small businessperson who lived nearby. By all accounts, it was the personalized service offered by these shops that gave the street its appeal. The notion that everyone knew everyone was real and lasted until well after La Bonte died in 1968.

The railway tracks were removed in 1955, and the 1960s brought innovations to the street like parking meters and street trees, which were heralded at the time but now pose a hazard, pulling up the concrete sidewalks. However, Larchmont retained much charm and quaintness thanks to the efforts of business owners who formed the Larchmont Boulevard Association in 1965 to beautify and promote the street. Early events included art shows, pet shows, parades, and holiday decorations along the street. The annual Larchmont Family Fair continues, as does the Taste of Larchmont, a fundraiser supporting efforts to end homelessness that highlights restaurants and food establishments and reflects another evolution in the composition of businesses on the street.

As real estate values and affluence increased in the sounding neighborhoods so did the value of Larchmont. The 1980s marked the disappearance of old-time, family-owned businesses. Increased rents priced out the wide variety of small businesses that offered typewriter ribbon, sewing needles, and screws.

In a 1990s effort to preserve the neighborhood and the stores residents used regularly, zoning restrictions were passed to limit the number of banks, escrow companies, real estate offices, and restaurants on the street. To some extent it has worked, but to a large degree change has come. Still, Larchmont remains quaint, charming, and beloved by residents and newcomers alike.

One

Early Larchmont

Los Angeles was rapidly growing, and real estate was the currency for expansion. Entrepreneurial developers invented idealized neighborhoods from barley fields along Wilshire Boulevard, transforming the landscape with trees and lawns.

Larchmont is nestled inside Windsor Square, which was envisioned by George A.G. Howard as a beautiful, tranquil park for family homes found in the English countryside.

Land records from around 1868 indicate that Canadians John C. and Cecilia Plummer acquired 640 acres for farming purposes. In 1885, during the height of Los Angeles's first big land boom, a syndicate of real estate investors bought 200 acres of the Plummer property. In 1911, they sold the land to Robert A. Rowan of the Windsor Square Investment Company, which began the subdivision called Windsor Square. The "Square" ran from Wilshire Boulevard to Third Street (later extended to Beverly Boulevard) and from Irving Boulevard to Plymouth Boulevard (later extended to Bronson).

Deed restrictions set a minimum cost of $12,550 on each home to be built in order to assure handsome homes in an exceptionally beautiful setting. Intervening walls or fences were discouraged so that one garden ran into another, creating a parklike setting. Windsor Square was the first area in the city to have power lines below grade, an extraordinary innovation for 1911. The English flavor was enhanced by the street names: Irving, Windsor, and Plymouth.

Nearby Hancock Park owes its name to developer and philanthropist G. Allan Hancock, who subdivided the property in the 1920s. Hancock, born and raised in a home near the La Brea Tar Pits, inherited the 440 acres that his father, Maj. Henry Hancock, had acquired from the Rancho La Brea property owned by the family of José Jorge Rocha. Hancock subdivided the property from Rossmore to Highland Avenues between Wilshire Boulevard and Melrose Avenue into residential lots. He leased 105 acres to the Wilshire Country Club with an option to buy. Hancock also insisted that his master plan include concrete streets and the location of utility lines at the rear of each development, out of sight of homeowners. Another condition was that homeowners build no less than 50 feet from the curb.

Hancock also gave $100,000 to the Los Angeles Railway to extend its tracks west along Third Street (which stopped at Larchmont Boulevard) to La Brea Avenue.

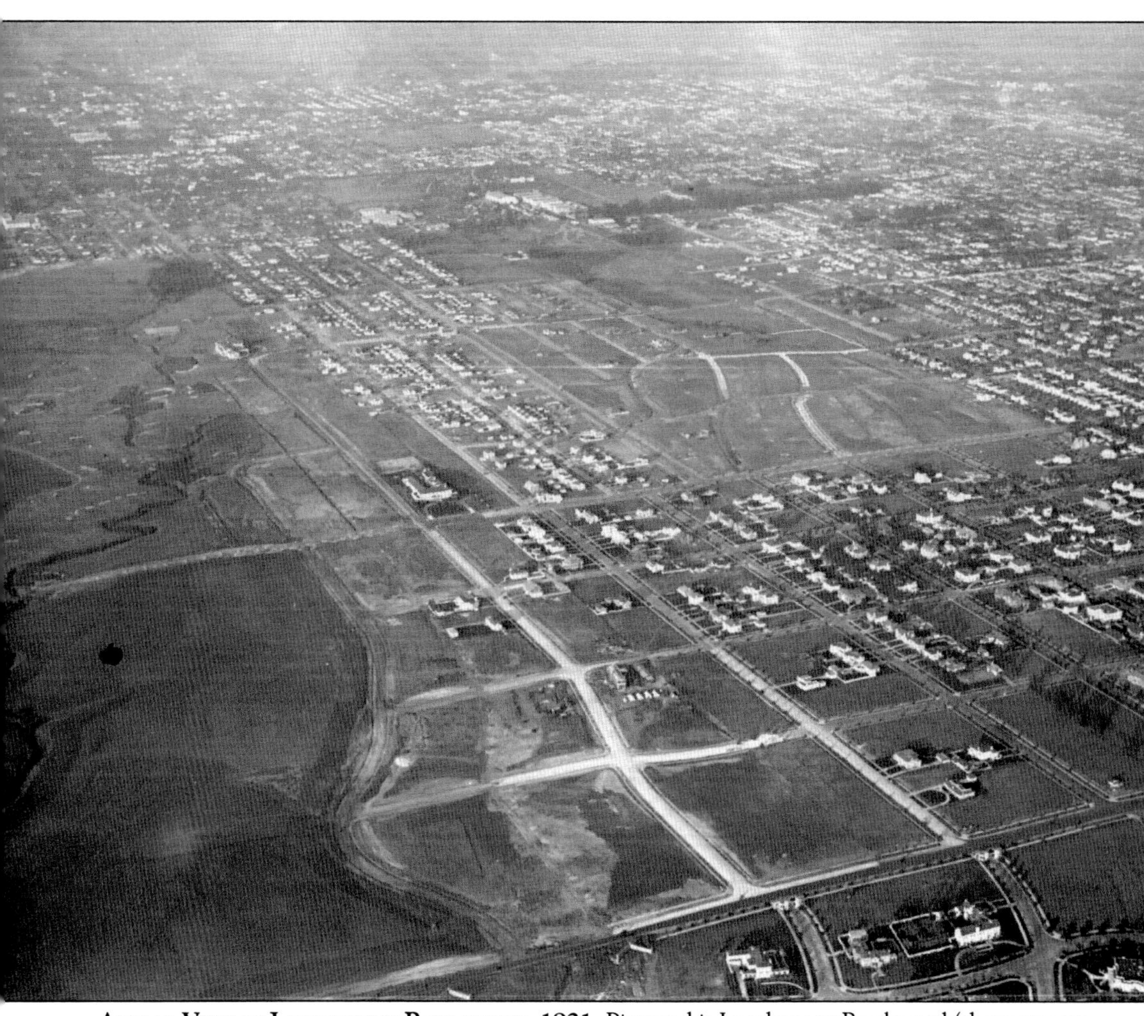

Aerial View of Larchmont Boulevard, 1921. Pictured is Larchmont Boulevard (three streets east of Rossmore Avenue) before any development. East is Windsor Square with its curving streets, and Hancock Park will be developed to the west. Marlborough School on Rossmore is in the center left, and Fremont Place is already landscaped with street trees and entry gates at Rossmore Boulevard and Arden Street. Wilshire Boulevard is shown along the bottom edge. (Courtesy of Marc Wanamaker at Bison Archives.)

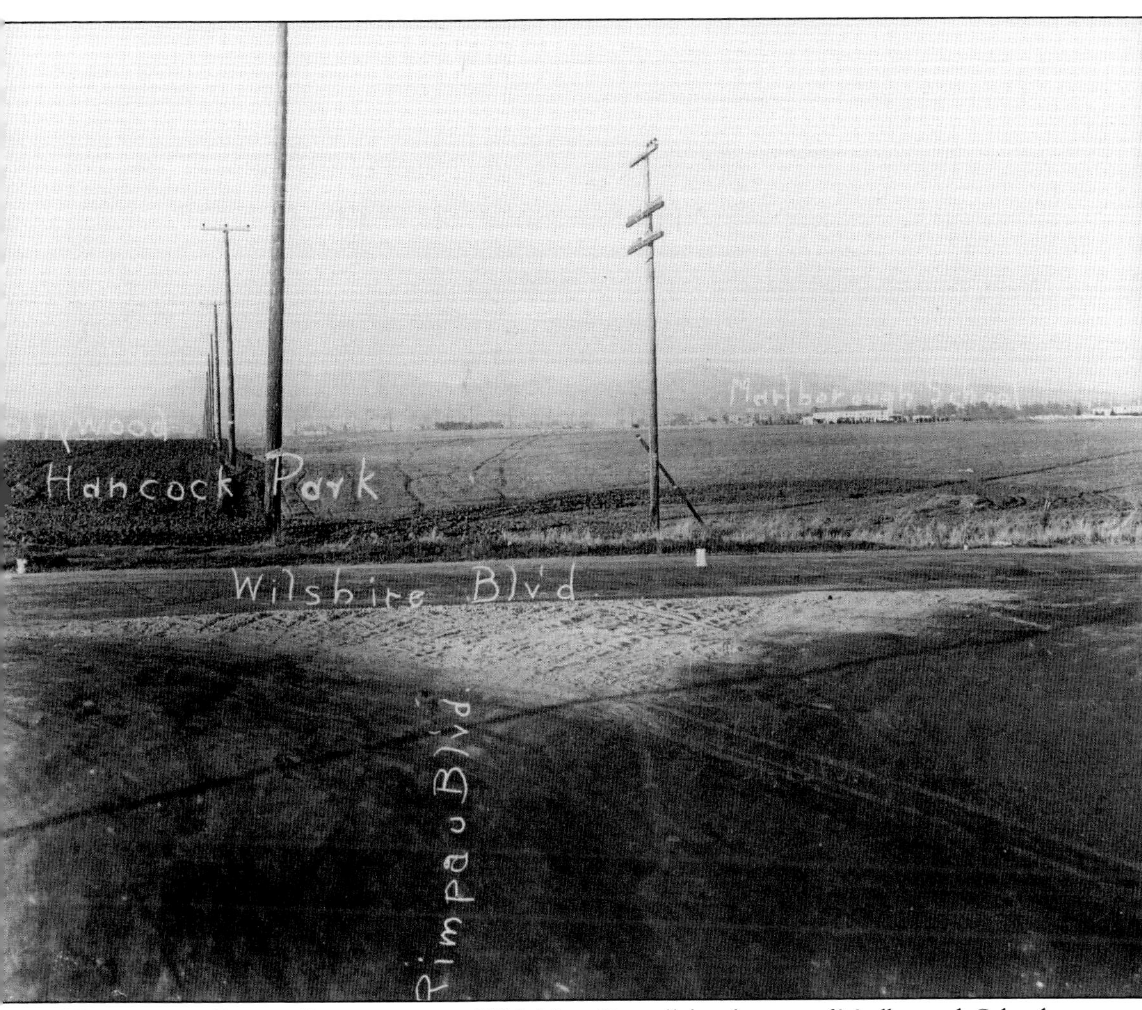

WILSHIRE AND RIMPAU BOULEVARDS, C. 1916. Mary Caswell, headmaster of Marlborough School, needed more space for the growing school. In 1916, she purchased land in the newly opened La Brea tract and built a new campus, surrounded only by bean and barley fields. Caswell knew the population of Los Angeles was slowly moving west. By the 1920s, much of this farmland would be developed into tree-lined streets with stately homes. G. Allan Hancock, for whom Hancock Park is named, would ultimately develop over 1,200 homes just north of Wilshire and west of Marlborough School. Windsor Square and Larchmont Village would take shape to the west of the school.

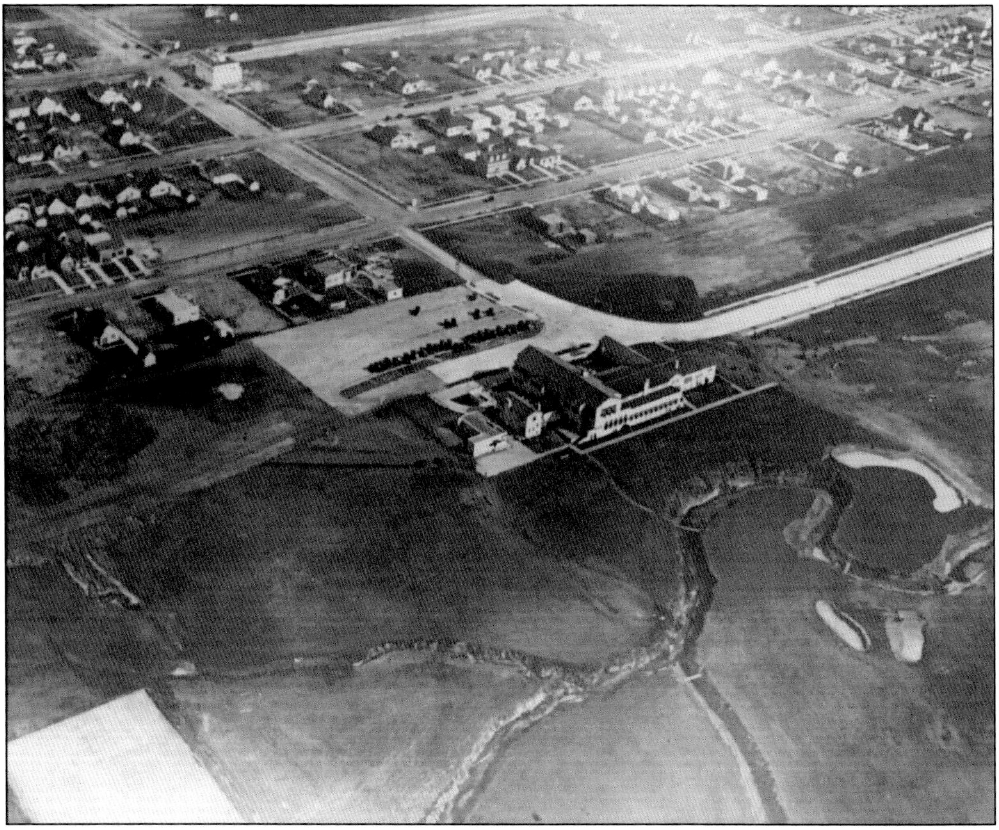

Aerial View of Wilshire Country Club. Developer and philanthropist G. Allan Hancock leased 105 acres to the Wilshire Country Club after he inherited 440 acres from his father, Henry Hancock. In the 1920s, he subdivided the property from Rossmore to Highland Avenues, between Wilshire Boulevard and Melrose Avenue, into residential lots. Temple Street, whose name was changed to Beverly Boulevard in 1921, ends at the clubhouse and heads south. By 1924, plans were developing to create a great east/west artery—from the ocean to the heart of downtown—that would bisect the golf course on its way to what would later become Sunset Boulevard.

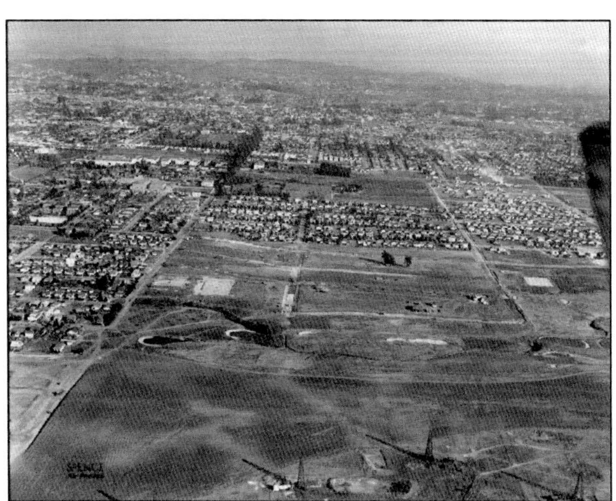

Aerial View of Melrose Avenue Looking East, 1921. Los Angeles was spreading west, and the neighborhoods around Larchmont were taking shape. In the foreground are Alan Hancock's oil fields, now the site of the La Brea Tar Pits and the Los Angeles County Museum of Art. The grove of trees is Melrose Avenue. (Courtesy of the UCLA Spence Air Photo Collection.)

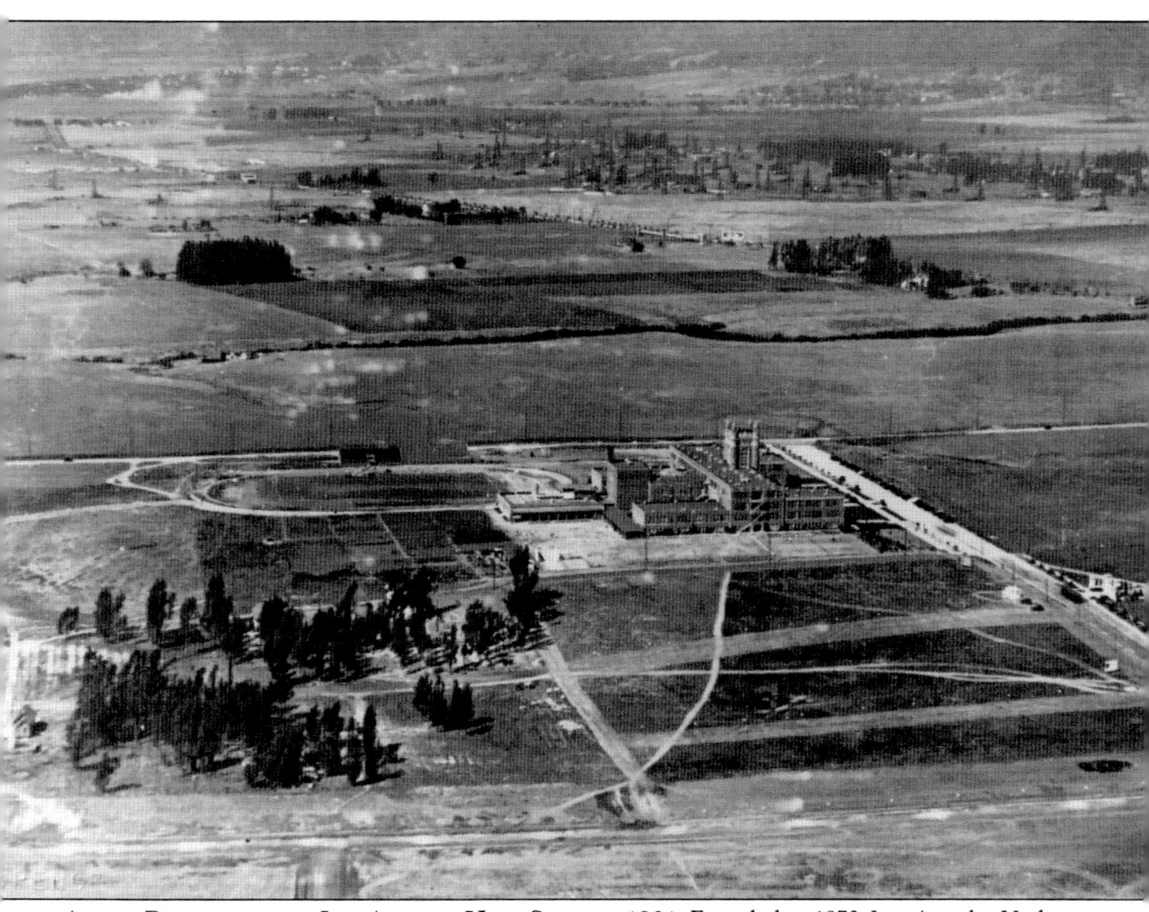

Aerial Photograph of Los Angeles High School, 1921. Founded in 1873, Los Angeles High School is the oldest public school in Southern California. The school moved from the corner of Rimpau and Olympic Boulevards to its current location in 1917 with 1,937 students. Olympic Boulevard was known as Tenth Street at the time of this photograph. The name was changed to commemorate the 1932 Summer Olympics that were held in Los Angeles. (Courtesy of Los Angeles High School.)

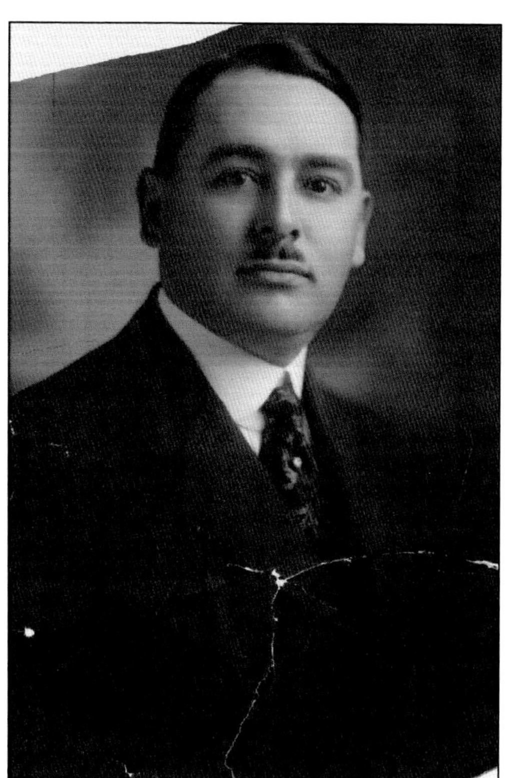

Julius J. La Bonte, Father of Larchmont Boulevard. Recognized as the "Father" of Larchmont, Julius La Bonte and his partner Charles Ramson retired from a successful business in Grand Rapids, Michigan, to Los Angeles. They purchased seven lots on Larchmont Boulevard in 1921. La Bonte, who built 70 percent of the structures on the street, is credited with creating the first neighborhood shopping street in the city that catered to the new neighborhoods of Windsor Square and Hancock Park. According to the *Los Angeles Times*, every store was leased before the buildings were finished.

La Bonte Building and Loan Association. Julius La Bonte and Charles Ramson operated their real estate and banking business out of one of their buildings at 126–132 North Larchmont Boulevard. La Bonte served as president, and Ransom served as vice president. The bank's safe is still in the location, now home of Chevalier's Books.

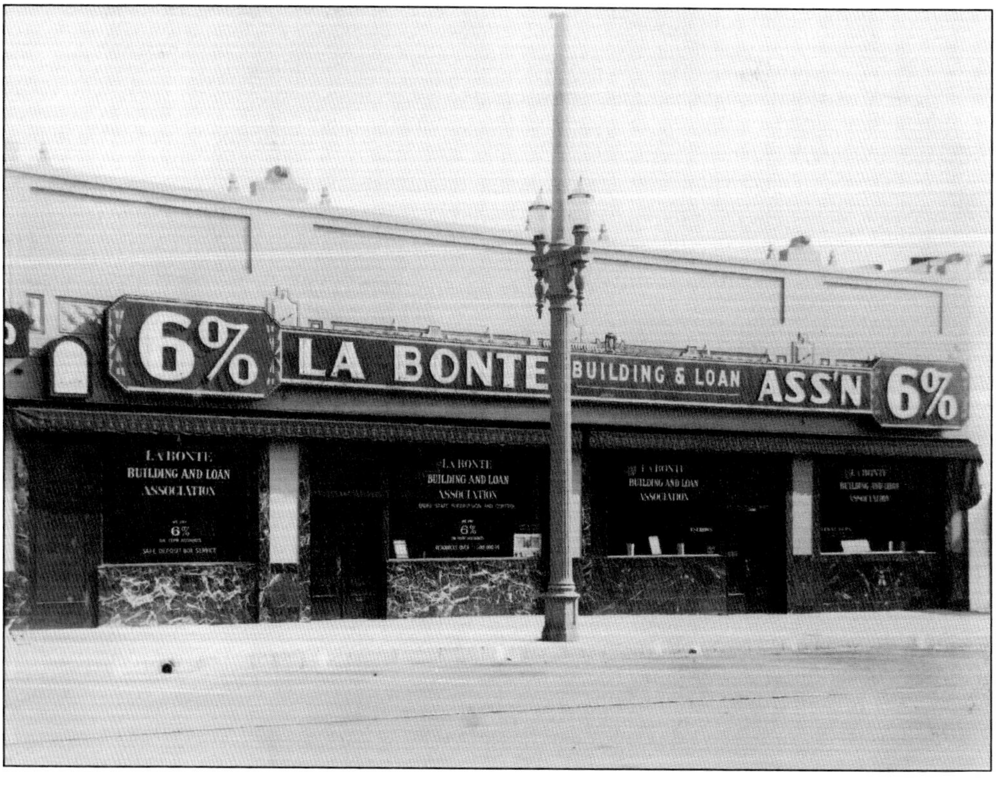

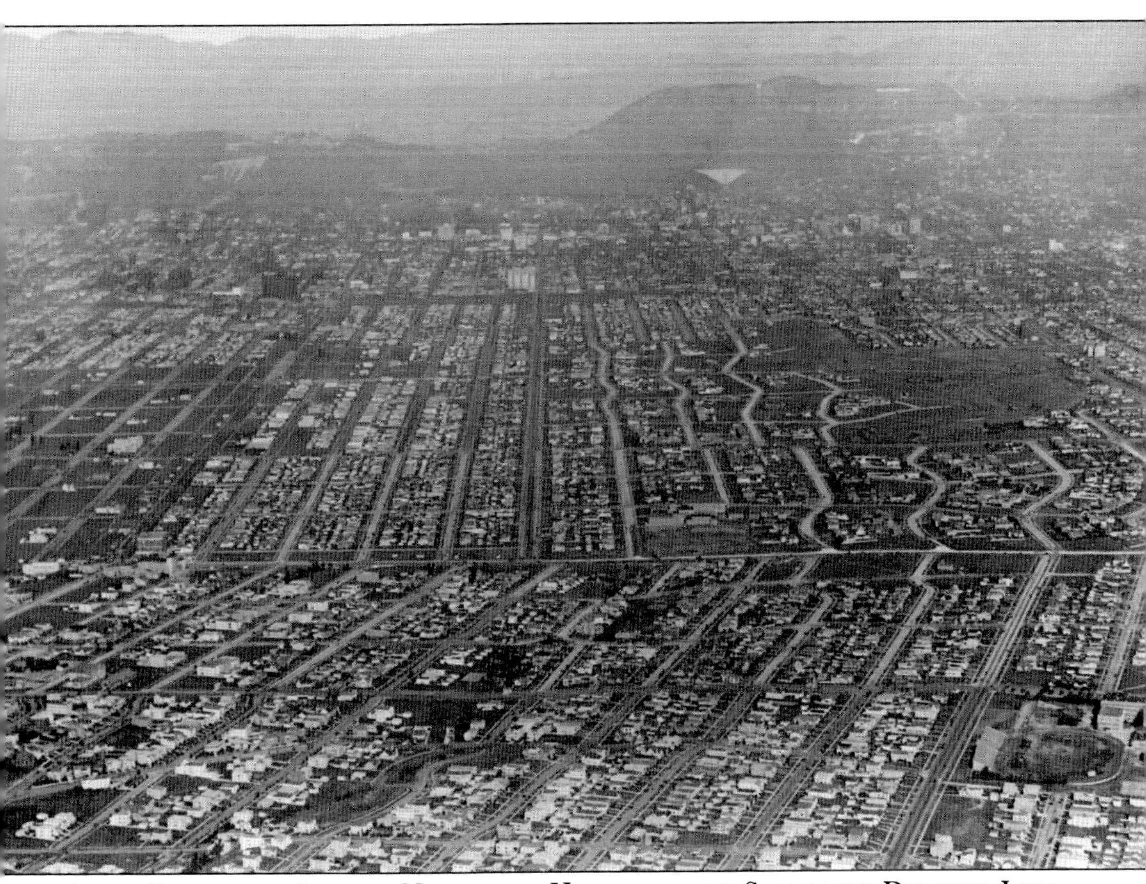

Aerial Photograph Looking North with Hollywoodland Sign in the Distance, Late 1920s. The Los Angeles High School track and football stadium can be seen in the lower-right corner of the image, and nearby is the neighborhood of Brookside. Originally called Wilshire Crest, Brookside is bound by Olympic and Wilshire Boulevards and Rimpau and Highland Avenues and was developed with tree-lined streets and diverse 1920s-style architecture like other nearby neighborhoods of Hancock Park, Windsor Square, and Fremont Place. The large undeveloped area is the Wilshire Country Club. A number of large Hancock Park estates were not yet built at the time of this photograph. In the distance on Mount Lee, the Hollywoodland sign (later shorten to Hollywood in one of its several restorations) beckons prospective buyers to the subdivision in the hills, formerly citrus groves. The original sign was lit with thousands of lightbulbs and could be seen for miles. (Courtesy of Los Angeles High School.)

La Blanche Ethel asst prod mgr Christie Film Co r6109 Afton pl
" Eunice usher Marcal Theatre
" Geo C (Bertha) asst formn LAG&ECorp r2995 San Marino
" Geo F h2995 San Marino
Labley Edwin (Jennie) h438 S Gates
La Boda Agnes waiter r672 S Rampart blvd
La Boissiere Albt J (Mamie I) mgr Weatherby-Kayser Shoe Co h1333 Maltman av
Labonde Julia B Mrs music tchr 1045 S Vmont
" Cora Mrs clk r2407 S Grand av
La Bonge Carl (Hanna) h1017 W 22d
La Bonte Building 136½ N Larchmont blvd
LA BONTE BUILDING & LOAN ASSOCIATION, Julius La Bonte Pres, Chas Ransom V-Pres, Stanley J Martineau V-Pres, Jay C Fisher, Treas, 130 N Larchmont Blvd, Phone Gladstone 2161
" Darrell A slsmn r3761 Bev blvd
" Frances H M h3761 Bev blvd
" Francis W police r3748 S Grand av
" Julius (Pauline) pres La Bonte Bldg & Loan Assn La Bonte & Ransom Co and Windsor Mtg Co h340 S Arden blvd
" Louis J curtain clnr 662 W Slauson av r4624 S Figra
" & Ransom Co Inc Julius La Bonte pres S J Martineau v-pres Chas Ransom sec ins 132 N Larchmont blvd
Laboon Bruce clk h210 N Kenmore av
Labor Service Bureau & Vocational Headquarters M F Mitchell pres F W Wells sec treas 3608 S Central av
LABOR UNIONS, See Classified Section of Directory under heading of Trade and

Los Angeles Telephone Directory Listing for La Bonte Building and Loan Association, 1929. The officers of the company and their titles are listed, along with Julius La Bonte's wife, Pauline. In July 1923, the *Los Angeles Times* reported the real estate firm was celebrating its second anniversary with a staff of more than 50 salesmen, draftsmen, architects, and engineers. By 1930, the firm announced it was expanding its offices to an adjacent space north of its location at 132 North Larchmont Boulevard. (Courtesy of the Los Angeles telephone directory.)

LaBONTE & RANSOM CO. LTD.

GLadstone 2161 132 N. Larchmont Blvd.

The desirability of Los Angeles Real Estate as an investment is not questioned by investors with vision. Many sound investments and fine homes are available today.

HANCOCK PARK RESIDENCE
The real beauty of Italian Architecture is revealed in this newly completed eleven-room home. There is an unusual appeal in its beauty, interior conveniences and superior construction. Located on a fine corner lot at McCadden Place and Second. It is moderately priced at $49,500.

ARCHITECT'S OWN HOME
An unusually attractive two-story eight-room Italian home at 2371 Live Oak Drive, Los Feliz Terrace. One-quarter of an acre of beautifully landscaped ground. Spacious enclosed patio with fountain and fireplace. Price $30,000.

HANCOCK PARK RESIDENCE
A charming eleven-room home of English Norman design on one of the finest corners in this district. An ideal arrangement of rooms combined with an artistic and beautiful finish makes this one of the most desirable homes in the city. Price $65,000. Shown only by appointment. 515 South Hudson ave.

LARCHMONT BLVD. STORE BUILDING
Modern two-story store and apartment building. Fully occupied with a yearly income of $5460.00. Price $55,000. We will gladly give full particulars to interested parties.

HANCOCK PARK RESIDENCE
This beautiful twelve-room Italian home is the best value in Hancock Park. Price $57,500. 625 South Rimpau Blvd.

Financing, designing and building homes to your own ideas and tastes, is only one of the many services we offer.

We offer unusual values in Hancock Park Homes.

La Bonte & Ransom Co. LTD. *Los Angeles Times* Display Advertisement. Serving as developers, bankers, and real estate brokers, Julius La Bonte and Charles Ramson successfully developed homes and commercial properties in the nearby vicinity, west of Western Avenue and between Melrose and Pico Avenues. This advertisement was in the *Los Angeles Times* in 1930.

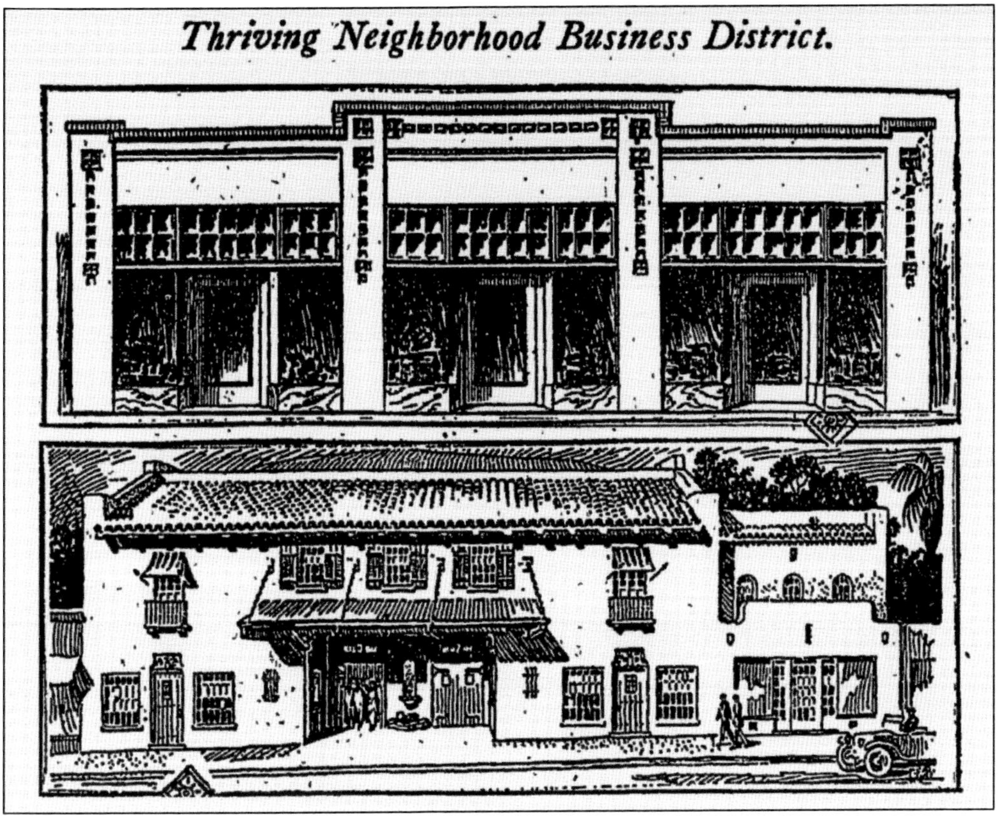

Thriving Neighborhood Business District.

New Business Center Grows. On September 25, 1921, The *Los Angeles Times* reported that a new business district was planned for Larchmont Boulevard between First Street and Beverly Boulevard. The stores were said to be "attractive . . . the building will be of colored pressed brick embellished with ornamental stucco work and . . . will be furnished with modern mercantile conveniences." The lower building depicted above is a motion picture theater of Mission Revival design, made with reinforced concrete and featuring modern acoustics and ventilation. The theater seated almost 900 people and featured a magnificent $40,000 organ. In addition, there was a "large, carefully selected string orchestra." (Both, courtesy of the *Los Angeles Times*.)

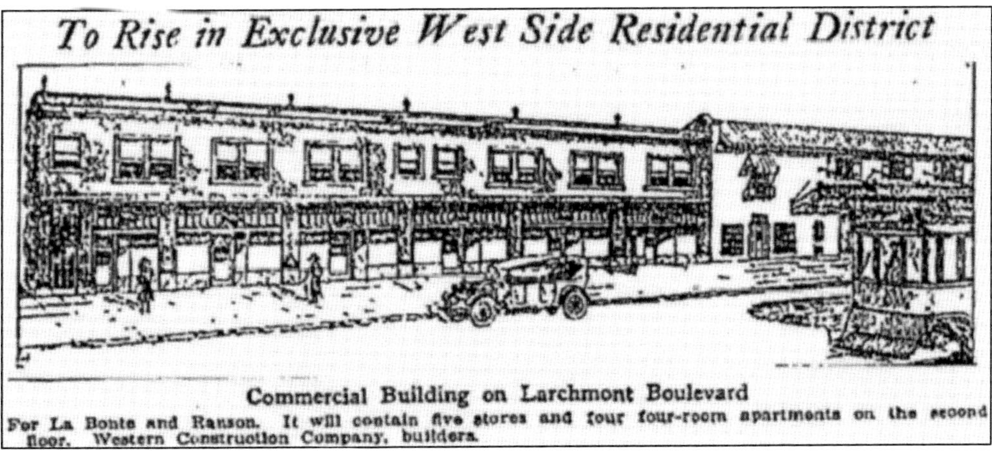

To Rise in Exclusive West Side Residential District

Commercial Building on Larchmont Boulevard

For La Bonte and Ranson. It will contain five stores and four four-room apartments on the second floor. Western Construction Company, builders.

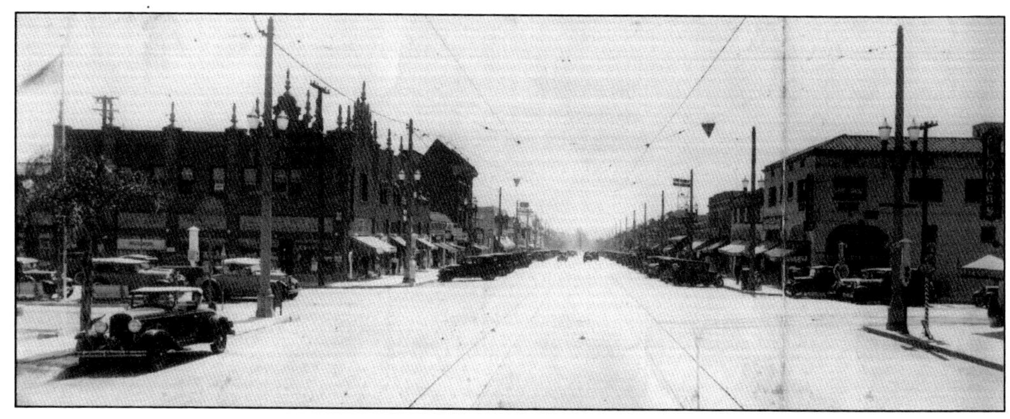

Larchmont Boulevard at Beverly Boulevard Looking South, c. 1920. Real estate developers Julius La Bonte and Charles Ramson purchased seven lots on Larchmont Boulevard to create a business district of 30 stores between First Street and Beverly Boulevard. Jack Lipson, whose collection this photograph is from, was the son-in-law of La Bonte, having married Charlotte La Bonte. According to notes on the back, this photograph was part of the historical collections of Security Pacific National Bank and was marked "Hollywood Street, Larchmont Boulevard at Beverly Boulevard 1930s." (Both, courtesy of the *Larchmont Chronicle* from the Jack Lipson Collection.)

From JACK LIPSON collection to Chronicle

Larchmont

Rep 4x6

This photograph is furnished on condition that whenever it is used CREDIT WILL BE GIVEN TO

HISTORICAL COLLECTIONS, SECURITY PACIFIC NATIONAL BANK

Please return this photograph to:

Historical Collections
Security Pacific National Bank
P. O. Box 2097 Los Angeles, Calif. 90054

File Reference: Hollywood Street.

LARCHMONT BLVD AT BEVERLY BLVD

1930's

crop marks

Sept 1982

10¼

1.71
.16
1.55

LARCHMONT CHRONICLE
542½ N. LARCHMONT BLVD.
LOS ANGELES, CALIF. 90004

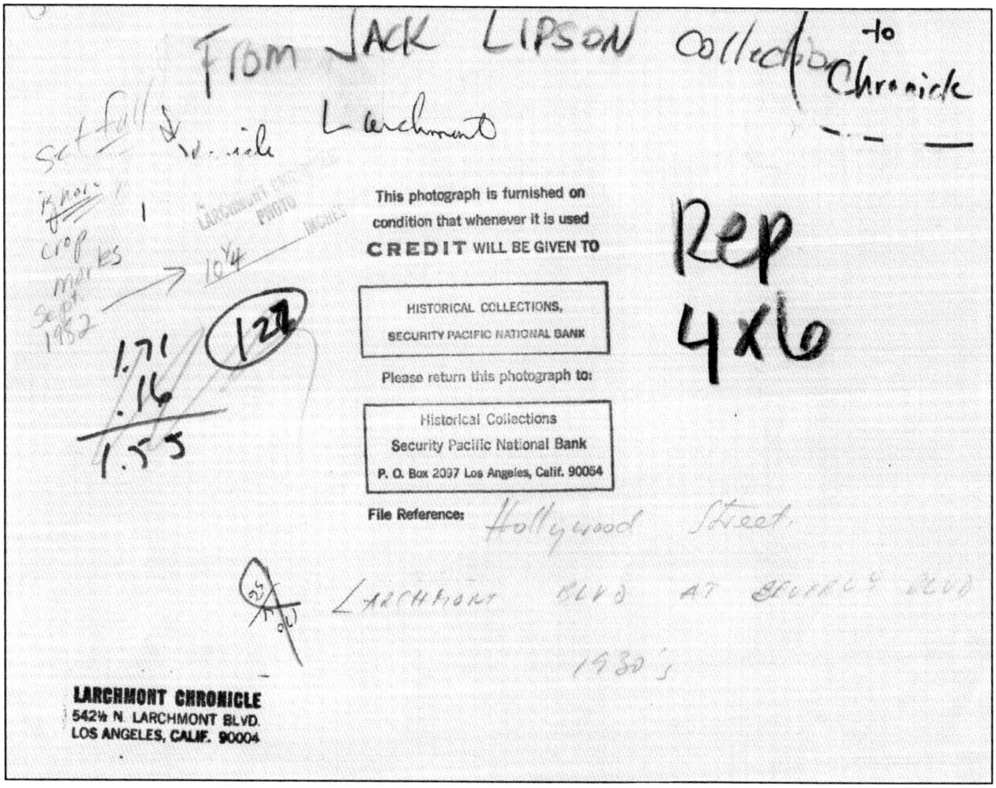

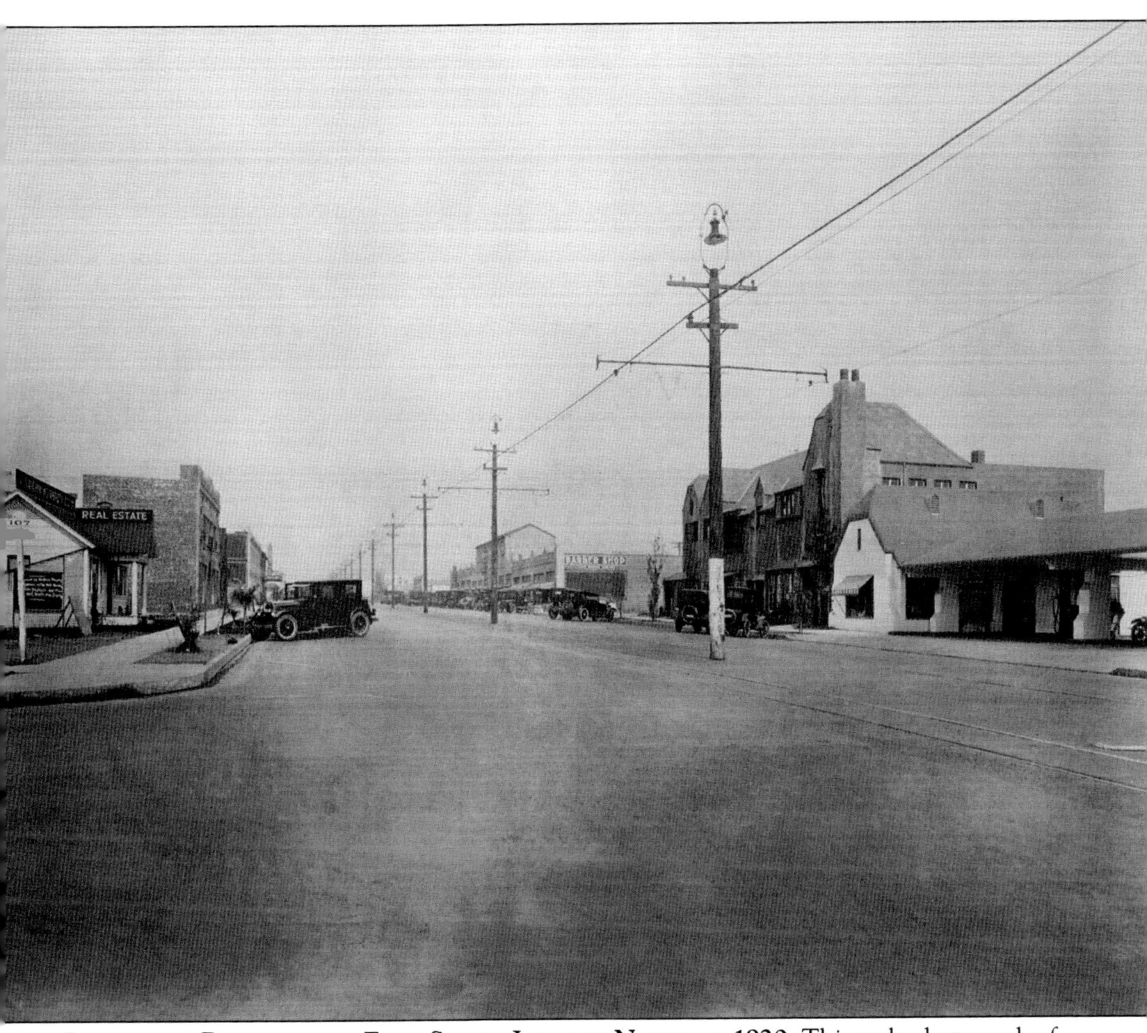

LARCHMONT BOULEVARD AT FIRST STREET LOOKING NORTH, c. 1920. This early photograph of Larchmont Boulevard was taken before all the stores were built. In 1922, Ben T. Cossart received a building permit to construct a real estate office for Larchmont Realty Company at 107 Larchmont. B.T. Cossart and J.P. Smith are listed in the 1923 Los Angeles telephone directory doing business at 107 North Larchmont.

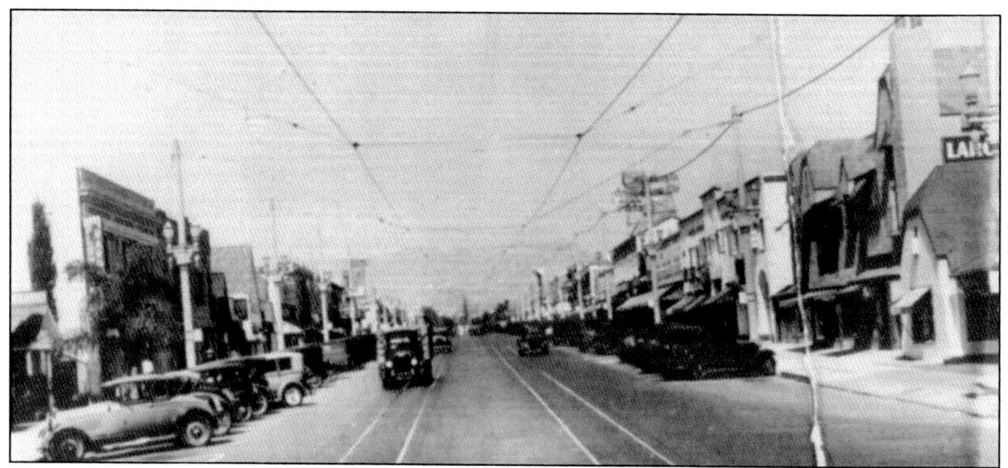

LARCHMONT BOULEVARD AT FIRST STREET LOOKING NORTH. This is a street view of Larchmont Boulevard from the 1920s. The street featured angled parking for easy access to shopping. The Yellow Car rail line, developed in 1911, offered convenient shopping for residents of nearby Windsor Square who did not want to go to Western Avenue or ride downtown. The *Los Angeles Times* speculated that the new shopping district would rival nearby Western Avenue by offering unique shops with "no duplication of mercantile establishments."

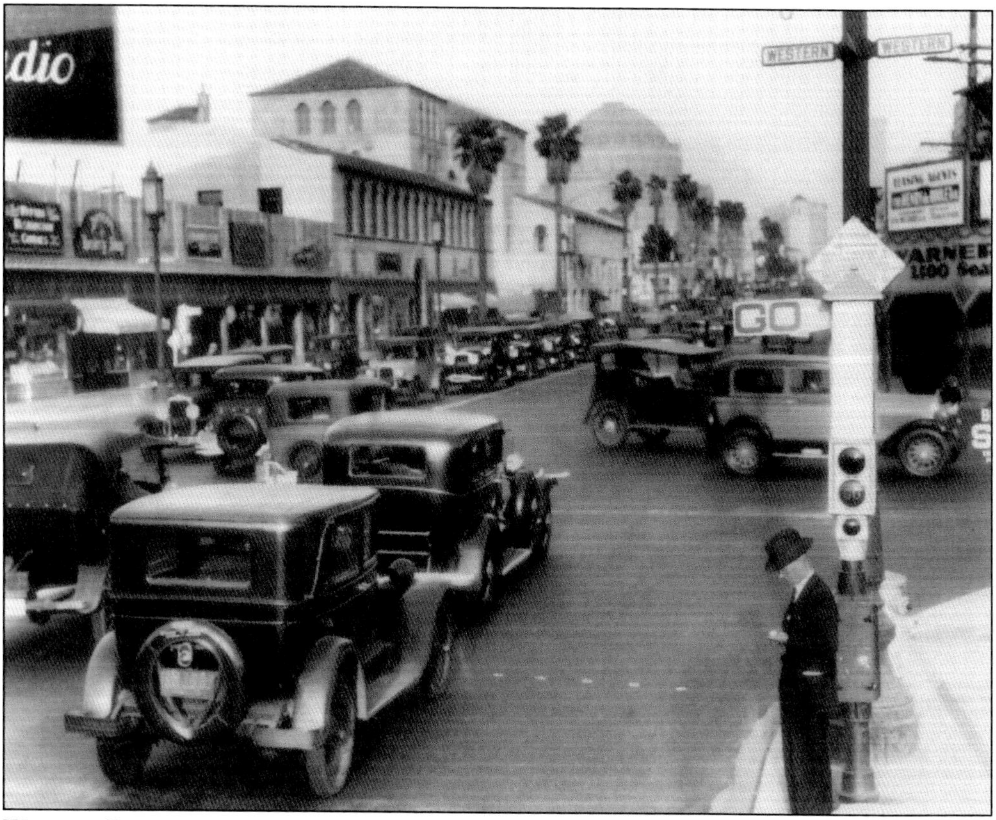

WILSHIRE BOULEVARD AND WESTERN AVENUE. This was considered one of the busiest intersections in the nation. Wilshire Boulevard Temple, a reform congregation that catered to the movie industry, can is visible at left (with the domed roof).

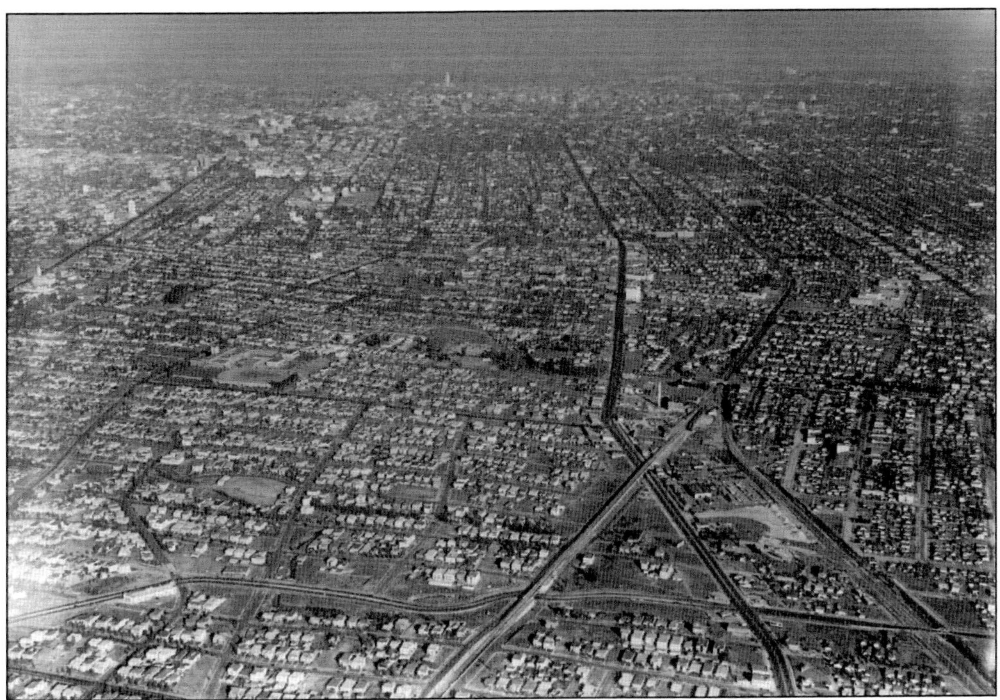

Aerial View Looking East, Late 1920s. Los Angeles High School is shown in the middle left of the photograph. Los Angeles City Hall can be seen off in the distance. By the end of the 1920s, much of the city had been expanded, starting from historic downtown and extending to the west. (Courtesy of Los Angeles High School.)

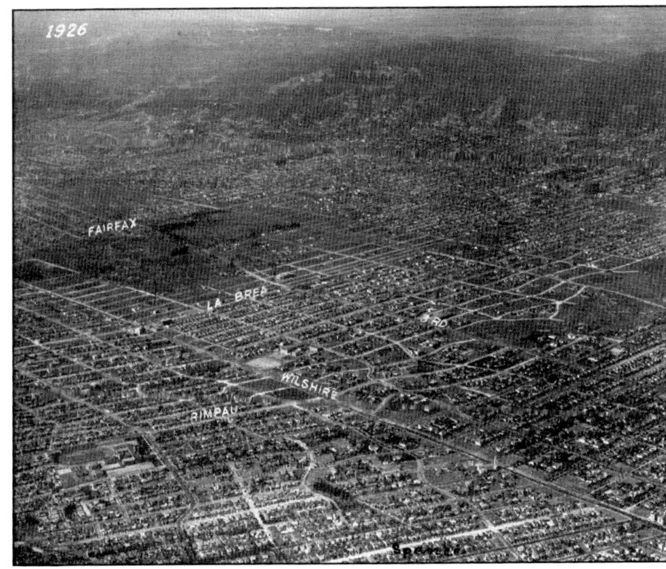

Aerial View of Rimpau and Wilshire Boulevards, 1926. The neighborhoods along Wilshire Boulevard were rapidly growing, providing many customers for Larchmont Boulevard merchants. This photograph shows the neighborhoods of La Brea, Hancock, Brookside, Windsor Village, Wilshire Park, and Windsor Square. The curving streets of Fremont Place (south of Wilshire) and Hancock Park (north of Wilshire) still had many vacant lots. (Courtesy of the UCLA Spence Air Photo Collection.)

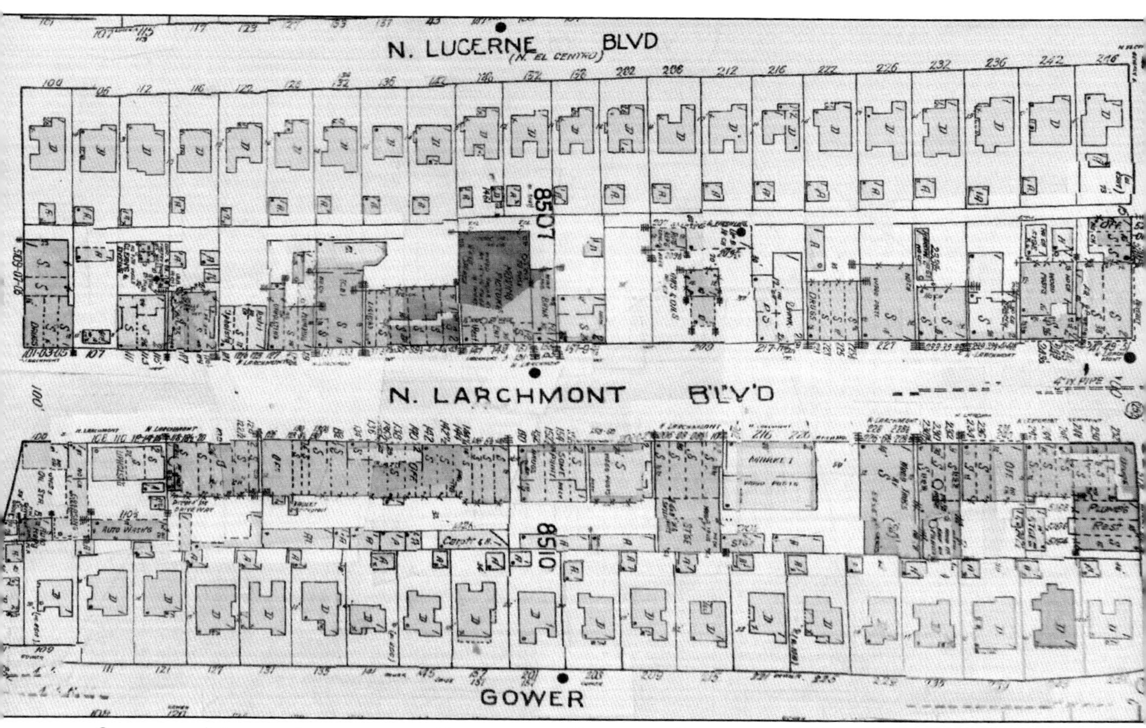

Sanborn Map of Larchmont Boulevard Business District, 1928. Originally created to assess fire insurance liability in US cities, Sanborn maps provide detailed information about each building and its occupancy. This is a photograph composite of the map in the Los Angeles Public Library collection. Many of the buildings shown here are still in use on Larchmont Boulevard today, with the notable exception of the two gas stations and the movie theater.

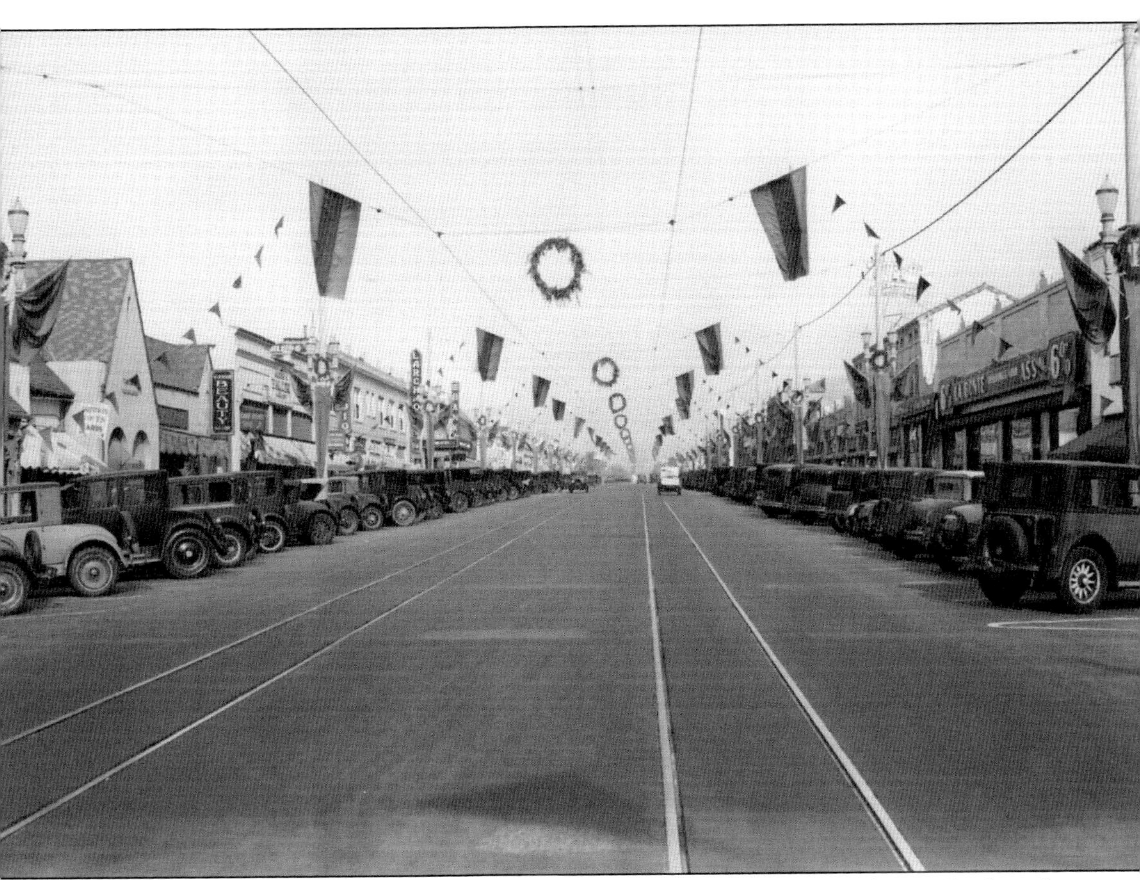

Larchmont Boulevard Looking South toward Third Street, 1929. Larchmont Boulevard was a busy mercantile street in very short order, with most construction taking place in six short years. This photograph shows the angled parking spaces, offering easy access and convenience for shoppers. The street is also decorated for the holiday season, with banners and wreaths suspended from the railway lines. (Courtesy of Marc Wanamaker at Bison Archives.)

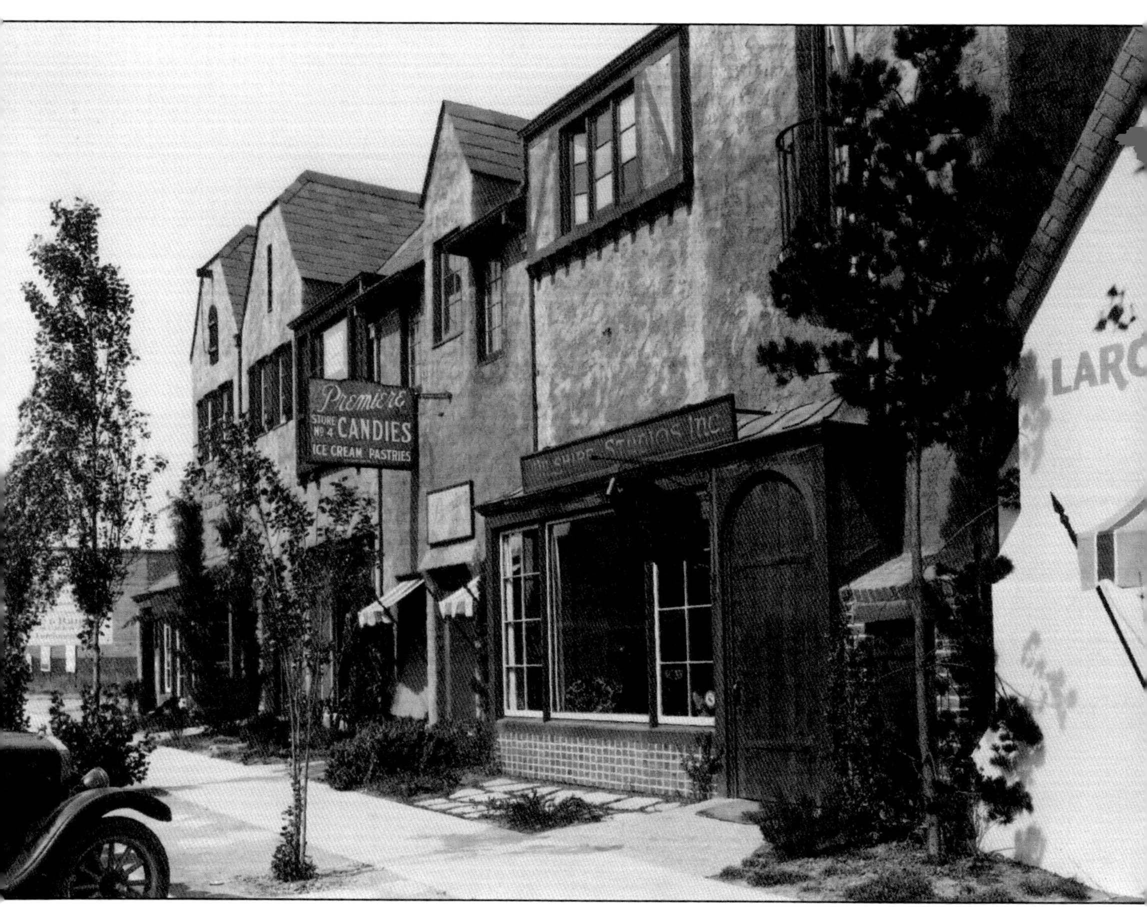

108–110 Larchmont Boulevard, 1923. Early tenants on Larchmont included the offices of Wilshire Studios. The 1929 Los Angeles telephone directory listed the upholstery company at 108 North Larchmont Boulevard. This building no longer stands. (Courtesy of Marc Wanamaker at Bison Archives.)

Weekly Topics

LOS ANGELES TRANSIT LINES

Published weekly by the Bureau of Public Service, Los Angeles Transit Lines, 1060 South Broadway, Zone 15

VOLUME 6 | JULY 16, 1945 | NUMBER 29

Go Places WITH THE... LOS ANGELES TRANSIT LINES

SECURE YOUR FUTURE

WE WANT VETERANS WHO WANT SECURITY AND STEADY WORK

Work with the Transit Lines does not depend upon changing seasons for the Transitliners must roll day and night, rain or shine, summer, winter, spring and fall.

GOOD PAY AND VACATIONS WITH PAY

The pay is comparable to most of the better paid industries. Allowances, such as travel time pay, dead head pay, signing on and signing off pay. After one year of service, you will receive a vacation with pay.

FREE TRANSPORTATION

A pass which entitles you to go wherever you wish at any time on all our lines is given you. After five years your wife or nearest dependent is granted the same privilege.

EMPLOYEE BENEFITS

These are provided through a special fund for medical and surgical treatment, nurses, hospitals, pharmacists, X-rays, examinations, etc., also life insurance, and sickness and accident insurance which pays benefits up to twenty dollars a week. These services, cost of which is partly borne by the Company, are made possible at a very small expense to employees.

GOOD FELLOWSHIP

Long and lasting friendships have been made through the various employee organizations, a few of which are the American Legion, Women's Club, Red Cross Auxiliary, Veterans' Club, etc. Before the war we had baseball leagues, golf tournaments, bowling tourneys, shows and dancing to the music of our own orchestra. These will be resumed after victory.

NO EXPERIENCE REQUIRED

We train you and pay you during the training period.

POSITIONS OFFERED—
TRAINMEN
COACH OPERATORS
CONDUCTORETTES
COACHETTES

Applicants between the ages of 18 and 55 (excluding those for coach service who must be 21) with good eyesight and no physical handicaps are eligible for employment. An Availability Certificate is required.

POSITIONS AVAILABLE AT DIFFERENT LOCATIONS (SEE MAP)

A. DIVISION NO. ONE

Located at Seventh and Central, handy by car line to South and Southeast homes.

B. DIVISION NO. THREE

Located at 28th and Idell. If you live in Highland Park, Glendale, South Pasadena, or Northeast Los Angeles this division is practically at your doorstep.

C. DIVISION NO. FOUR

Right down town at 12th and Sentous, it is within walking distance of numerous apartments. Served by the P, W, and U cars. Easily accessible for the West Siders.

D. DIVISION NO. FIVE

If you live in Inglewood, Hawthorne, or in the Southwest section of Los Angeles,

APPLY 1056 SO. BROADWAY NOW

WORK NEAR YOUR HOME

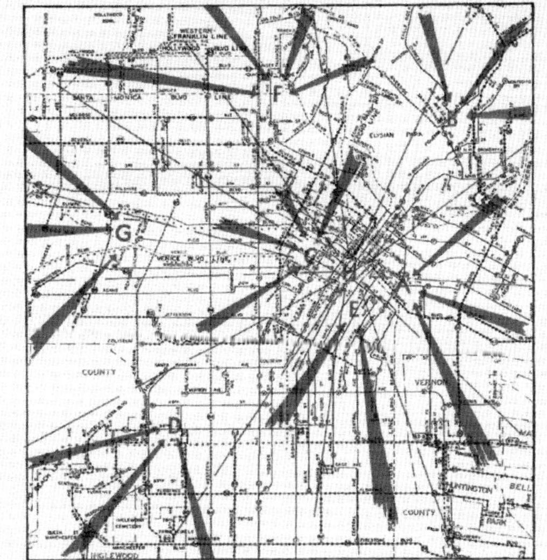

this division, located at 2300 West 54th Street, is the place for you.

E. LOS ANGELES TRANSIT LINES COACH DIVISION

Located at 758 East 16th Street.

F. VIRGIL MOTOR COACH

1023 North Virgil Street. Convenient for those living in Hollywood or San Fernando Valley. You may apply here for work.

G. VINEYARD MOTOR COACH

4810 West Pico Street is the address—and for people living near or towards the beach, this is the place to work. You may apply at 1023 North Virgil for work at this division.

H. MAIN OFFICE BUILDING

This is where you apply for work. Take any Broadway car except the "5" to 11th and Broadway. Step into 1056 where a courteous interviewer is waiting for you. The doctor's office, personnel department are in the same building for your convenience. It won't take long. Come down today —open from 8:30 to 5:00.

APPLY 1056 SO. BROADWAY NOW

Map of the Service Area of the Los Angeles Railway. The Pacific Electric Railway provided a network of rail lines, enabling Los Angelenos to travel all over their growing city. It was a great boon to Larchmont, bringing shoppers and customers to local businesses. It helped create one of the most enduring pedestrian shopping streets in the city.

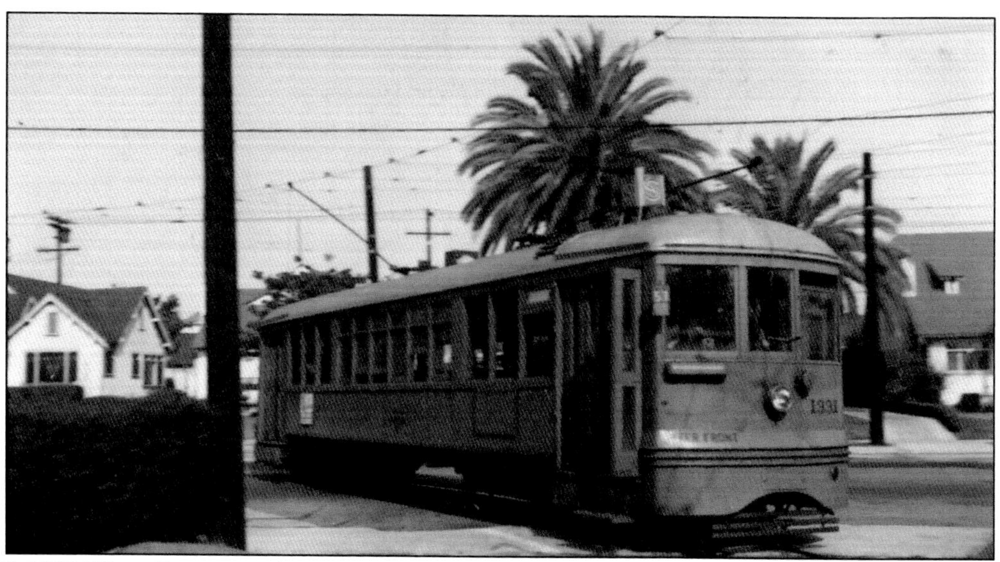

LARY S Line Railcar. The Los Angeles Railway served the city proper, and the S Line was one of the lines that operated along west Third Street and Larchmont Boulevard. The tracks were laid to carry people up Larchmont to the Hollywood Mineral Hot Springs at 5626 Melrose Avenue.

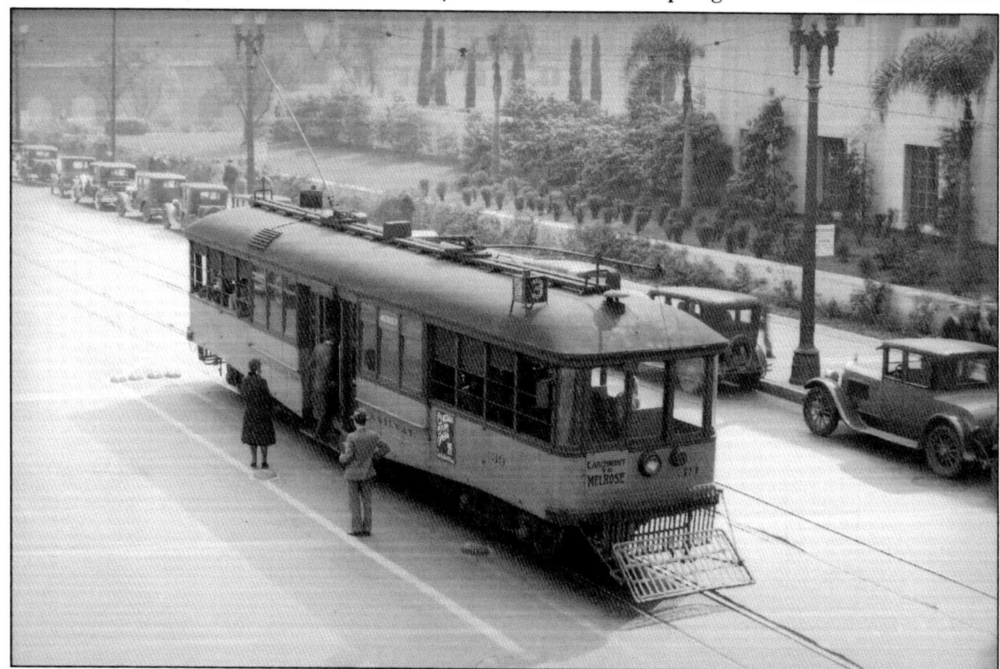

Larchmont to Melrose Cable Car, 1932. This photograph is of men and women entering the Larchmont to Melrose cable car. By 1948, the S Line was replaced with the LARY 3 Line. The rail service had gone as far west as La Brea Avenue. According to Pacific Electric, "Rail service along West Third Street past Wilton Place and up Larchmont Boulevard was now operated as the R line. The rail service along Larchmont Boulevard was unique in that the trolley wire center poles were left in place in the pavement after the private right of way along the boulevard was paved over. The lower portion of the poles were painted silver with black stripes in an effort to keep LA motorists from crashing into them." (Courtesy of Dick Whittington Studio/Corbis.)

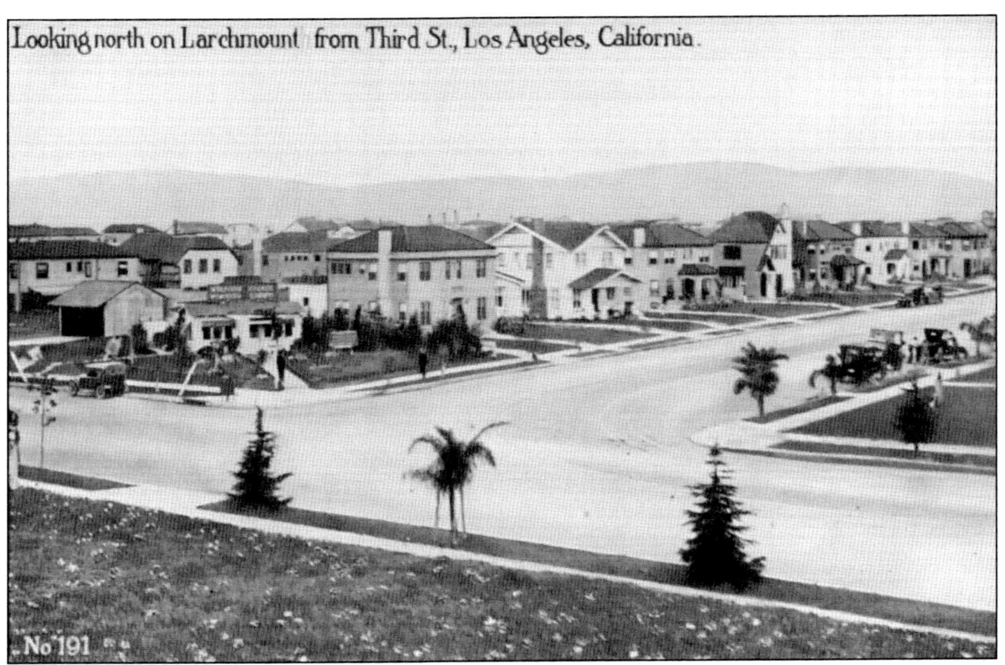

SOUVENIR POSTCARD OF LARCHMONT, C. 1930. This picturesque view of Larchmont is looking north from Third Street. The idealized neighborhood perspective has softened the railway tracks turning up Larchmont Boulevard.

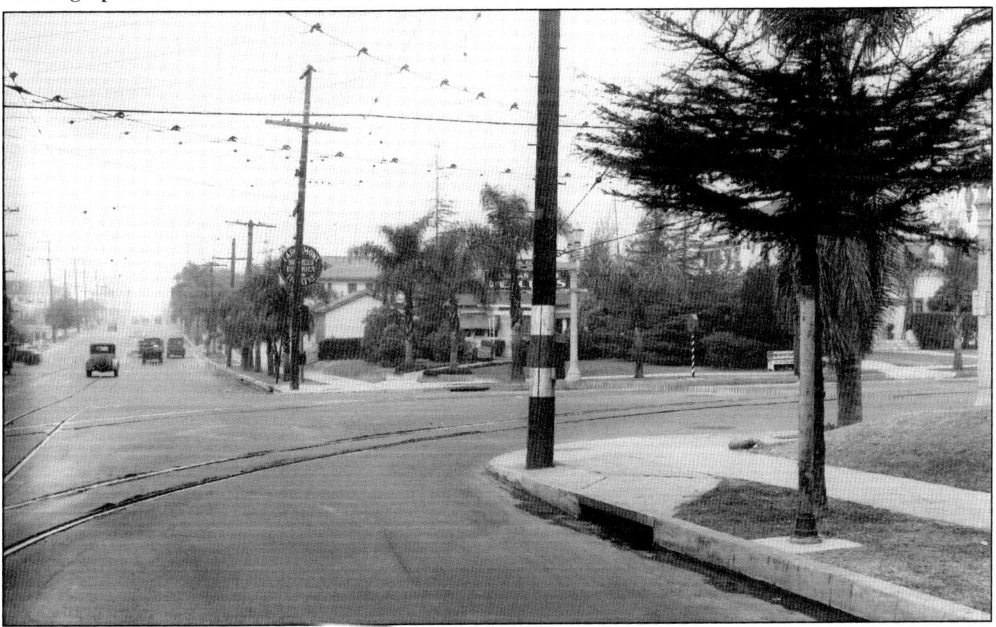

LARCHMONT BOULEVARD AND THIRD STREET. This photograph shows a street view of Third Street turning north on Larchmont Boulevard. The Larchmont business district and theater sign is next to the original real estate office of La Bonte and Ramson. In this photograph, it is the office for the Larchmont Tract, operated by Shoults and Company at 269 South Larchmont. It later became the Wilshire YMCA until relocating to 225 South Oxford Street in 1964. (Courtesy of Marc Wanamaker at Bison Archives.)

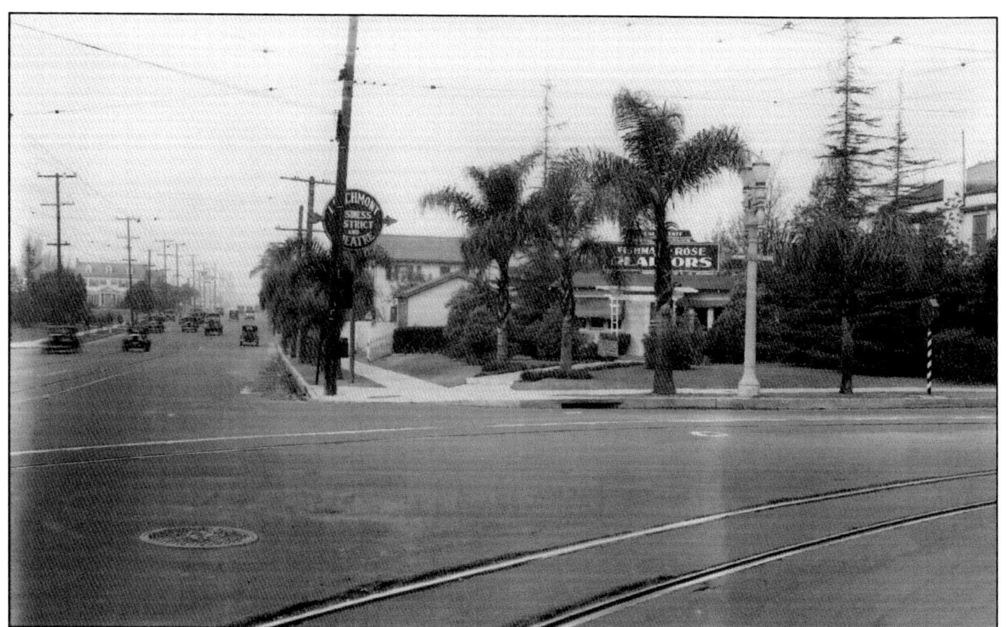

Northwest Corner of Third Street and Larchmont Boulevard, 1932. Here is a view turning north on Larchmont Boulevard from Third Street. Rail tracks are visible on both thoroughfares. (Courtesy of Marc Wanamaker at Bison Archives.)

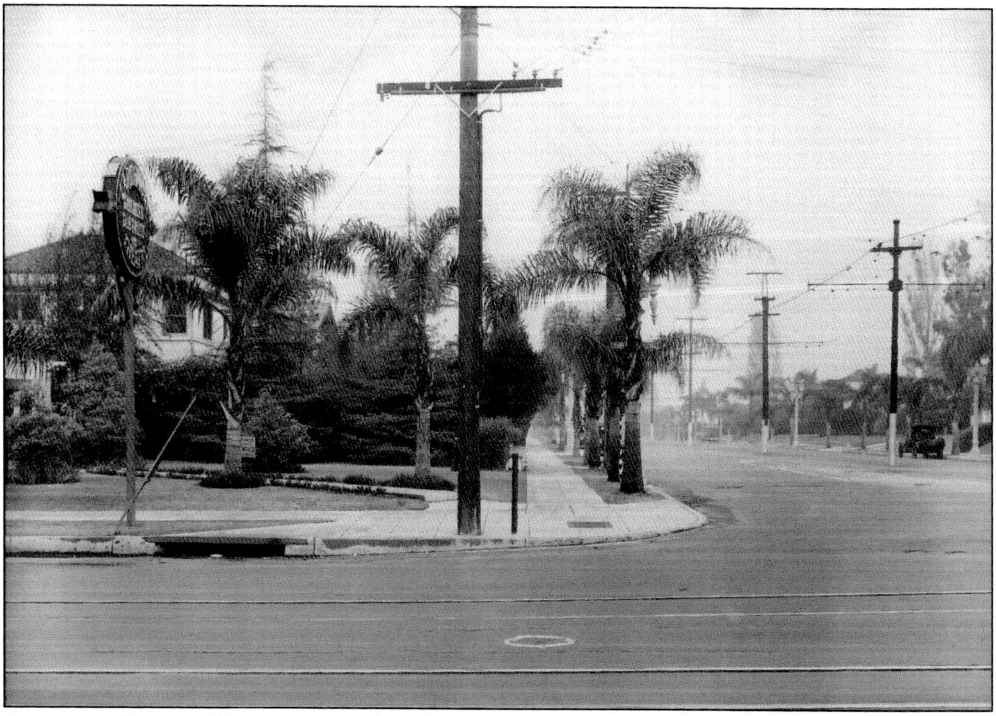

Another Corner View, 1932. This photograph was taken from the southwest side of the intersection. It shows a closer view of the Larchmont business district and theater sign and the railway poles in the center of Larchmont Boulevard. Also shown are the palm trees planted in the parkways lining both sides of the street. (Courtesy of Marc Wanamaker at Bison Archives.)

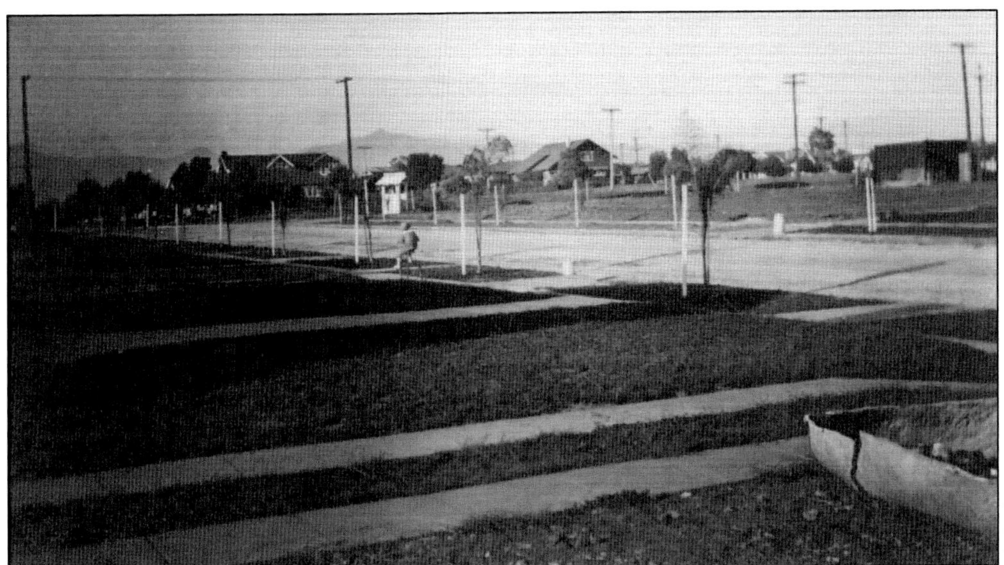

PHOTOGRAPH OF NEIGHBORHOOD, 1920s. This is an early image of a child riding a three-wheeled bike on the sidewalks of the yet undeveloped neighborhoods around Larchmont Boulevard. Also visible are recently planted, young palm trees.

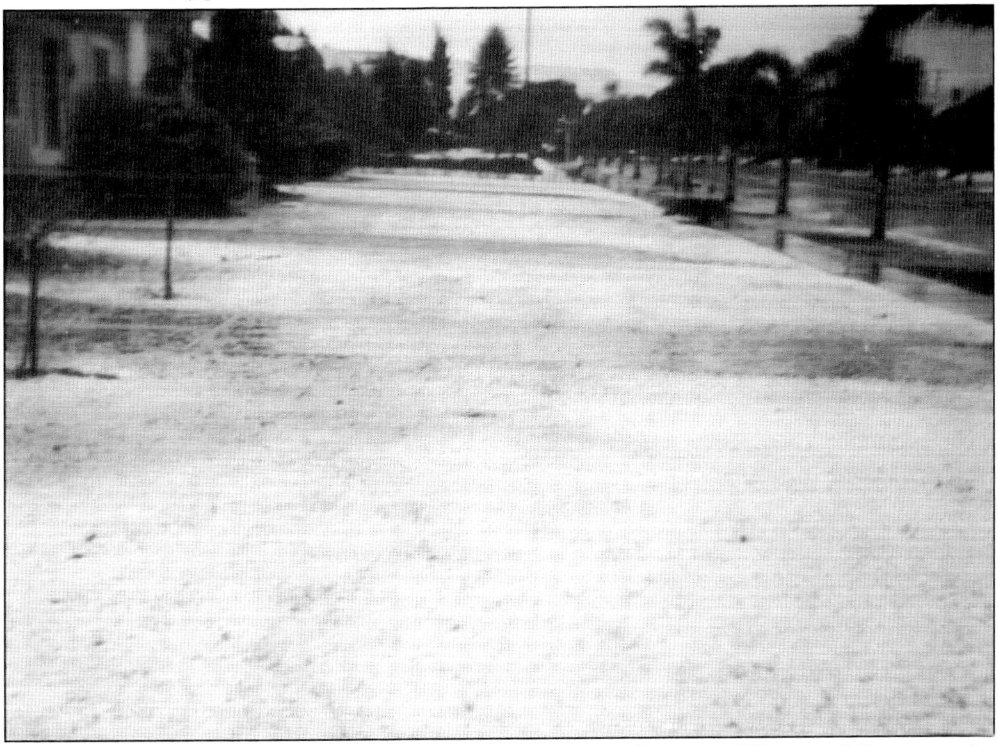

SNOW ON LARCHMONT AREA LAWNS, JANUARY 1932. Snow began to fall around 5 a.m. on the morning of January 15, 1932, according to the *Los Angeles Times*. Residents awoke to find two inches of snow covering their lawns. This was the first record of snow in the 56-year history of the city's bureau. Snow fell in downtown Los Angeles, Hollywood, and Westwood, where UCLA students made snowballs and enjoyed a snow day.

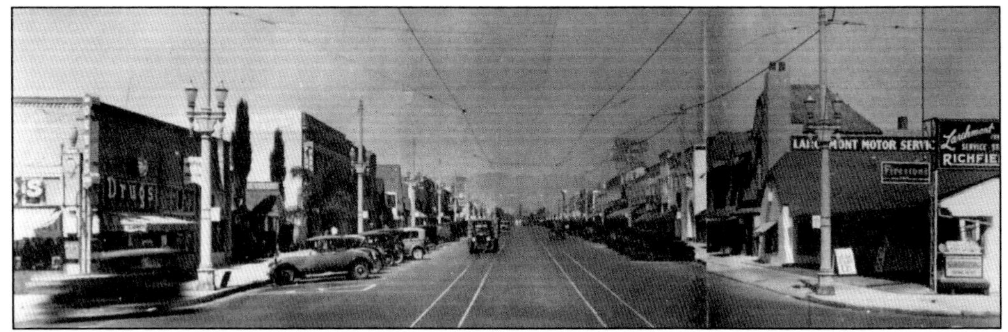

LARCHMONT AND FIRST STREET LOOKING NORTH. By the 1930s, the Larchmont business district was built out. In 1924, 101–103–105 North Larchmont Boulevard was built of brick on the northwest corner. On the opposite side of the street is Larchmont Motor Service station, which sold Richfield gasoline. Streetlights attached to the railway, power poles, power lines, and streetcar tracks can also be seen.

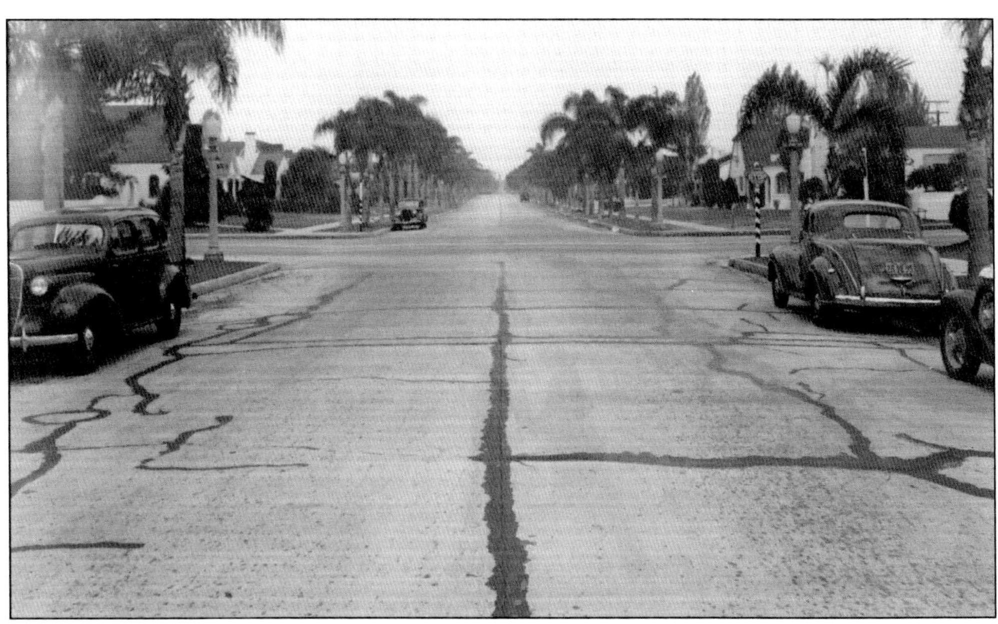

BEVERLY BOULEVARD AND LUCERNE STREET, 1938. Pictured is the intersection of Beverly Boulevard (the cross street) and Lucerne Boulevard in 1938. This photograph shows the concrete streets and homes in the neighborhood just one block west of Larchmont Boulevard. (Courtesy of Marc Wanamaker at Bison Archives.)

Two

LARCHMONT LIFE

Mayberry, the fictional town of *The Andy Griffith Show*, is often used to describe Larchmont. It is fitting that Hollywood would help define Larchmont, as their histories are intertwined with nearby Paramount Studios and Sunset Gower Studies. Larchmont's small-town appeal comes in part from the business plan envisioned by Julius La Bonte in 1921, when he populated the street with neighborhood-serving stores operated by owners committed to personalized service.

First, there were grocery stores and dry goods stores like Landis Department Store that catered to the large estates nearby. There were also banks and real estate offices, helping newcomers purchase homes. For everyday life, there were dry cleaners, bakeries, coffee shops, and toy stores. Then came specialty shops like Balzer's Market that offered the finest selection of gourmet foods and Chevalier's Books that catered to the well educated. As businesses took root on Larchmont Boulevard, they became civic leaders, caring for the community with the shared values of service and excellence instilled by La Bonte in those early years.

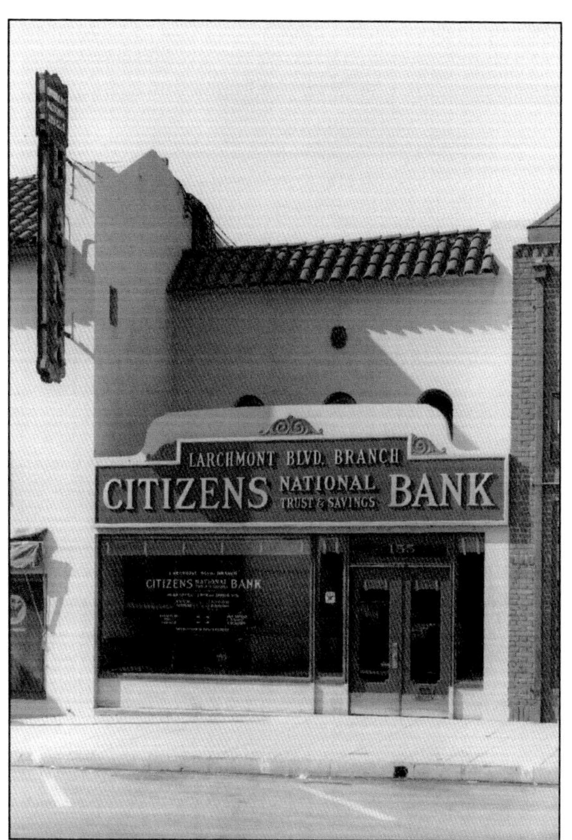

CITIZENS TRUST AND SAVINGS BANK AT 155 LARCHMONT BOULEVARD, 1927. Citizens Trust and Savings Bank was a Los Angeles–based bank incorporated in 1911. C.E. Toberman, a real estate developer known as "Mr. Hollywood," served as a director of the bank. He was called "Mr. Hollywood" for his role in developing Hollywood and many of its landmarks, including the Hollywood Bowl, Grauman's Chinese Theater, and the Roosevelt Hotel. (Courtesy of Marc Wanamaker at Bison Archives.)

CITIZENS NATIONAL TRUST AND SAVINGS BANK AT 155 LARCHMONT BOULEVARD, 1933. In 1928, the bank changed the name to Citizens National Trust and Savings Bank, reflecting the consolidation with Citizens National Bank. The bank operated in the northwest corner of the building, which was constructed by Julius La Bonte in 1921 as a moving picture theater and store. (Courtesy of Marc Wanamaker at Bison Archives.)

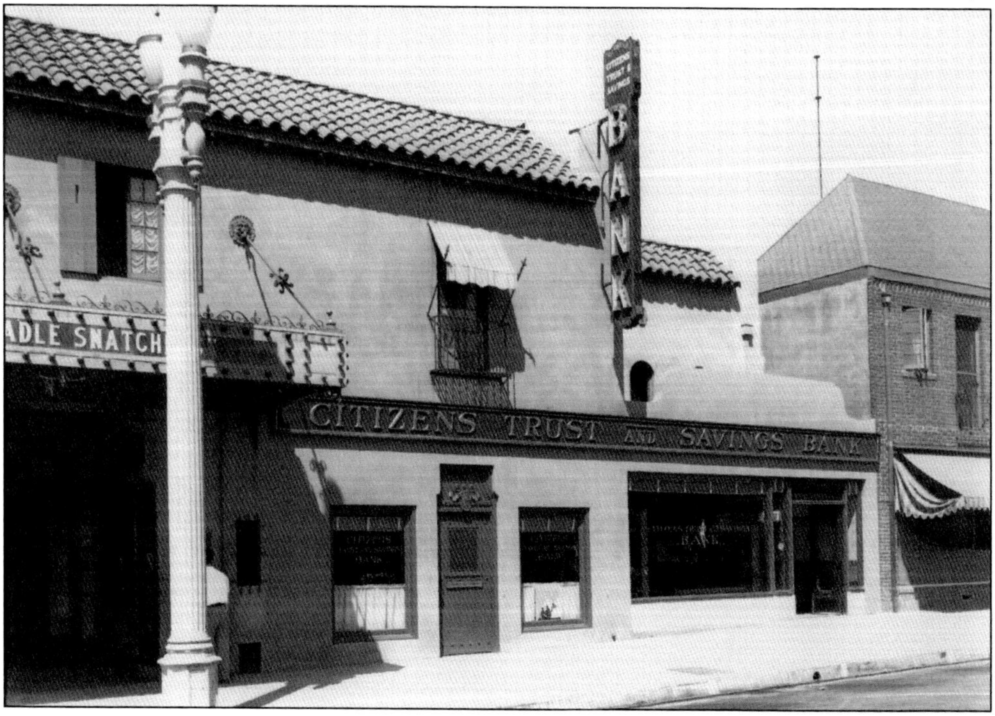

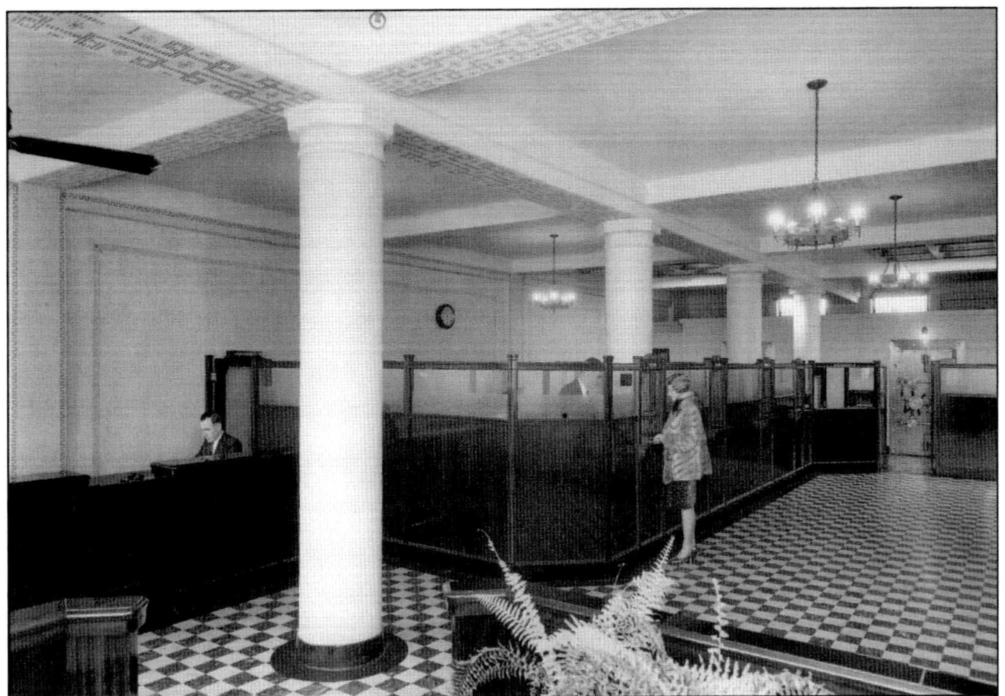

Security First National Bank of Los Angeles, 1929. Pictured is the elegant interior of the Security First National Bank branch on Larchmont Boulevard. (Courtesy of Marc Wanamaker at Bison Archives.)

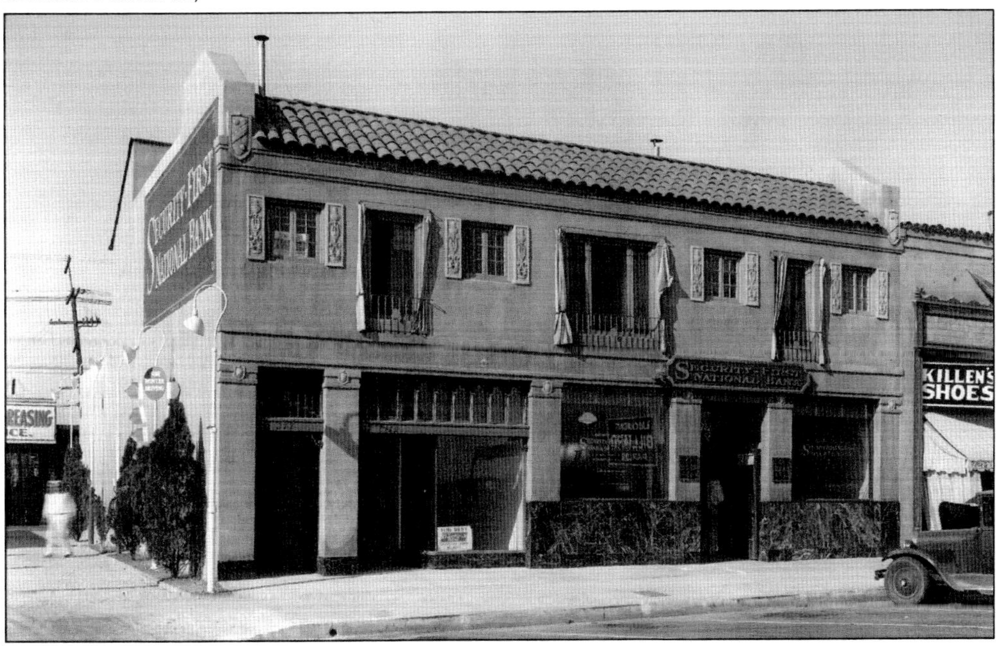

Security First National Bank of Los Angeles, 1930. Security First National Bank, founded in Los Angeles in 1889 as Security Savings Bank and Trust, merged with First National Bank in 1929, becoming Security Pacific in 1968 and finally Bank of America in 1991. (Courtesy of Marc Wanamaker at Bison Archives.)

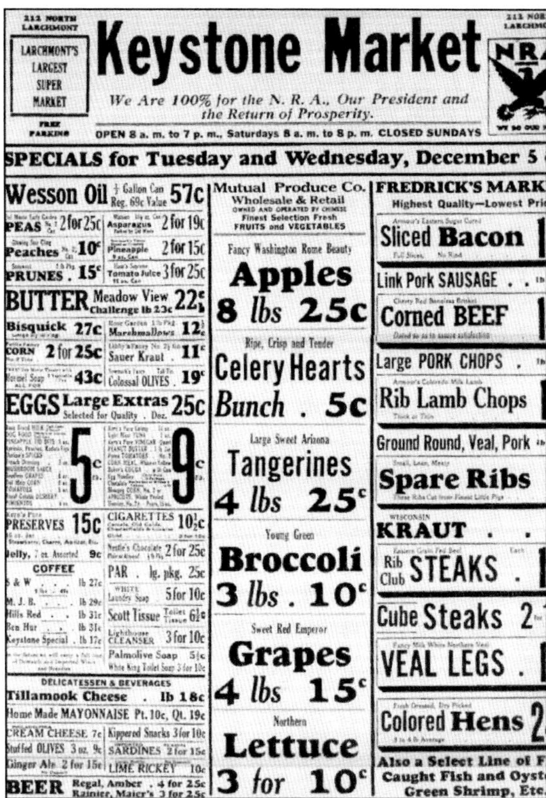

KEYSTONE MARKET AT 212 NORTH LARCHMONT. Over the years, Larchmont shoppers had many choices when it came to shopping and groceries. This advertisement from the Keystone Market boasts that it is the largest supermarket on the street and features the National Recovery Administration (enacted in 1933) symbol, showing support for the New Deal program intended to promote economic recovery after the Great Depression.

CARDER AND HESS IGA GROCERY AT 245 NORTH LARCHMONT, DECEMBER 16, 1932. The Independent Grocers Alliance (IGA), founded in 1926, was a consortium of local independent grocers across the United States. Each store was locally owned and operated like a franchise. This photograph shows the staff during the holiday season in 1932. This was one of several grocery stores on Larchmont Boulevard. (Courtesy of the Los Angeles County Natural History Museum.)

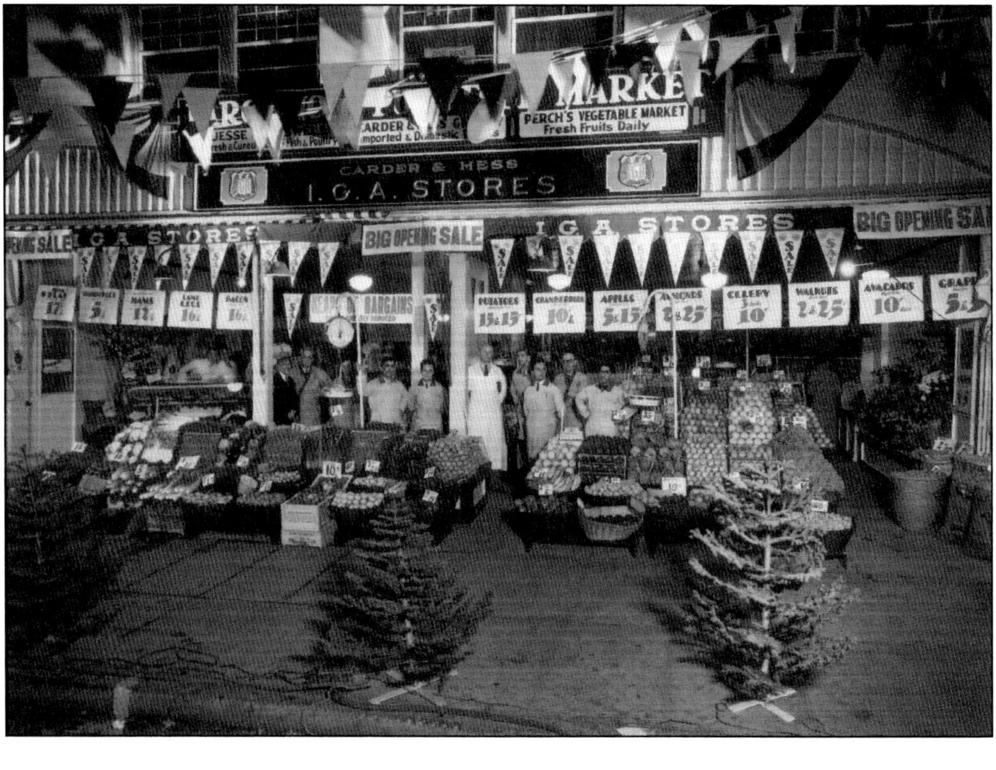

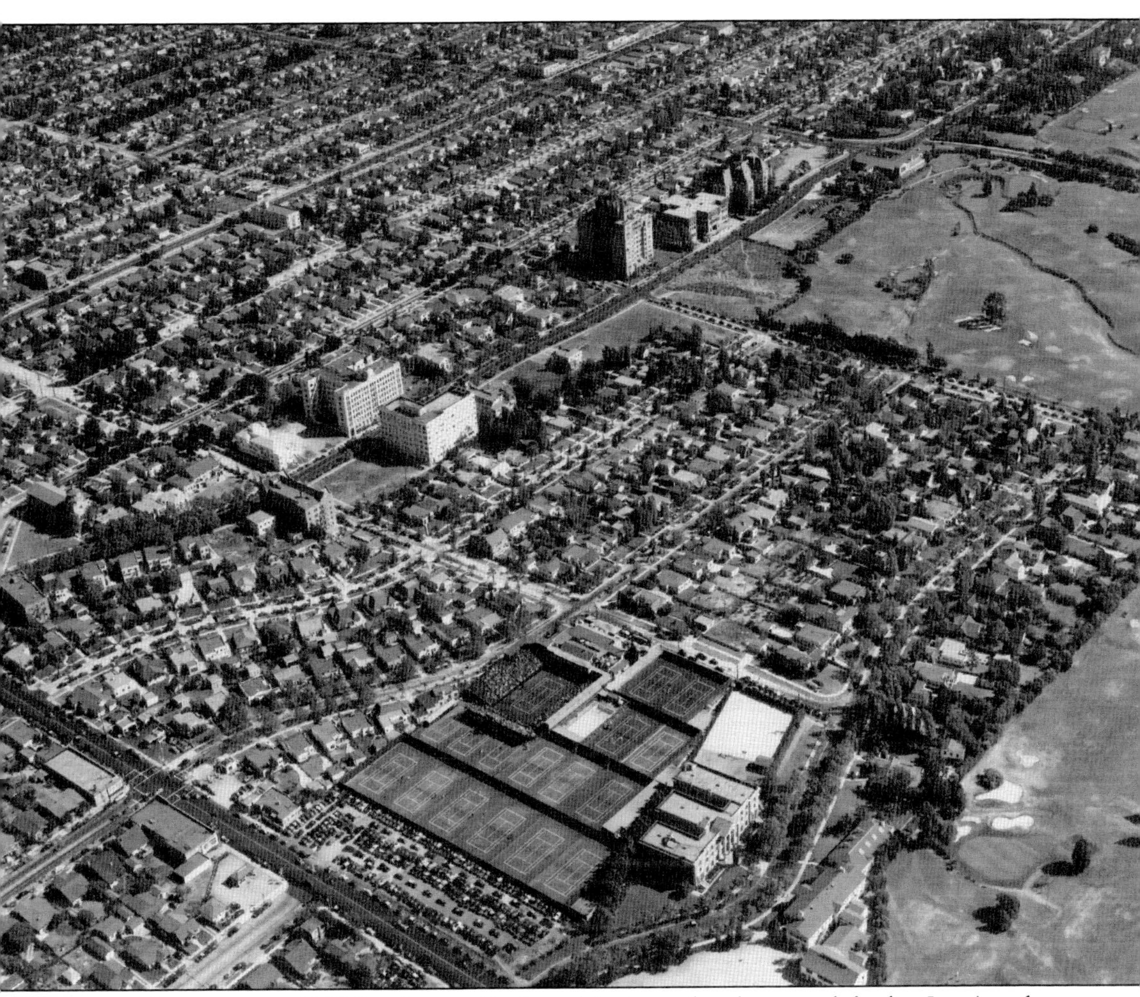

Aerial Photograph, 1937. Larchmont Boulevard is pictured at the upper-left edge. Los Angeles native Thomas Bundy—three-time US doubles champ, member of two Davis Cup teams, winner of three Southern California Tennis Association titles, and newlywed to May Sutton (the first non-British woman to win Wimbledon)—organized the purchase of five acres of lemon groves along Melrose Avenue to build the Los Angeles Tennis Club in 1927, adjacent to the elite, new residential neighborhood of Hancock Park and the Wilshire Country Club. (Courtesy of the UCLA Spence Air Photo Collection.)

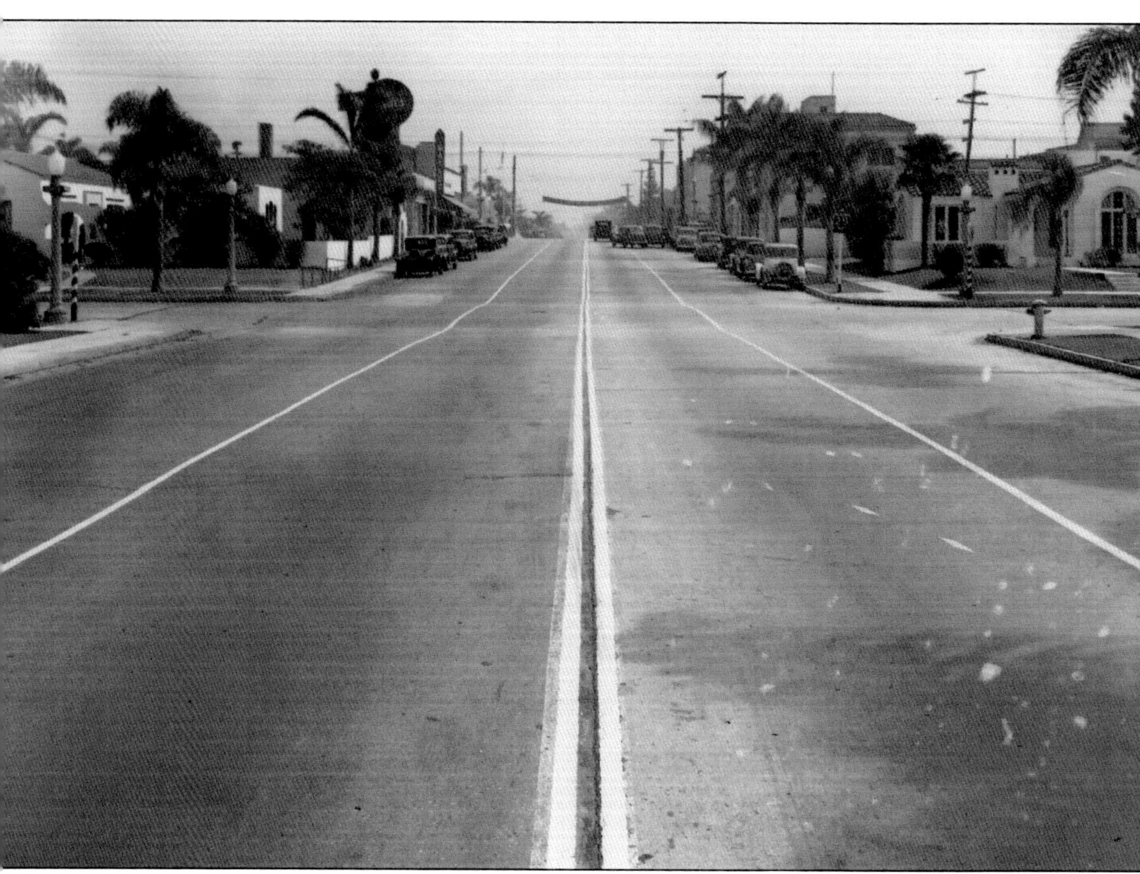

Beverly Boulevard Looking East toward Larchmont Boulevard, 1938. Here is a view of the approach to the intersection of Larchmont and Beverly Boulevards, passing Lucerne Boulevard. Ahren's Kitchen is located in the Spanish-style building on the corner of Larchmont and Beverly. Other businesses on the corner include Chapman's Ice Cream, Beverly Cleaners, and a florist on the corner next to Ahren's. (Courtesy of Marc Wanamaker at Bison Archives.)

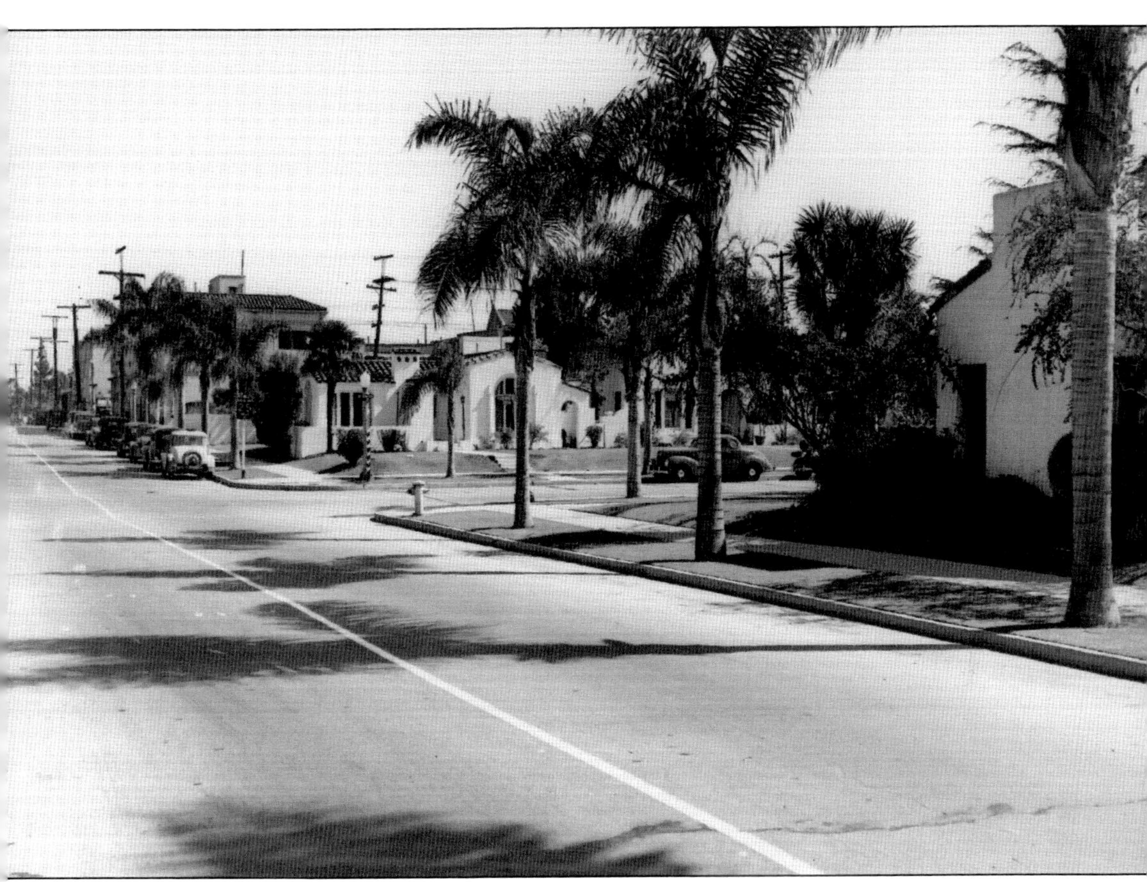

BEVERLY BOULEVARD AND LUCERNE STREET, 1938. This view looks east along Beverly Boulevard at the corner of Lucerne Street. The quaint Spanish Bungalow–style homes of the Larchmont Village neighborhood, with their concrete streets located just one block west of Larchmont, can be seen. Many of these homes look just as they did when they were constructed in 1920s. The Windsor Square Historic Preservation Overlay Zone, enacted in 2007, preserves the architectural heritage from this period.

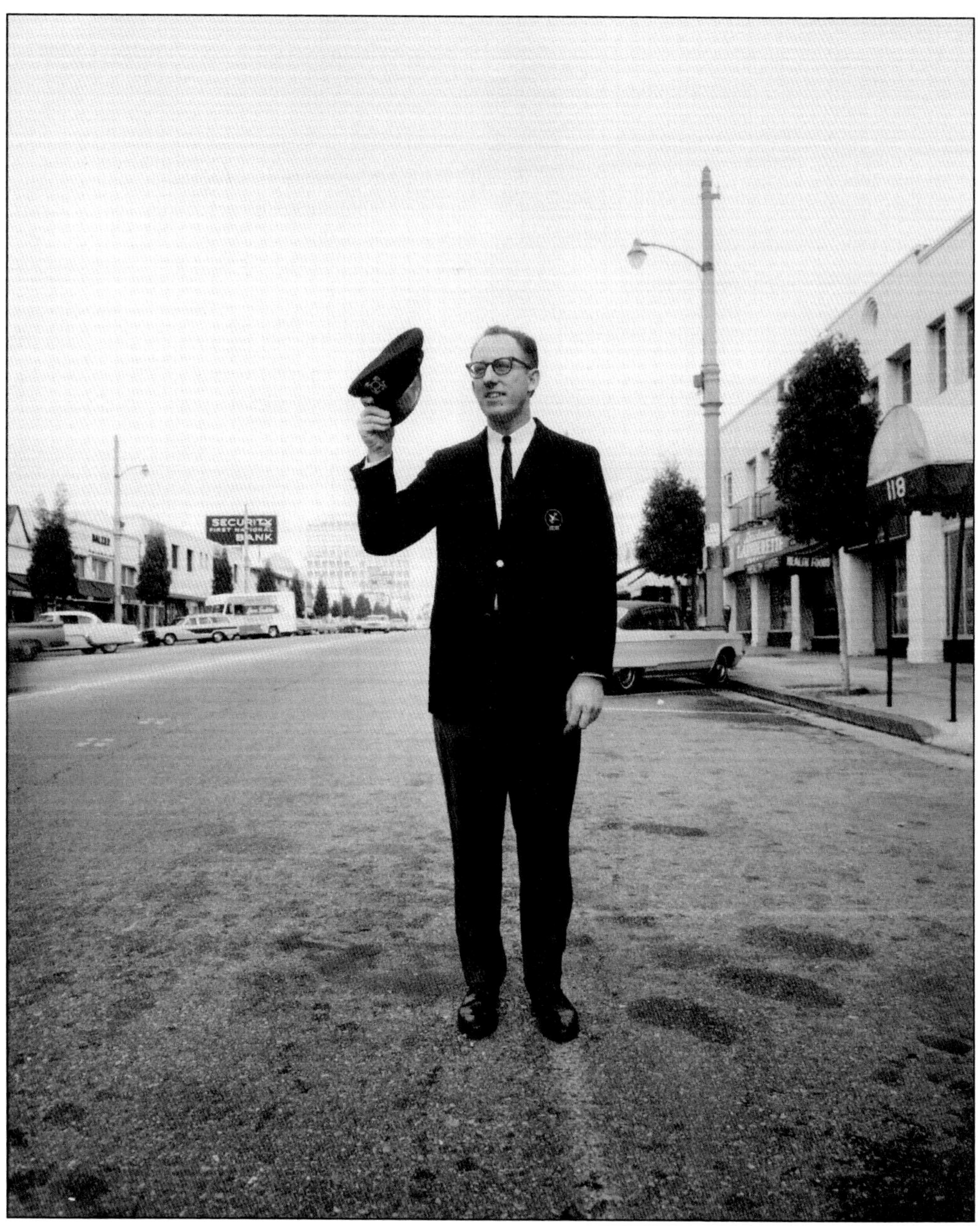

ALBERT DIPPELL. Realtor Albert Dippell is pictured in nautical attire on Larchmont Boulevard. Dippell was one of the most important realtors in developing and maintaining the residential character of Larchmont Boulevard and the surrounding neighborhoods. He came to Larchmont in 1923 after attending the School of Commerce at the University of Southern California. After exploring other parts of the city, Dippell concluded that the Wilshire district offered both stability and potential for further growth. Dippell was very active in civic affairs.

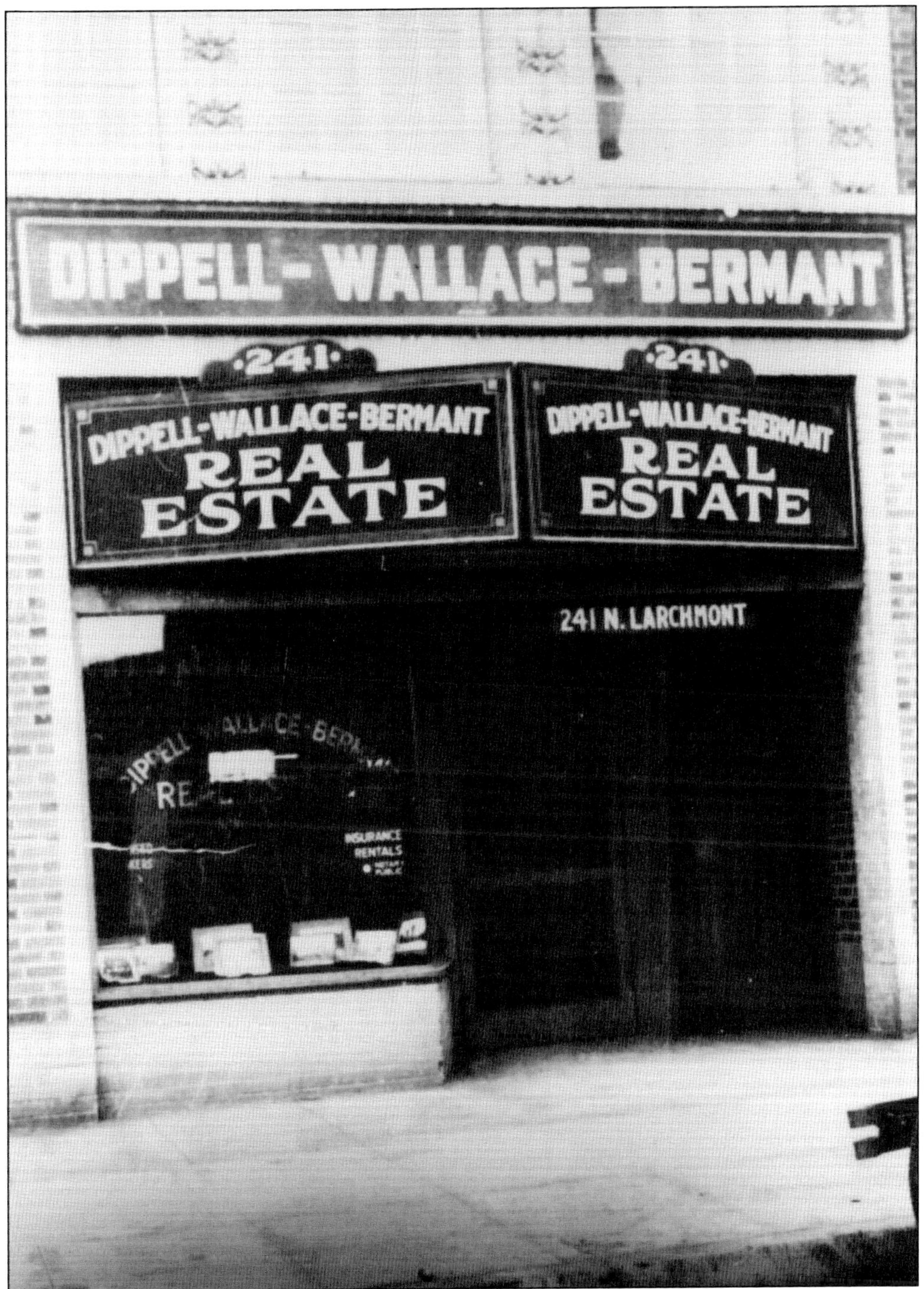

DIPPELL, WALLACE, AND BERMANT REAL ESTATE OFFICE AT 221 NORTH LARCHMONT BOULEVARD. Here is the early office of Albert Dippell, Ira Bermant, and Harry Wallace. The partnership lasted 15 years before the men went their separate ways. In 1932, Dippell moved his office to 107 North Larchmont Boulevard. His son Howard joined the family business in 1955, followed by his brother Cutler two years later.

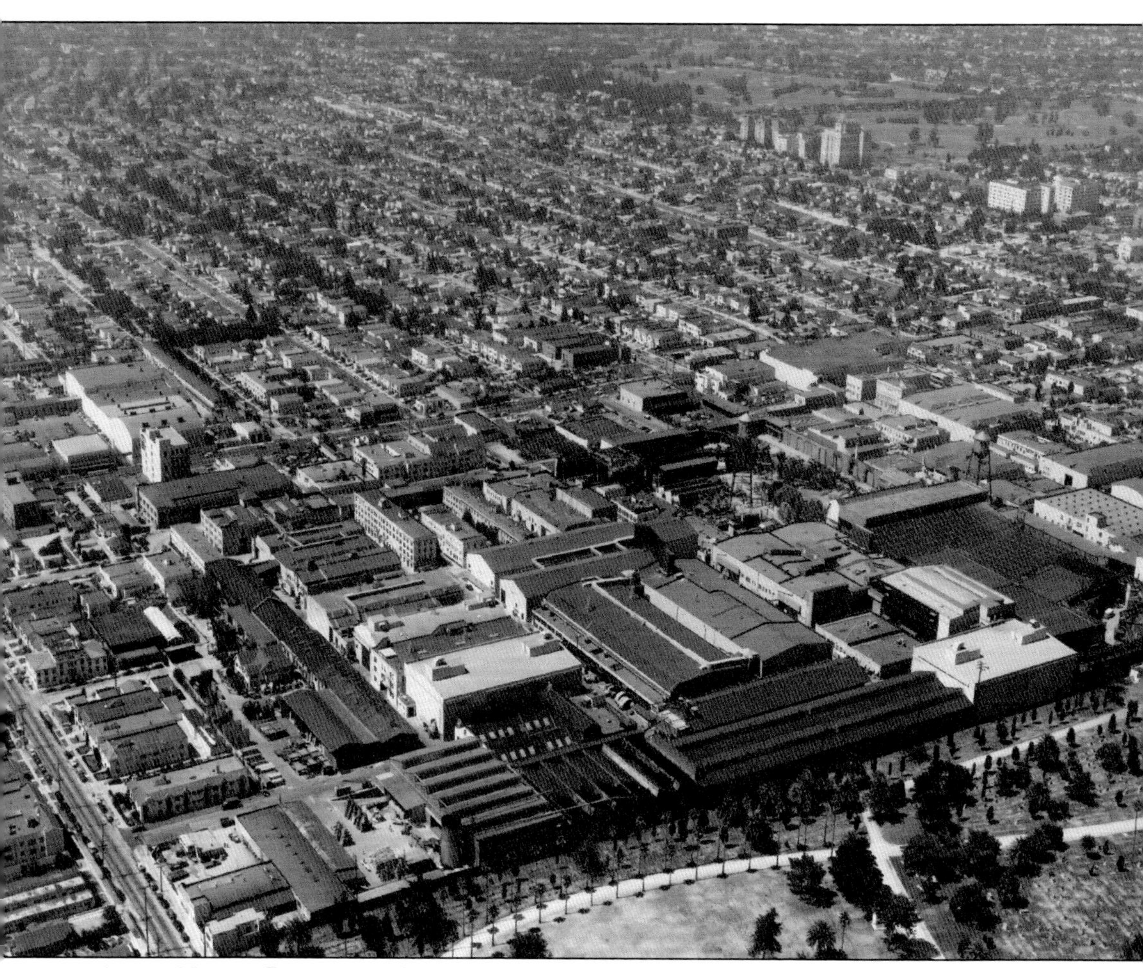

Aerial View of Paramount Studios, 1947. North of Larchmont Boulevard, at Melrose Avenue, is Paramount Studios. (Courtesy of the UCLA Spence Air Photo Collection.)

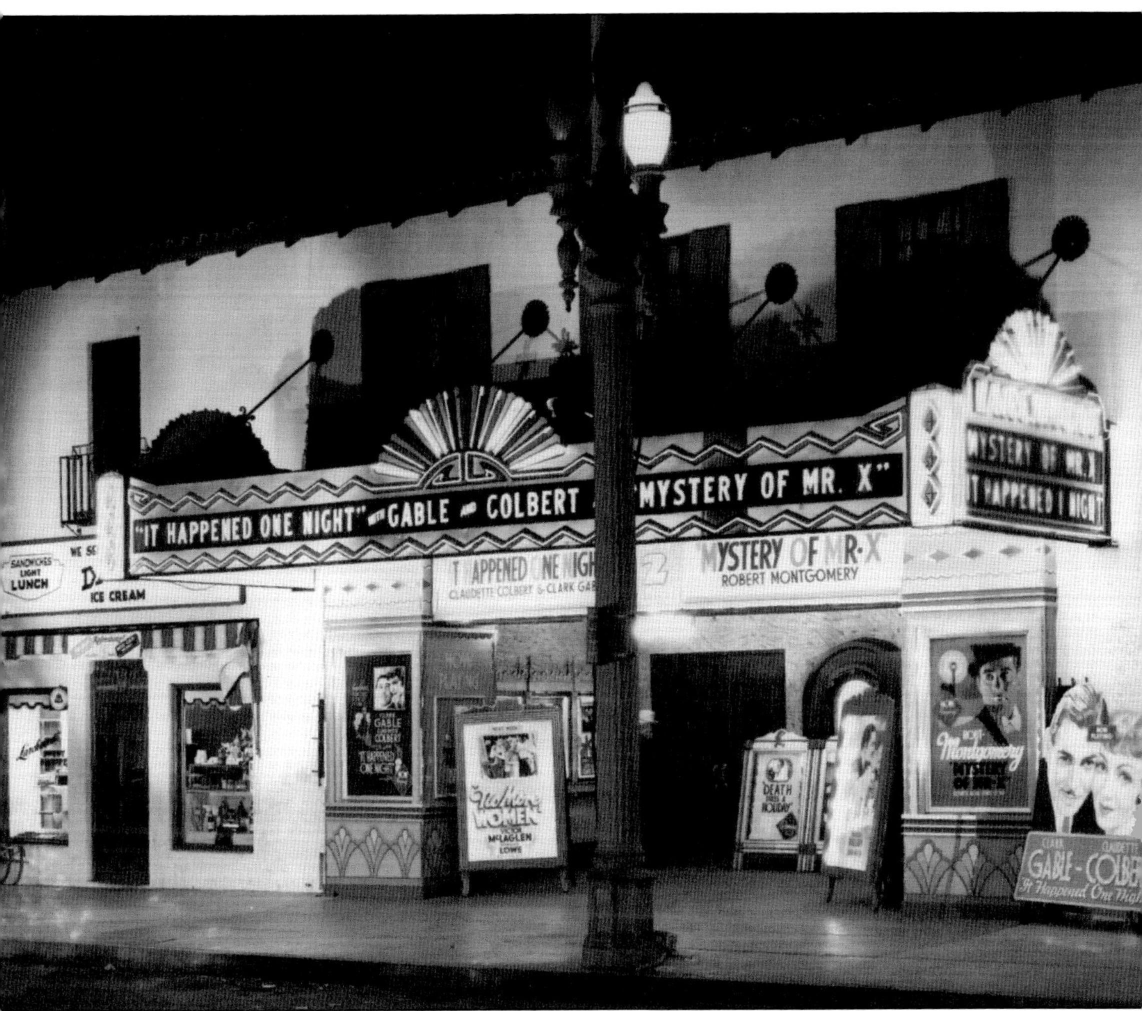

The Larchmont Theater, 1938. Built by Julius La Bonte at 155 North Larchmont Boulevard, the Larchmont Theater was a reinforced concrete construction of Mission Revival design. It was leased by Heinrich von Stein, founder of Von Stein's Academy of Music. The auditorium seated 900 people and featured an organ that cost $40,000 according to local news reports at the time. A string orchestra was brought in for movie presentations. The theater operated until the 1950s. Charlotte Lipson, daughter of Julius La Bonte, told UCLA student Michael Scott Copper in a 1975 oral history that the theater was her father's only architectural failure. In order to provide sloped seating, the floor of the theater was below the water table. Despite sealing the building, the theater flooded every time it rained. According to Lipson, her father filled in a stream that used to run along the west side of Larchmont and continue between Arden and Lucerne Boulevards. Perhaps this is the modern-day Arroyo del Jardin de las Flores that still flows through the Wilshire Country Club then underground until it surfaces in nearby Brookside. (Courtesy of Marc Wanamaker/Bison Archives.)

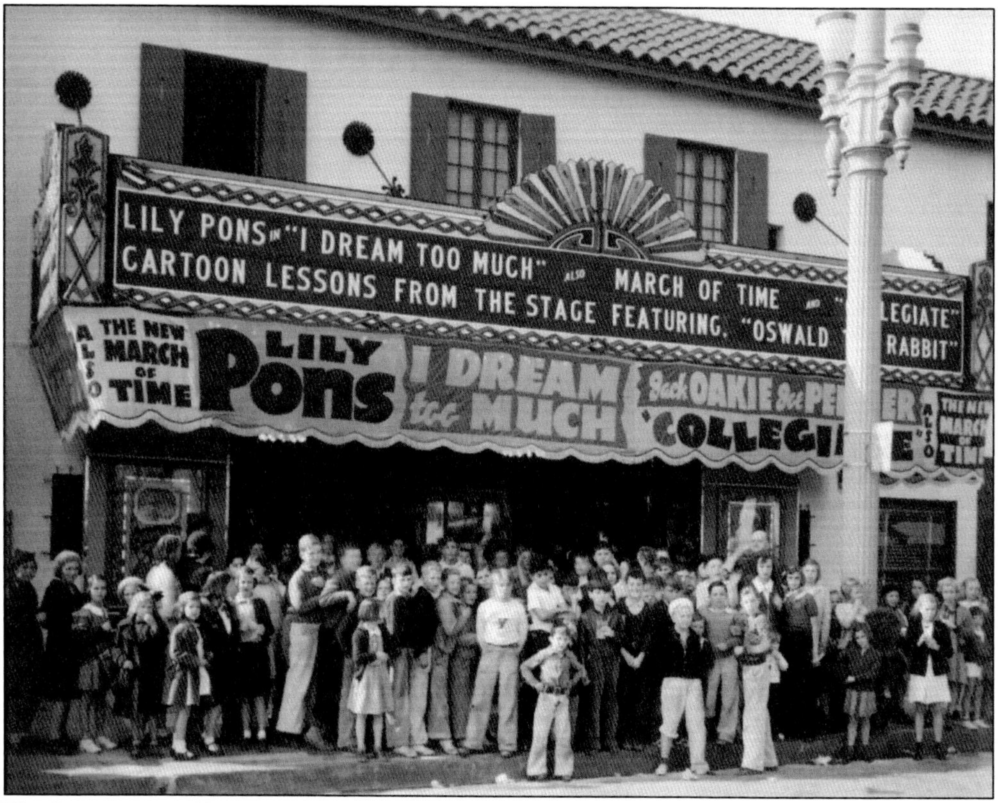

The Larchmont Theater, 1935. Children are waiting outside the theater for admission. The marquee promises "Cartoon Lessons from the Stage Featuring Oswald the Rabbit." Oswald the Rabbit was created by Ub Iwerks and Walt Disney for funny animal films distributed by Universal Pictures in the 1920s and 1930s. Also screening was *I Dream Too Much*, a 1935 romantic comedy directed by John Cromwell and starring Henry Fonda, Lily Pons, and Lucille Ball in one of her earliest roles. American radio news series broadcast *The March of Time* aired from 1931 to 1945. There was a companion newsreel series shown in movie theaters from 1935 to 1951. The marquee advertises presentation of the newest feature. (Courtesy of Bison Archives.)

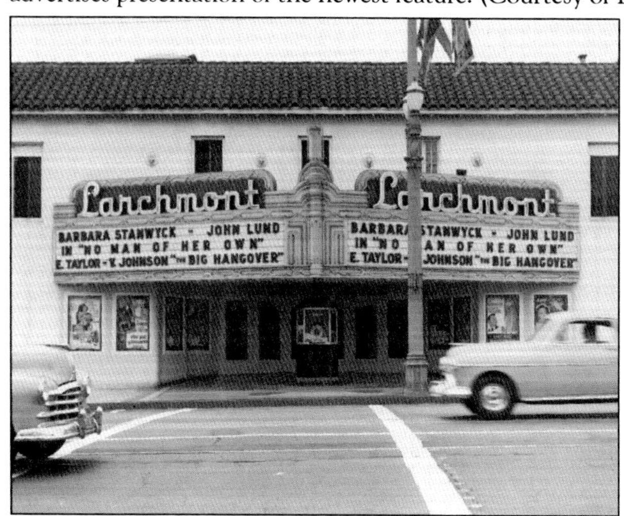

Larchmont Theater, c. 1950. The marquee advertises 1950 film noir feature *No Man of Her Own* with Barbara Stanwyck, John Lund, Phyllis Thaxter, Jane Cowl, and Lyle Bettger. It was directed by Mitchell Leisen. (Courtesy of Marc Wanamaker at Bison Archives.)

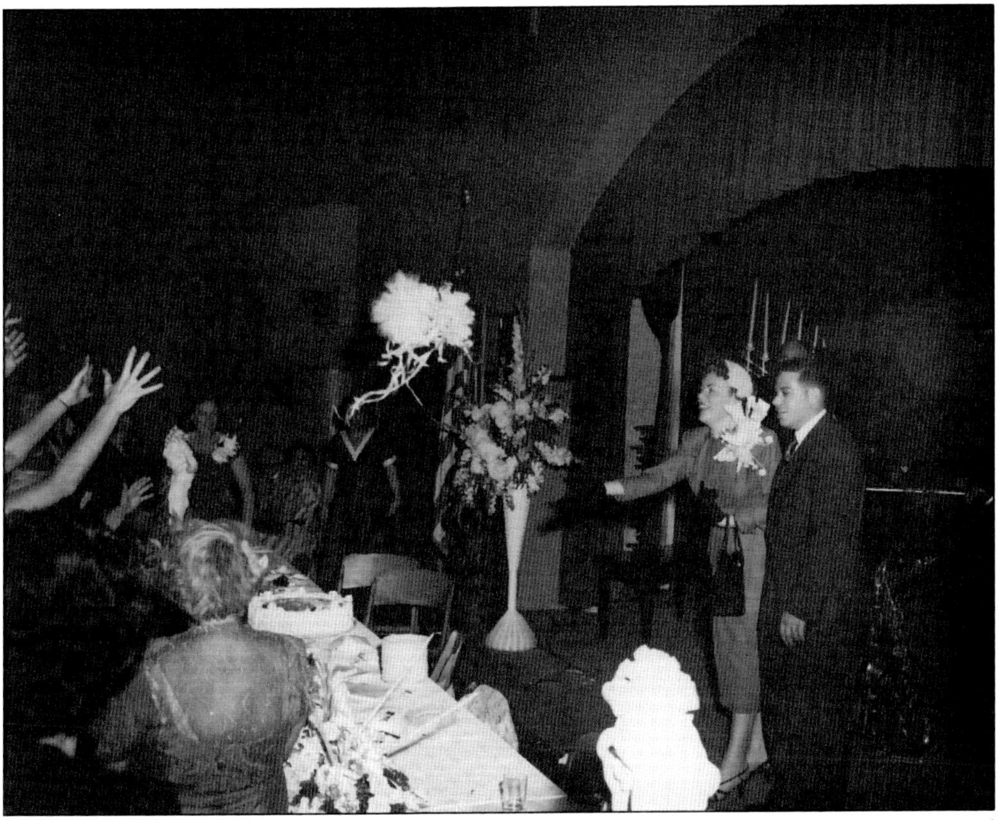

Finnerman-Lavitt Wedding at Larchmont Hall, 1954. Florence Shirley Lavitt married Harris Wayne Finnerman on October 2, 1954, at 7:30 p.m. in the Larchmont Hall at 118 North Larchmont Boulevard. Larchmont Hall was built in 1947. The original building on the site, constructed in 1928, held retail and offices. This image shows the interior of the hall, which featured a small stage that is still intact, though the current use of the building is an office. (Courtesy of Jason Lavitt.)

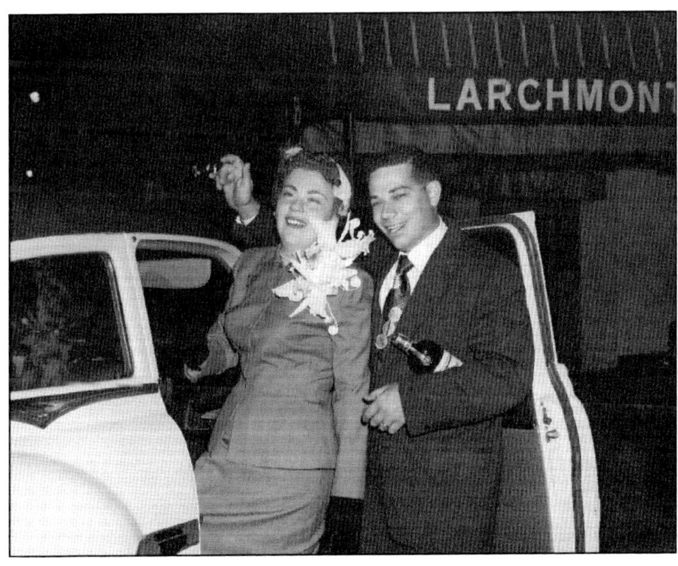

Mr. and Mrs. Finnerman Leaving Larchmont Hall. This photograph from the Finnerman wedding album shows the happy couple leaving the reception at Larchmont Hall. (Courtesy of Jason Lavitt.)

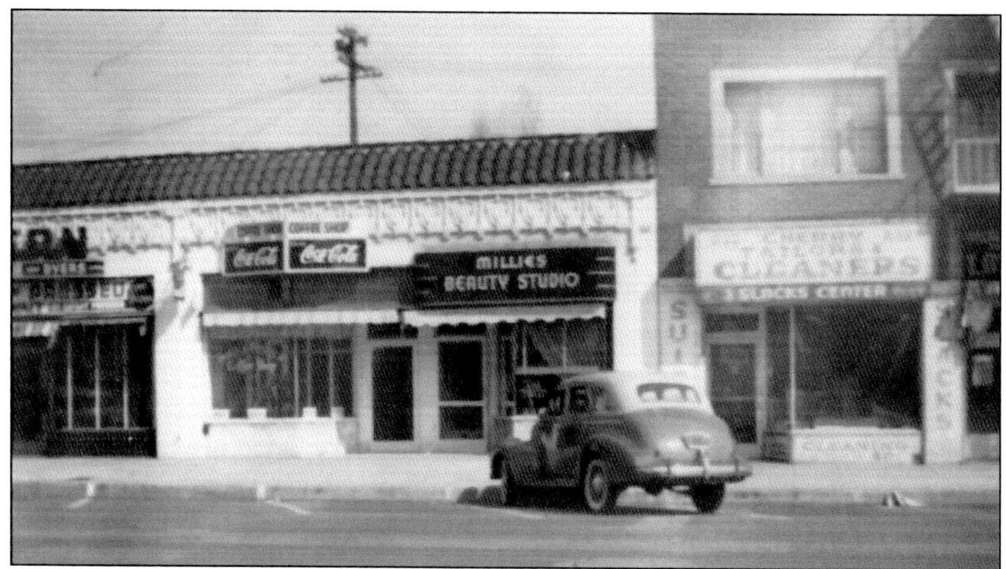

MILLIE'S BEAUTY STUDIO, c. 1942. This photograph displays a section of the east side of Larchmont Boulevard near the corner at Beverly Boulevard. The address of Millie's Beauty Studio is not shown, but the tailoring shop next door is 232 North Larchmont, so it is likely Millie's was at 234. The year is likely to be 1942, as the tailor, Morris Cohen, is listed in the 1942 Los Angeles telephone directory. The barrel tile roof and decorative plaster on the facade of the building are no longer there.

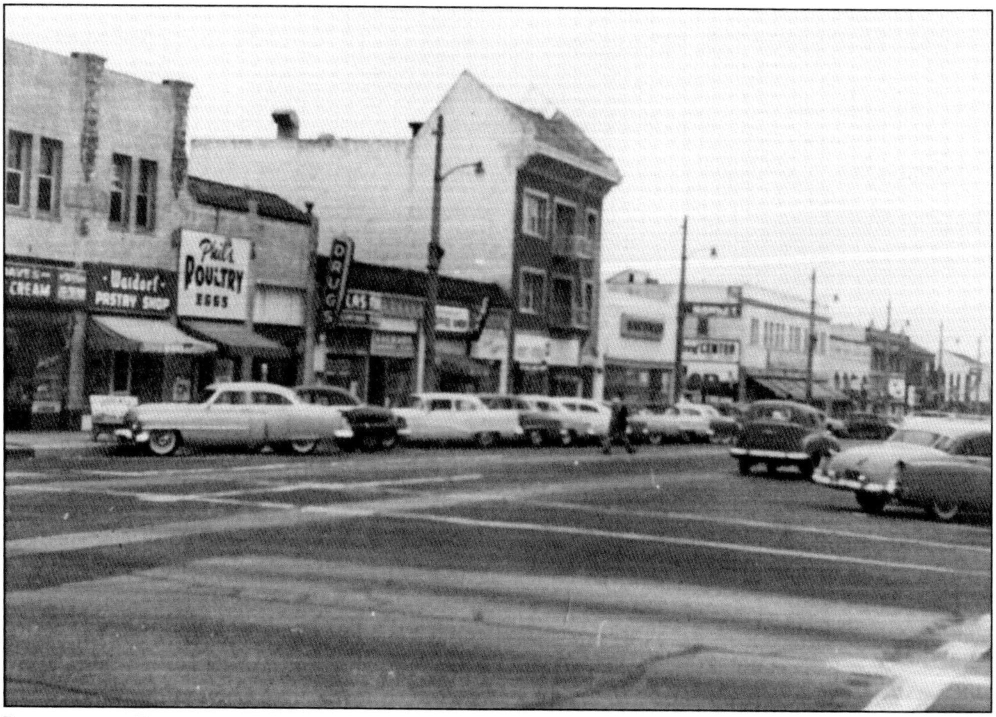

LARCHMONT BOULEVARD, c. 1950. Angled parking added to the village charm and made it easier for shoppers. This photograph shows the shops near Beverly Boulevard on the east side of the street. Phil's Poultry at 244 North Larchmont is listed in the 1956 Los Angeles telephone directory.

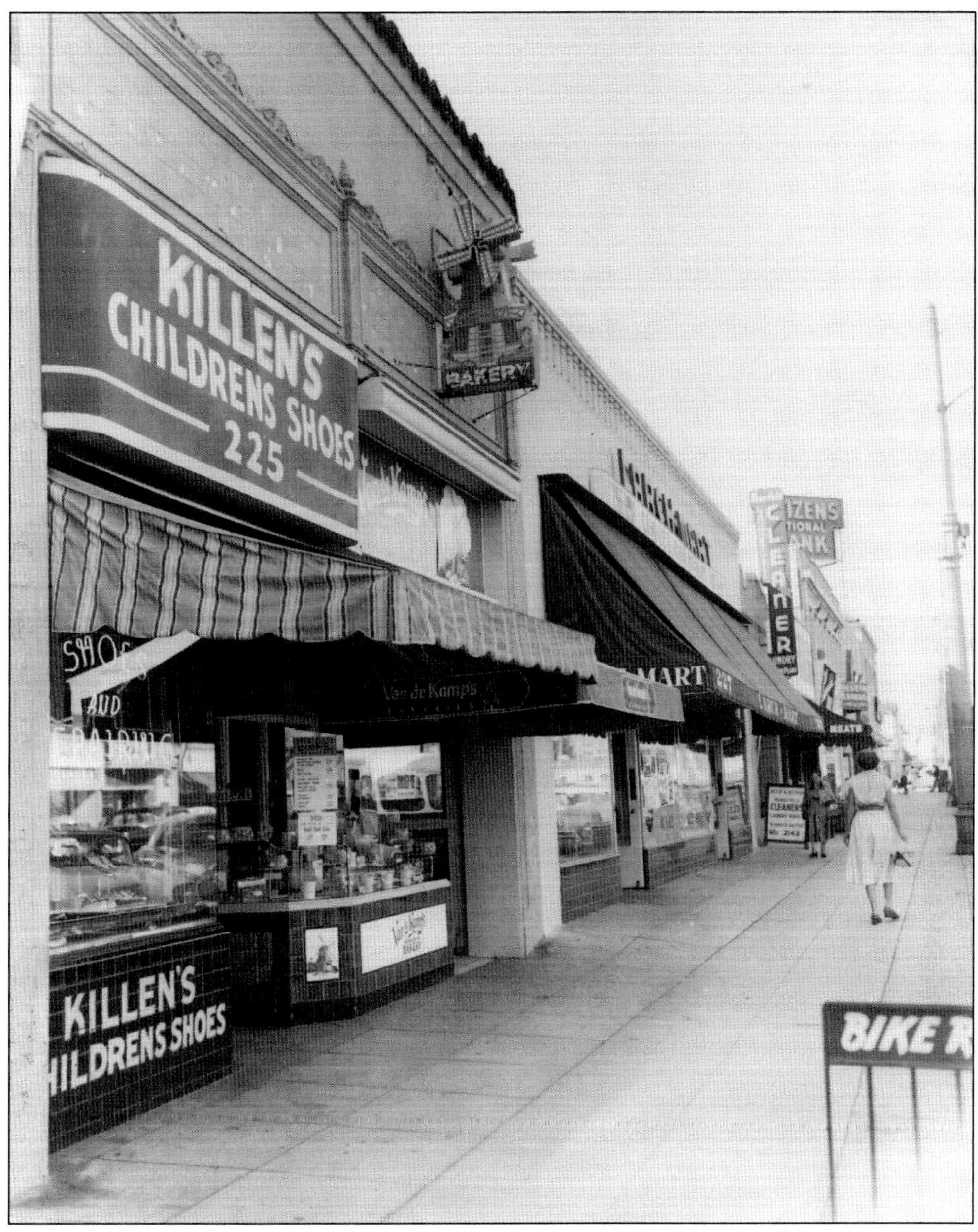

Killen's Children's Shoes at 225 North Larchmont, 1955. Shops and businesses moved up and down the street. Killen's Children's Shoes was listed in the 1936 Los Angeles telephone directory at 217 North Larchmont Boulevard and then in 1942 and 1956 at this location on Larchmont Boulevard.

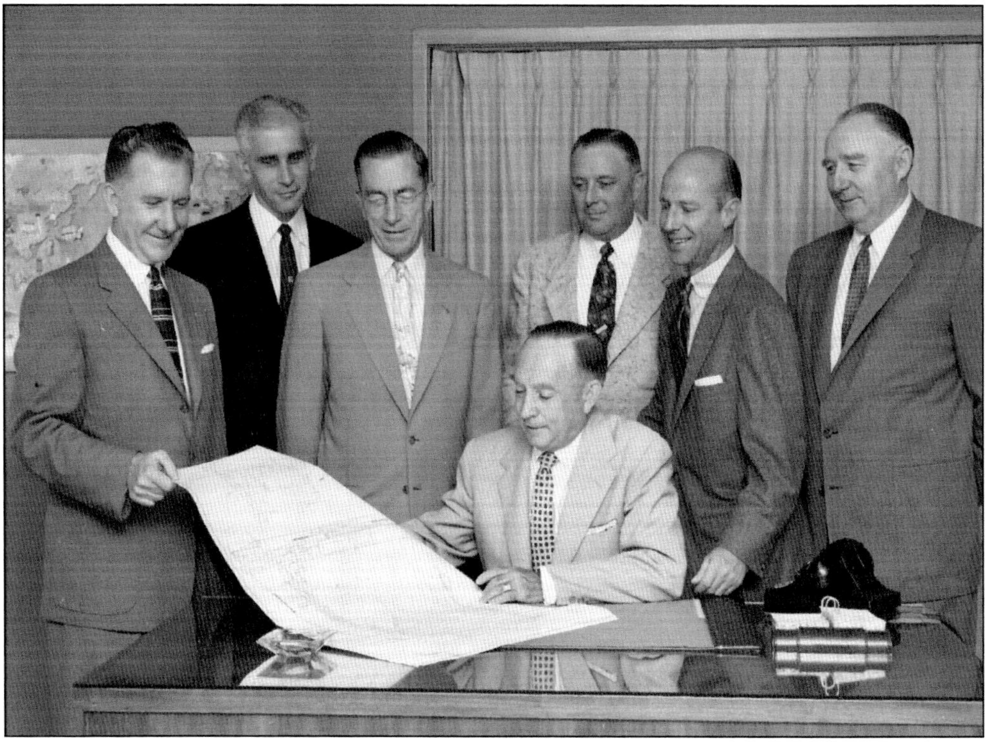

Los Angels City Councilman Harold Henry and Larchmont Leaders Review Plans for Larchmont Boulevard Improvements, 1955. With the help of city councilman Harold Henry and the Wilshire Chamber of Commerce, business leaders implemented improvements that included removing the streetcar tracks and utility poles, repaving the streets, and planting over 40 trees. Pictured with city councilman Harold Henry (seated at desk) are, from left to right, Lee Etheridge, manager of Security First National Bank; Joe Chevalier, owner of Chevalier's Books; Frank Mann, chairman of the chamber's small business committee; Jack Killingsworth, vice president and manager of Citizen National Bank; Robert Balzer, owner of Balzer's; and Albert Dippell, owner of Dippell Realty Company. (Courtesy of the *Larchmont Chronicle* and *Los Angeles Times*.)

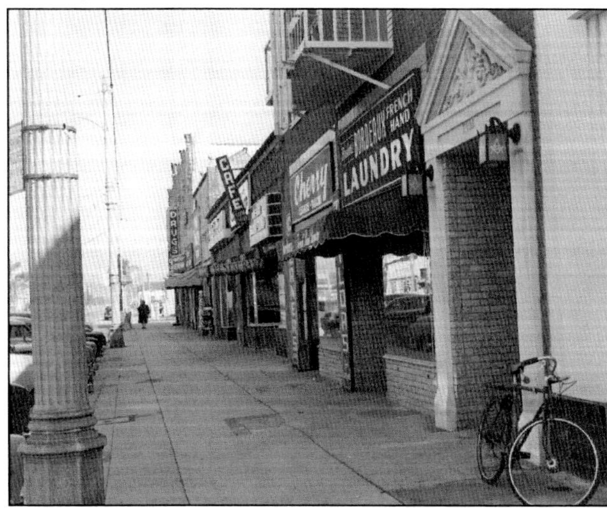

230 North Larchmont Boulevard, 1952. Here is a view of the east side of Larchmont, near Beverly Boulevard, before the installation of trees.

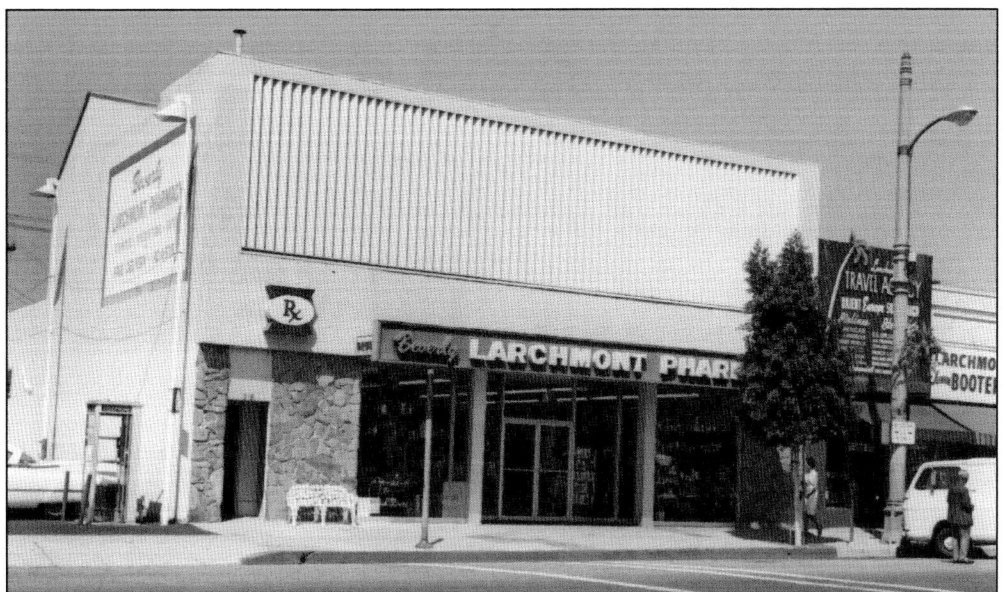

Beverly Larchmont Pharmacy at 217 North Larchmont. The Beverly Larchmont Pharmacy, owned by Bill Schulhoff, was the place for all things medical and a wide array of beauty products. The store had 15,000 to 20,000 different items and 11 salespeople to offer personalized service.

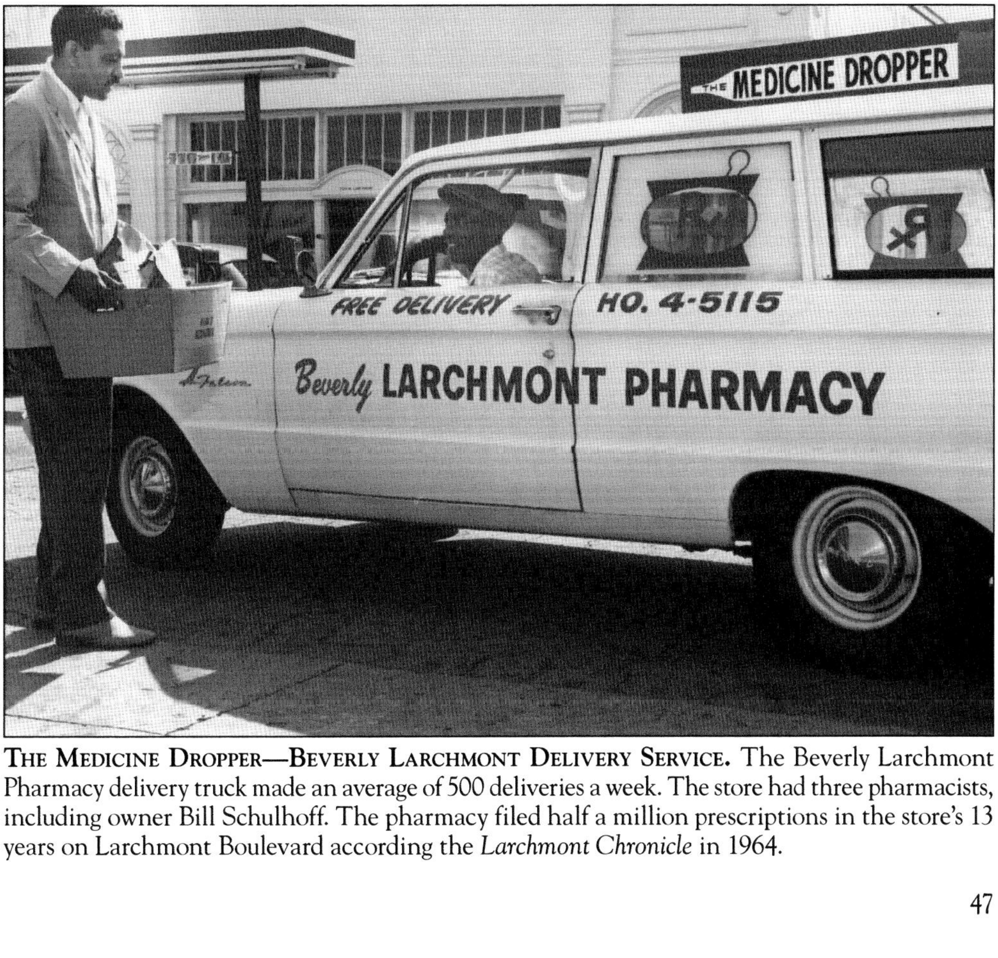

The Medicine Dropper—Beverly Larchmont Delivery Service. The Beverly Larchmont Pharmacy delivery truck made an average of 500 deliveries a week. The store had three pharmacists, including owner Bill Schulhoff. The pharmacy filed half a million prescriptions in the store's 13 years on Larchmont Boulevard according the *Larchmont Chronicle* in 1964.

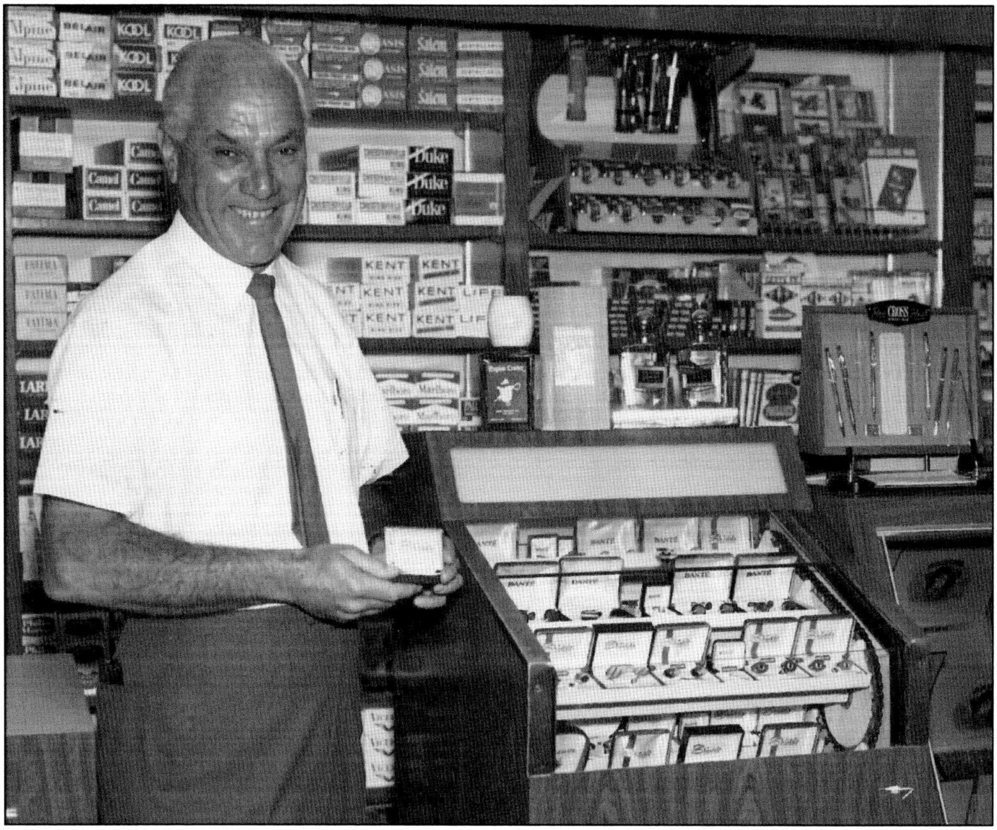

At the Shields Jewelry Display, Bill Schulhoff Suggests a Money Clip as a Suitable Gift for a Man. Bill Schulhoff graduated from the University of Southern California School of Pharmacy in 1939. He established the pharmacy in 1951 at the corner of Larchmont and Beverly Boulevards before relocating to 217 North Larchmont in 1960. In the October 1963 edition of the *Larchmont Chronicle*, Schulhoff urged parents to get vaccines for their children in his "To Your Health" advice column. He also served as president of the Larchmont Businessmen's Association in 1964.

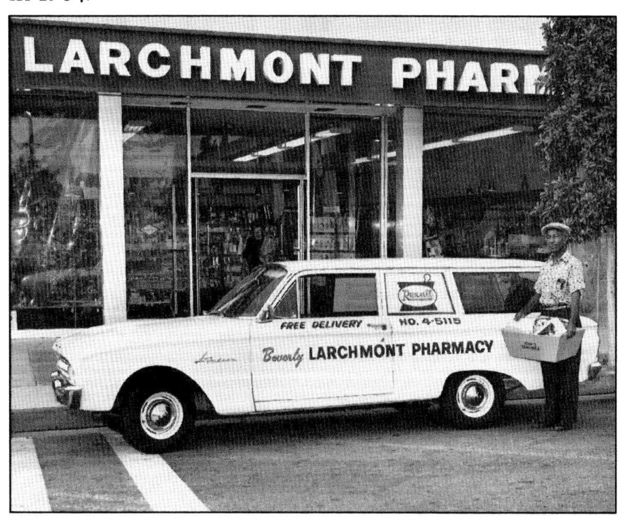

The Beverly Larchmont Pharmacy Delivery Truck. The delivery truck prepares for a daily run of deliveries to customers in the neighborhood.

FAMILY ON LARCHMONT BOULEVARD, C. 1960. Larchmont Boulevard shops and businesses always catered to families, with a number of shops offering fine clothing and shoes for children. This photograph was taken in front of 205 North Larchmont Boulevard at Naomi Price Gary Fashions, which carried elegant clothing for women.

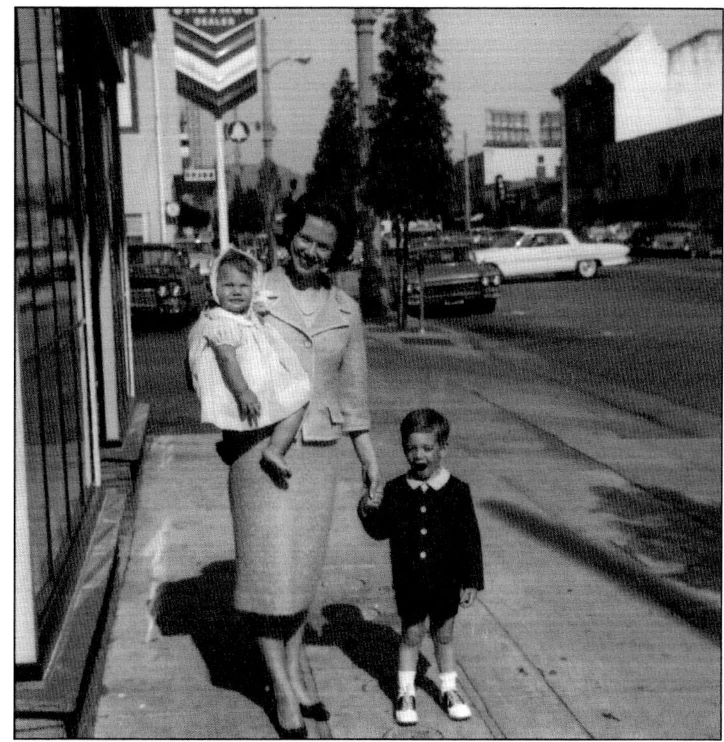

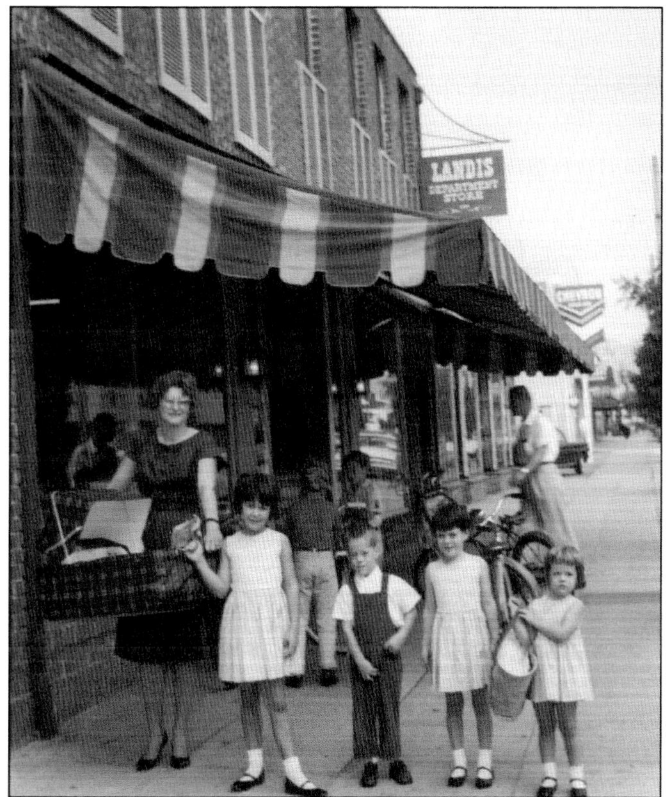

FAMILY SHOPPING ON LARCHMONT BOULEVARD, 1960. Landis Department Store carried everything a growing family needed, from clothing to toys. Children were welcome to shop in the store since the Landis staff knew everyone. Children were also very well behaved.

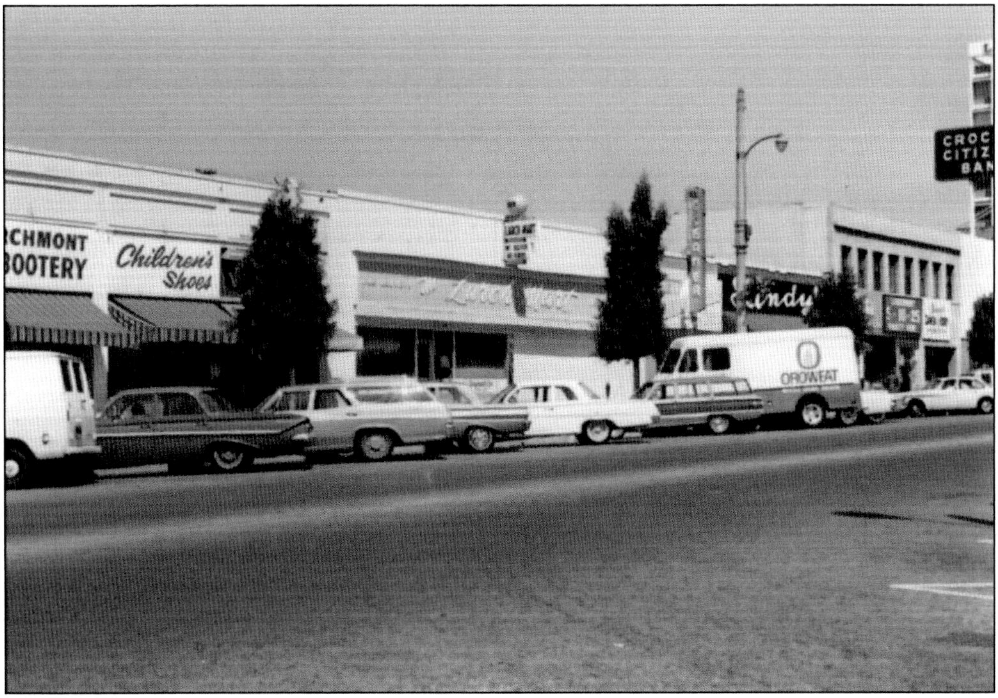

SHOPS ON THE WEST SIDE OF LARCHMONT BOULEVARD NEAR BEVERLY BOULEVARD, C. 1960. Larchmont Boulevard was populated with retail shops and businesses that served the neighborhood. Travel agents, tailors, dry cleaners, banks, and grocery stores were the mainstay of the street.

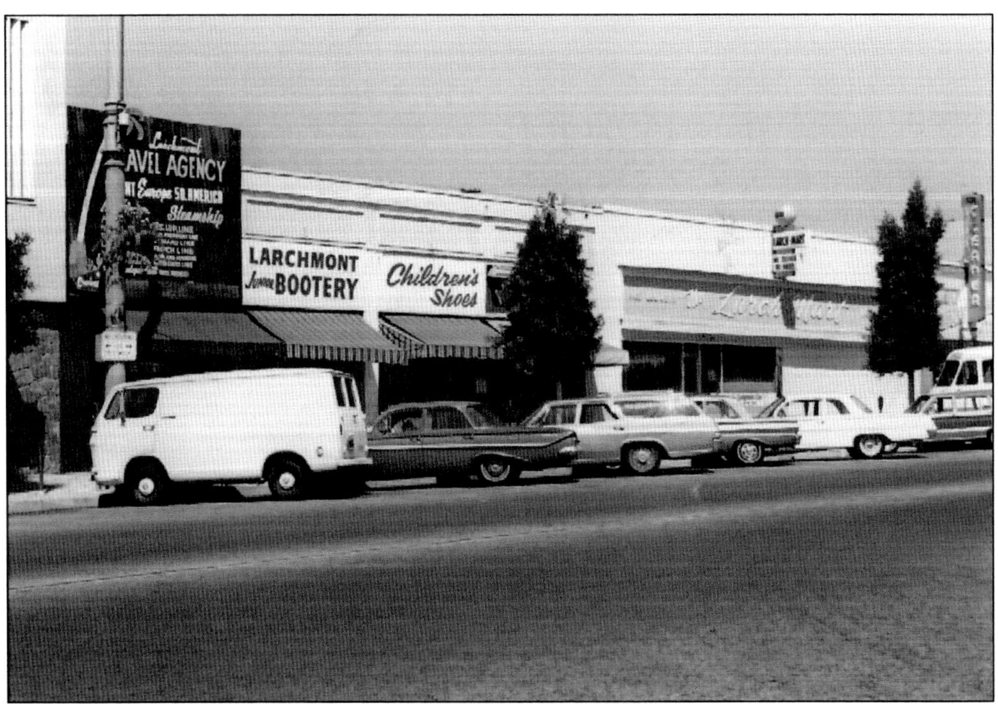

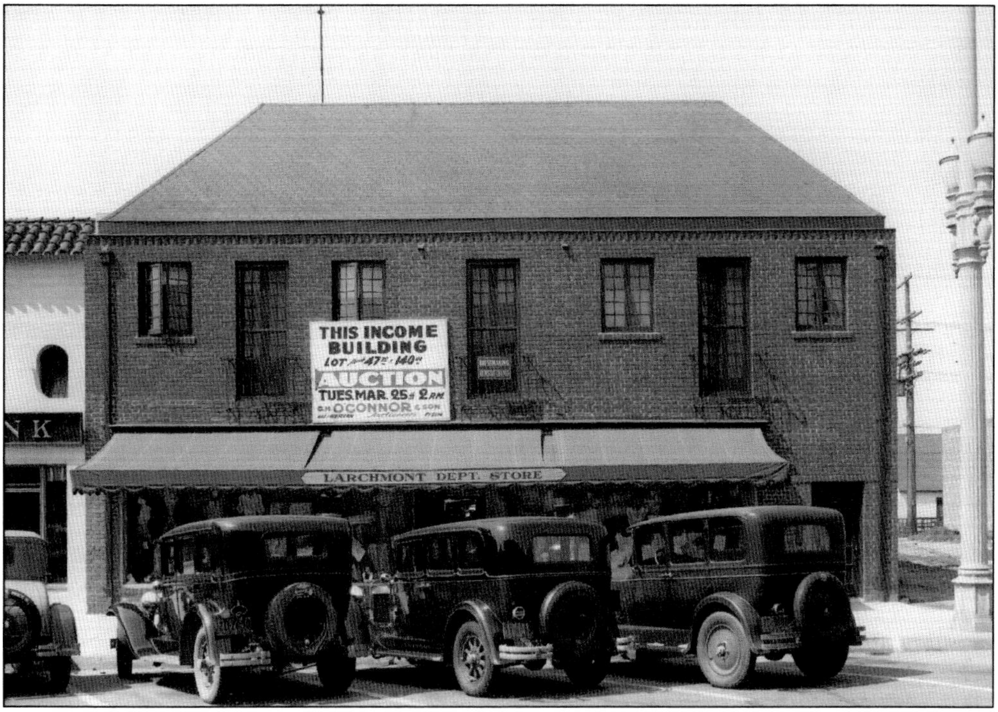

LARCHMONT DEPARTMENT STORE, 1930. Arthur Landis, considered a Larchmont pioneer, purchased the dry goods store with a loan of $400 and doubled the floor space by 1938. Born in Sterling, Illinois, in 1894, Landis moved to Los Angeles in 1905 and graduated from Los Angeles High School. He opened his first store in 1926 at Fifty-Ninth Street and Broadway and eventually operated seven stores until the Depression hit. (Courtesy of Marc Wanamaker at Bison Archives.)

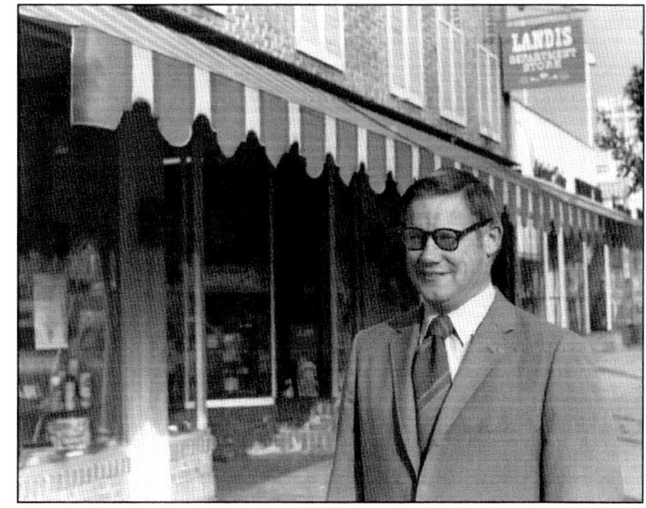

BOB LANDIS, OWNER OF LANDIS DEPARTMENT STORE, FORMERLY LARCHMONT DEPARTMENT STORE. Bob Landis grew up working in the store founded by his father, Arthur. He officially joined the family business in 1948 and devoted the rest of his life to the store and the Larchmont Boulevard community. Landis served as president of the Larchmont Boulevard Association and was supported by his wife, Betty, and their children, who all worked in the store and knew every customer by name.

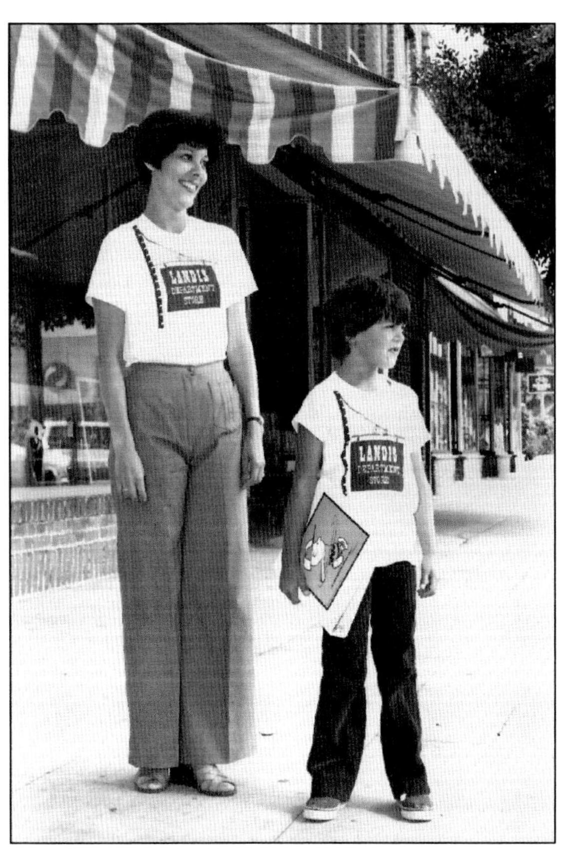

LANDIS DEPARTMENT STORE CUSTOMERS. Landis family members were good advertising for the family-run store that served the street until it closed in 1990. The name and the tradition of personal service continue at 138 North Larchmont Boulevard at Landis Gifts and Stationary, operated by Edie Frere, who Landis allowed to use the name.

LANDIS FAMILY AT CHRISTMAS. The Landis Department Store Christmas open house was a holiday season highlight, featuring sherbet punch and butter cookies.

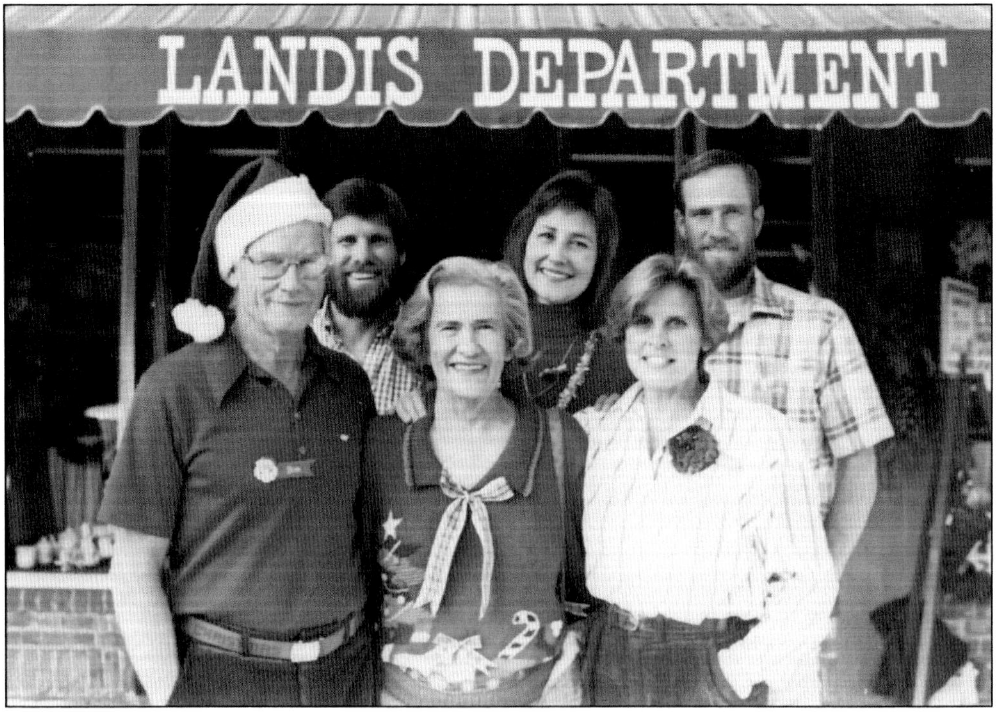

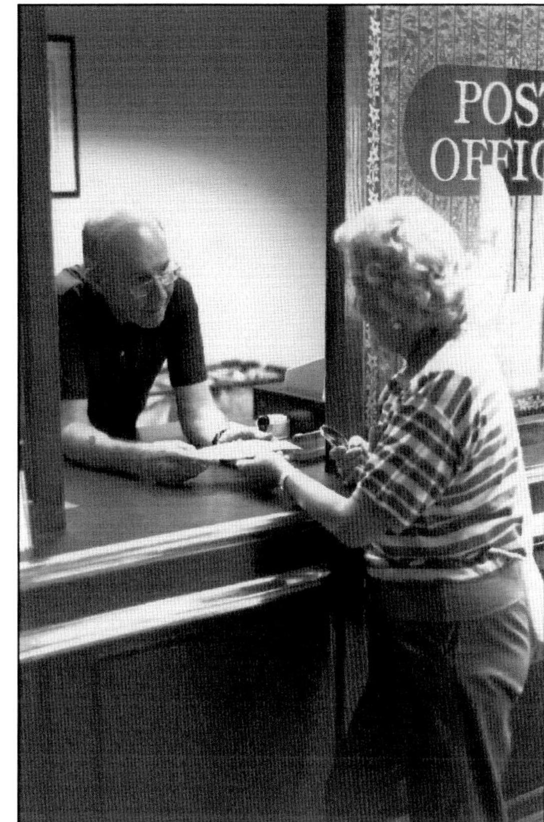

Landis Department Store Post Office. A small post office branch was located in Landis Department Store as a service for neighborhood customers.

Bob Landis Honored for Years of Service to Larchmont Community. In this image, city councilman John Ferraro (second from left) presents the Landis Lane sign to Bob Landis (far right), along with Tim Grogan (far left) and Bettie Landis. Landis served as president of the Larchmont Boulevard Association in 1985.

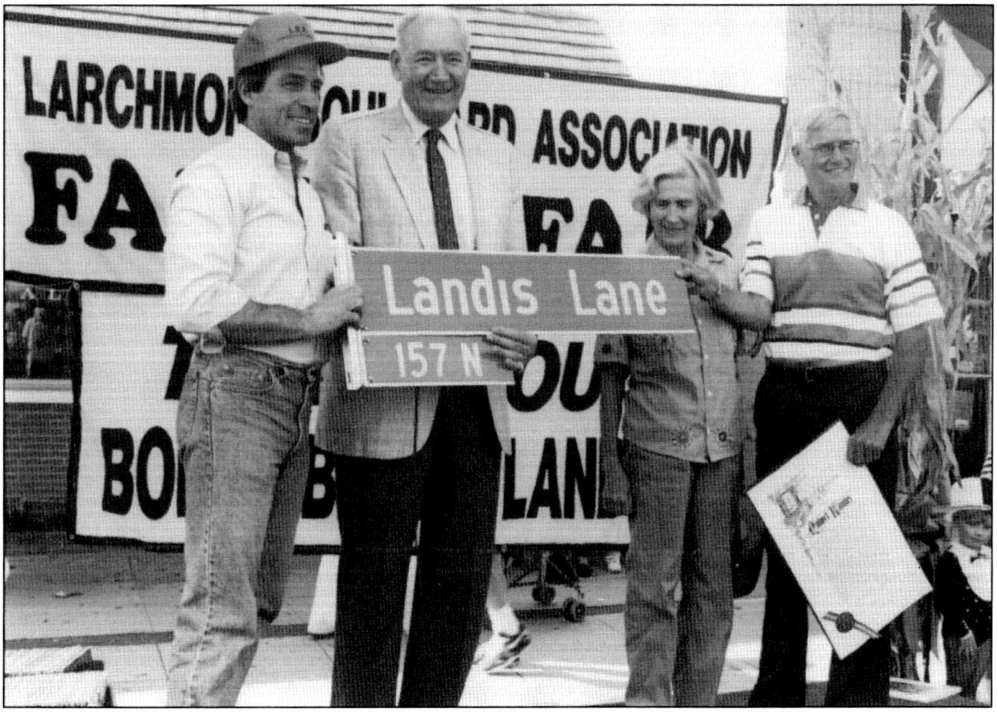

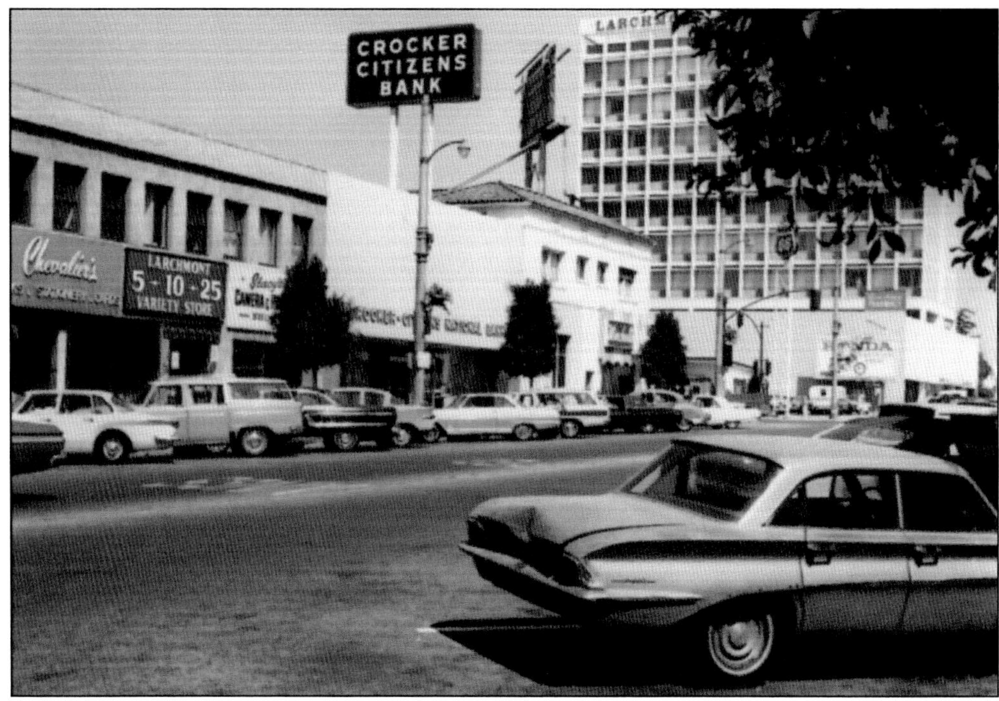

CHEVALIER'S AT 239 NORTH LARCHMONT, 1964. J.W. "Joe" Chevalier moved to Larchmont in 1940, when he opened his bookstore at 239 North Larchmont Boulevard. Chevalier was a director of the Larchmont Boulevard Association and former president of the Southern California Booksellers Association from 1962 to 1963.

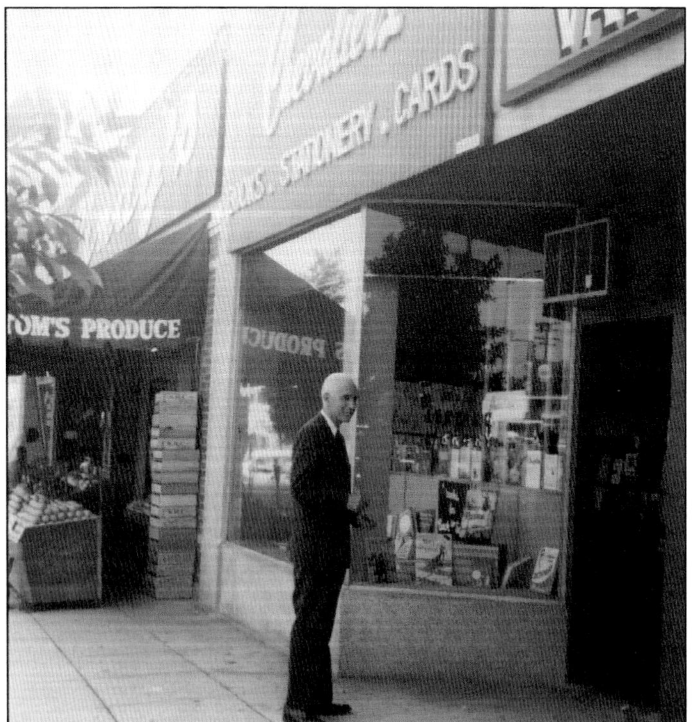

JOE CHEVALIER IN FRONT OF HIS STORE. Chevalier's became one of the most important independent book stores in the city. New York publishing houses regularly paid visits to Chevalier, seeking his advice on how to successfully market their books in Los Angeles.

JOE CHEVALIER AT 126 NORTH LARCHMONT. Chevalier was an avid reader and loved books. His home library contained close to 1,900 books, including some rare editions.

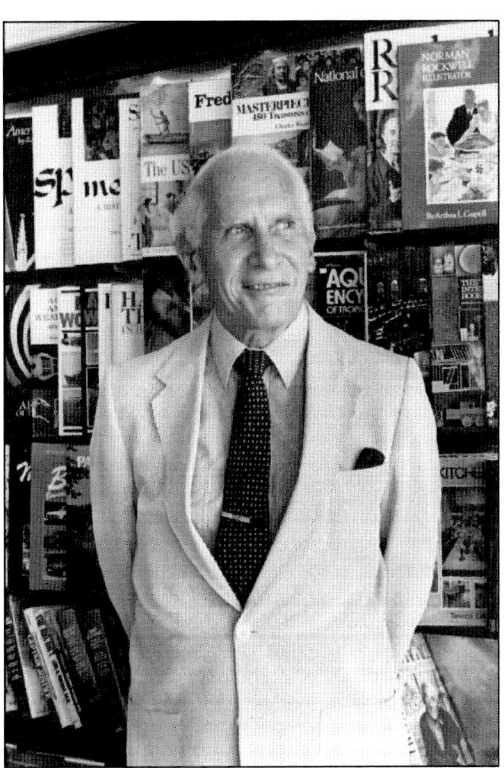

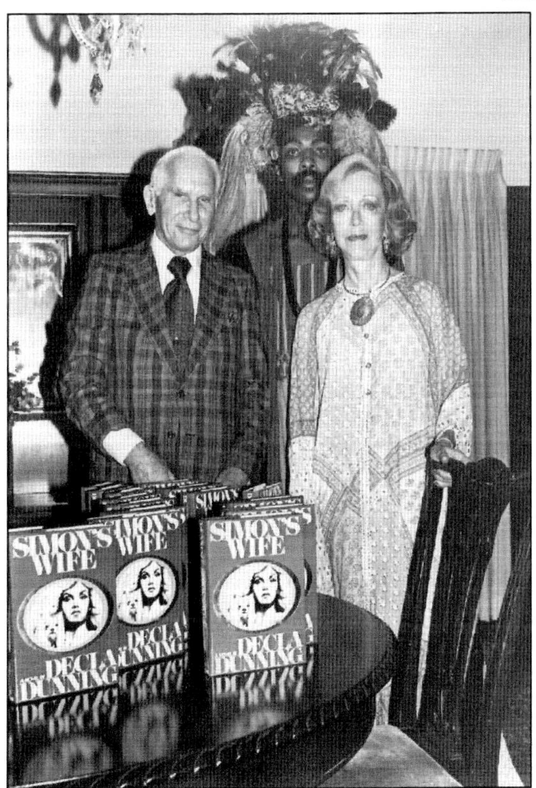

JOE CHEVALIER WITH DECLA DUNNING. Chevalier is pictured with Decla Dunning at a book signing for *Simon's Wife: A Novel*, published in 1980. Dunning was a screenwriter, and her most famous feature was *The Stranger*, which she cowrote with Anthony Veiller and Victor Trivas. The film was directed by Orson Welles and released in 1946.

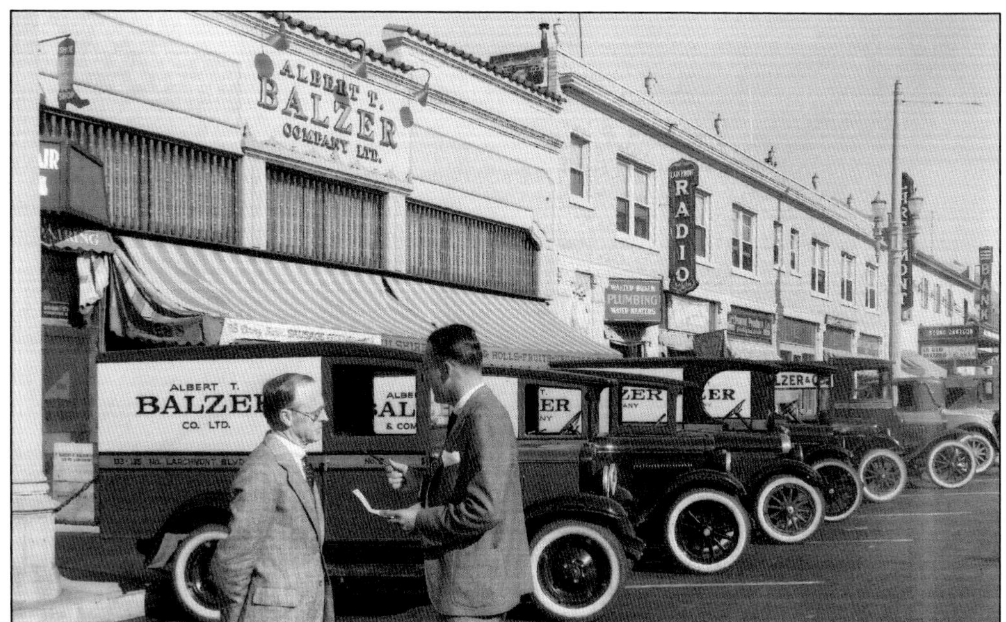

ALBERT T. BALZER COMPANY DELIVERY FLEET. Balzer and Company catered to wealthy residents, offering personal service and the finest selection of quality gourmet foods. Business was conducted by charge and delivery, and customers bought in quantity and quality. Canned goods were sold by the case. Sugar and flour were sold in sacks of 100 and 200 pounds, making delivery essential. The store sold a ton of cheddar each month. In this image, Balzer's executives are shown in front of their delivery truck fleet for what was most likely a photograph for an advertisement. This image was taken by a photographer from Dick Whittington Studio for the firm Nelson & Price, Inc., who sold automobile tires in Los Angeles. (Courtesy of Dick Whittington Studio/Corbis.)

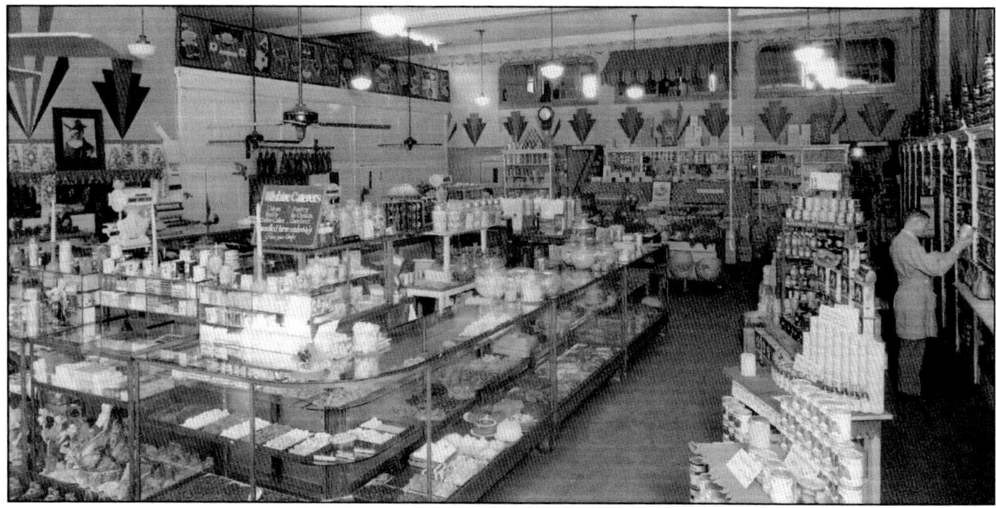

INTERIOR OF BALZER AND COMPANY AT 133 NORTH LARCHMONT. Albert Taylor Balzer started his career in the grocery business in Des Moines, Iowa. He sold his business and moved to California to get away from the cold. Balzer became part of the westward expansion of the city and purchased Hughes Market at 133 North Larchmont Boulevard in 1923. In 1926, after outgrowing the space, he moved the market—now called Albert T. Balzer Company—to a larger facility at 133–135 North Larchmont. (Courtesy of Marc Wanamaker at Bison Archives.)

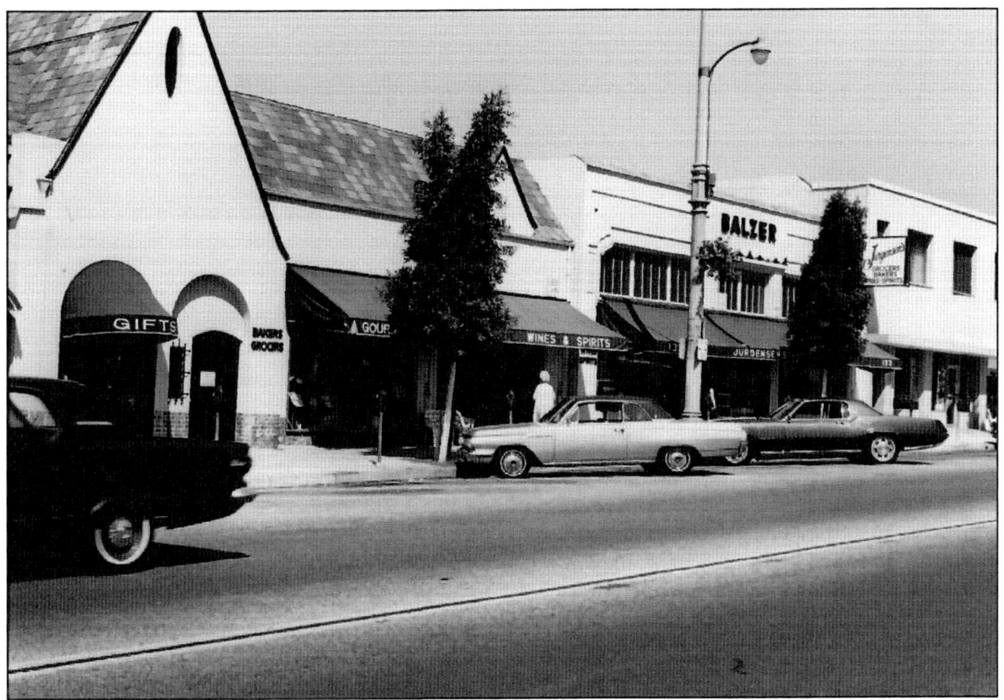

Street View of Balzer's at 133–135 North Larchmont. Balzer's was operated by family members who learned the business and then went off to start their own stores in Hollywood and the San Fernando Valley. Balzer's operated on the simple principle of honest business ethics and quality in every endeavor. Balzer died in 1952 at the age of 75. In 1959, Robert Balzer sold the store to Harold Jurgensen.

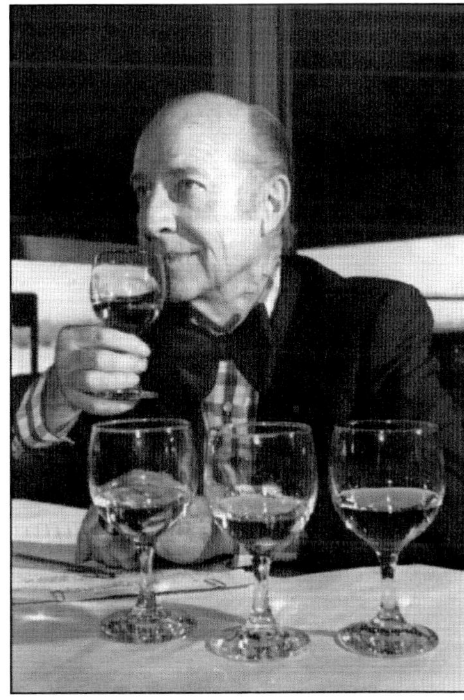

Robert Lawrence Balzer. In an autobiography in *Friends of Wine* magazine, Balzer notes that his great-grandfather, confectioner G.A. Balzer, catered Abraham Lincoln's second inaugural. He joined his father's business in 1936 after studying at the Royal Academy of Dramatic Arts in London. His father told him to buy wines, so Balzer became a student of wine and, eventually, a very influential wine columnist for the *Los Angeles Times*. Balzer championed the California wine industry. During his tenure, he expanded the store, opening a wine cellar and gift shop. Balzer was considered the dean of American wine writers by *Wine Spectator* magazine, which honored him in 2002 on his 90th birthday. Balzer was invited to oversee the inaugural party for Ronald Reagan in 1985 and George Bush in 1989.

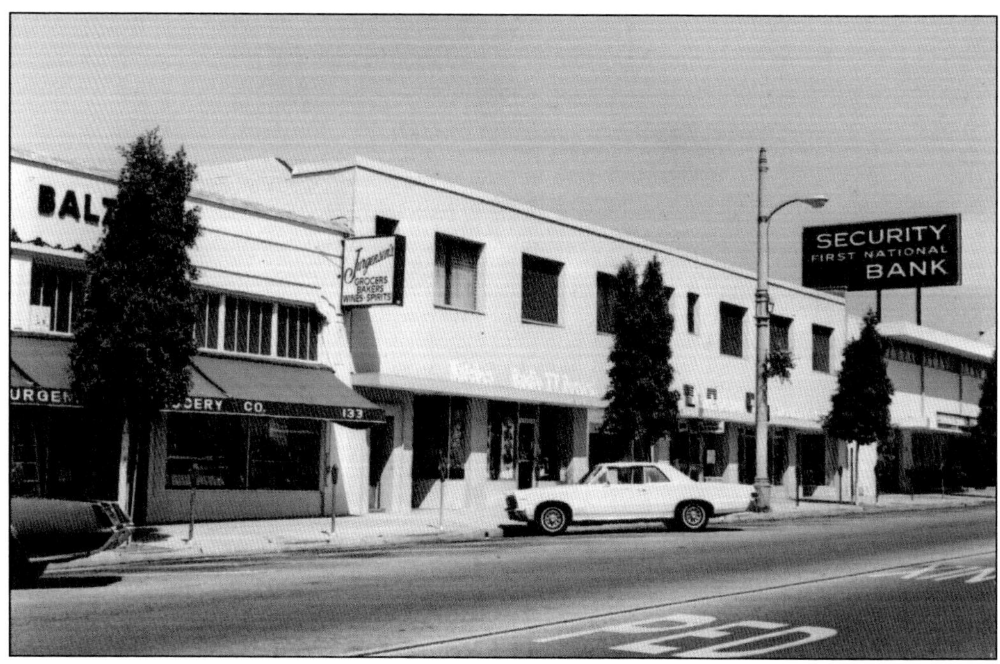

Jurgensen's Market at 133 North Larchmont. Customers appreciated Jurgensen's as they had Balzer's. Actress Mae West was reported to be a frequent shopper. Jurgensen's was founded in Pasadena in 1935 and catered to wealthy families and celebrities who preferred to have their gourmet delicacies and groceries delivered. At one time, there were 22 stores; the last one closed in 1993. The Larchmont store closed in the late 1980s.

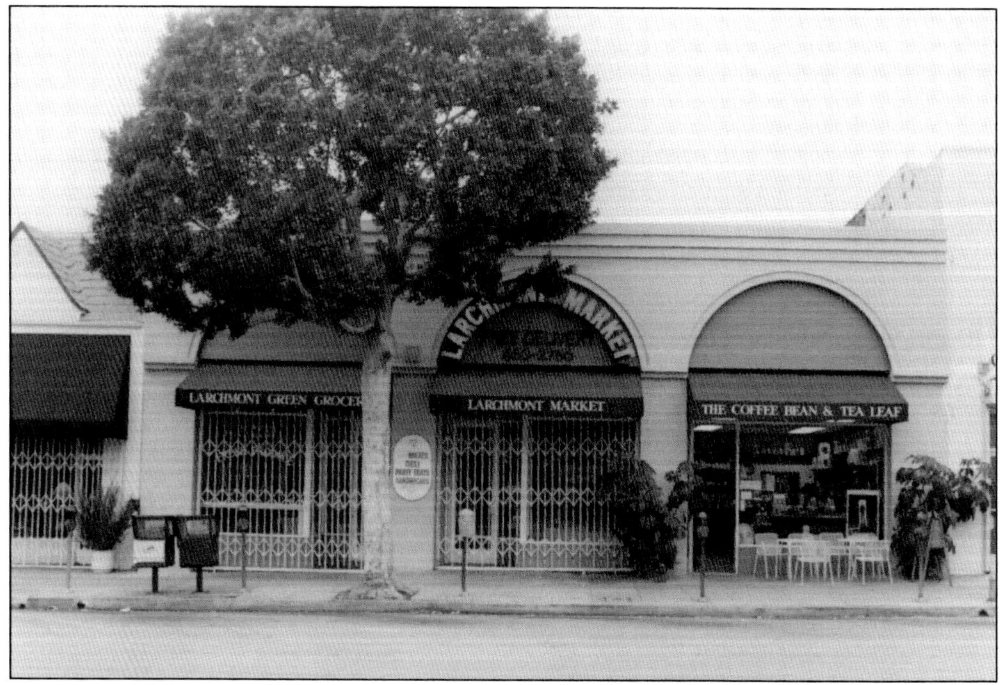

Larchmont Market at 133 North Larchmont, c. 1990. Various grocers tried to fill the shoes of Balzer's and Jurgensen's, but none had the longevity of their predecessors.

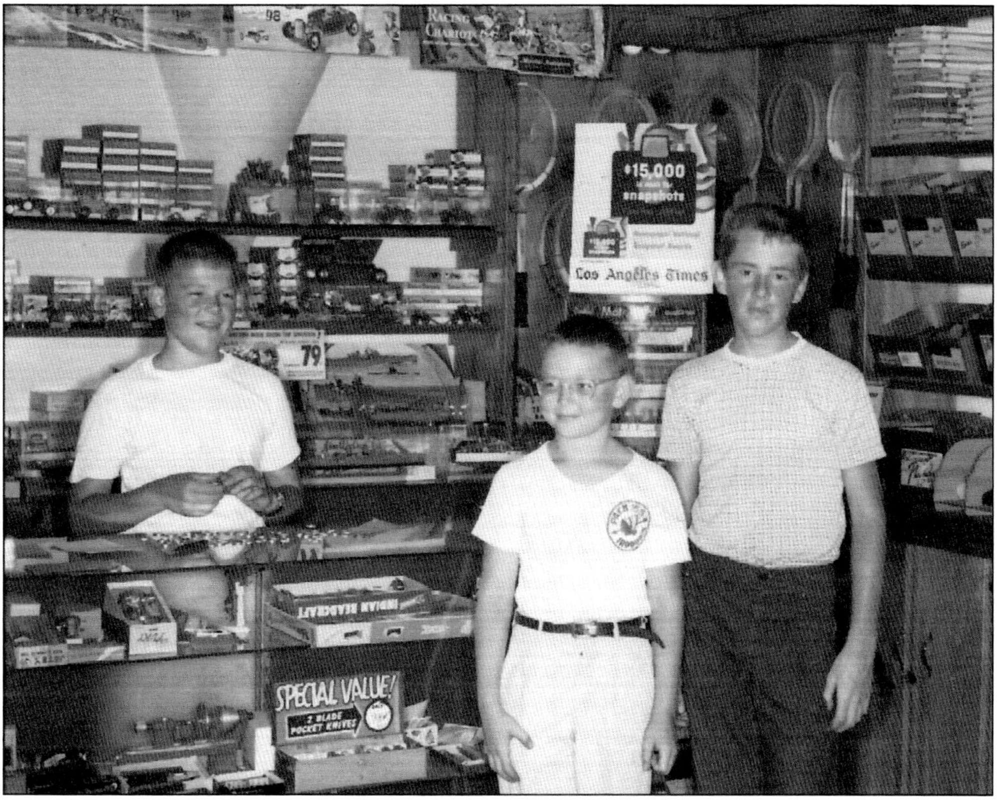

WESTERN CAMERA SPORTS AND HOBBIES AT 241 NORTH LARCHMONT, C. 1956. Enthusiastic shoppers from the neighborhood enjoy the offerings of a great hobby and sports shop.

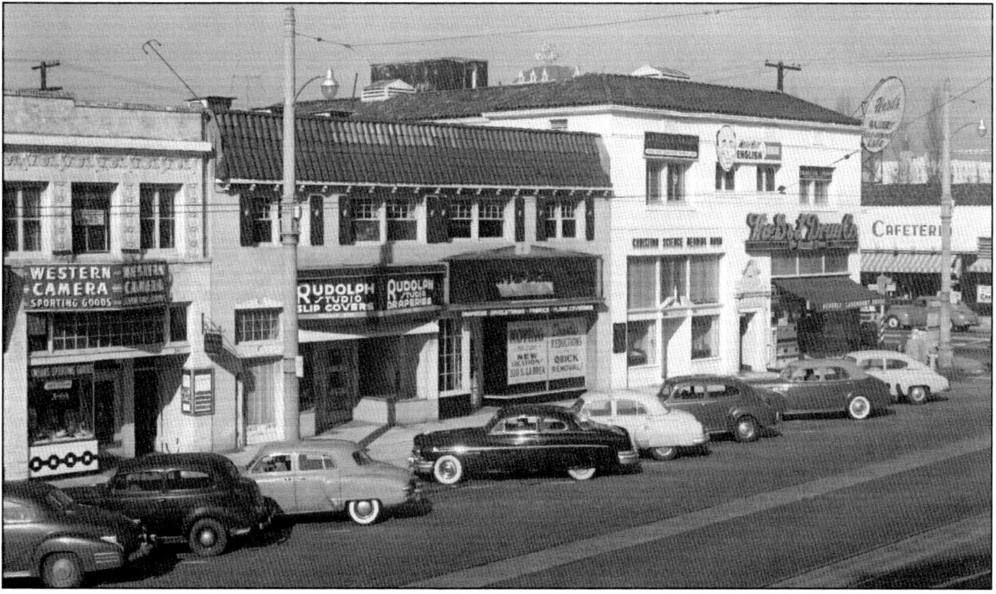

STREET VIEW OF THE WEST SIDE OF LARCHMONT NEAR BEVERLY BOULEVARD, 1952. Storefronts along Larchmont included services for the home as well as a Christian Science reading room. (Courtesy of Marc Wanamaker at Bison Archives.)

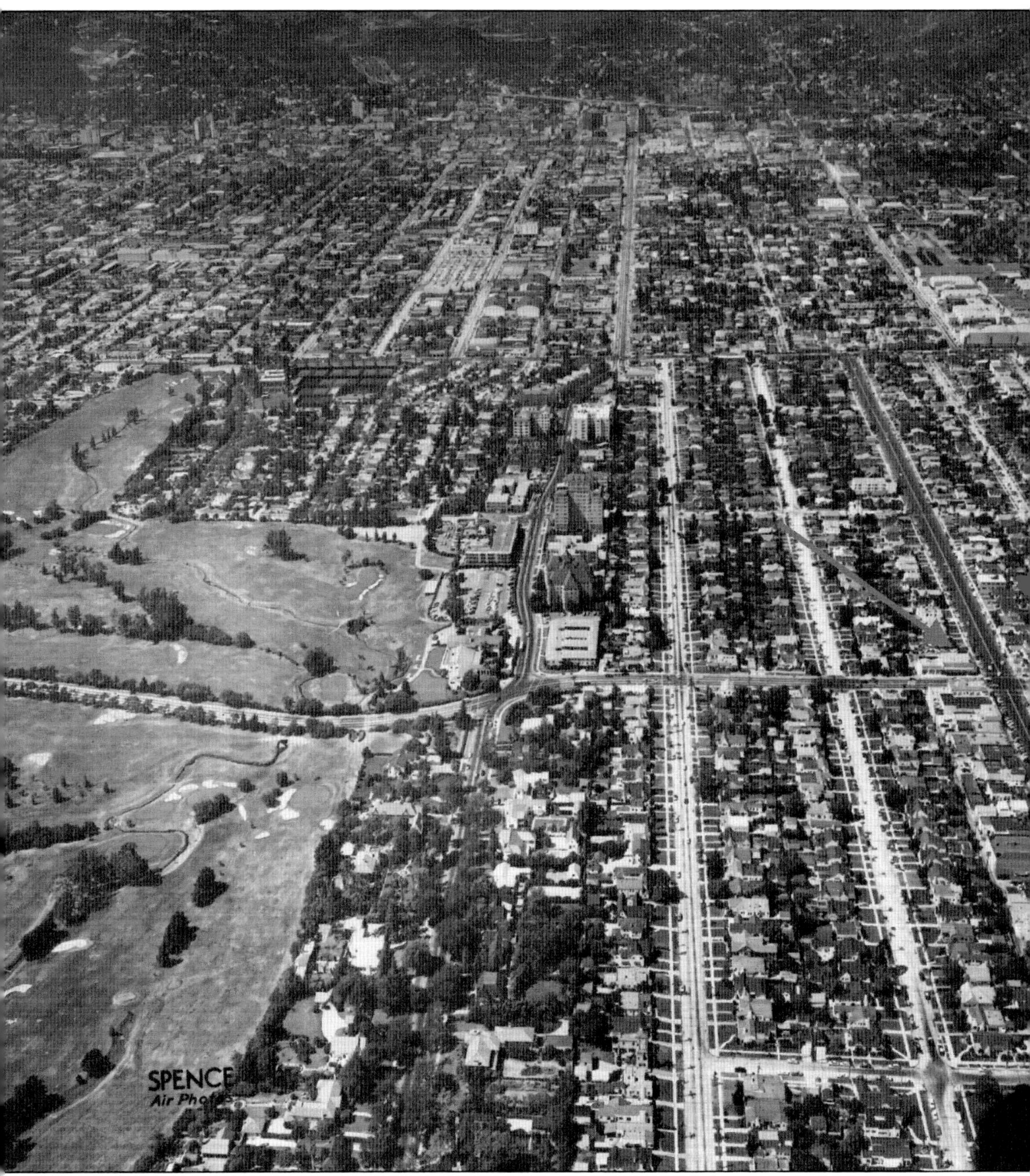

Aerial View, 1958. This image of the neighborhood looks north from Wilshire Boulevard and shows the continual growth of the neighborhoods around Larchmont. The Wilshire Country Club is on the left. (Courtesy of the UCLA Spence Air Photo Collection.)

Three

Modern Larchmont

As Los Angeles emerged as a national trendsetter, Larchmont was still a charming, quaint neighborhood with shops and restaurants where everyone knew everyone. Children were welcome to ride bikes and skateboard on the sidewalks, listen to records at the local record store after school, or stop by for ice cream. Many of the city's important political and business leaders who lived in nearby Hancock Park, Windsor Village, and Fremont Place enjoyed the privacy and friendliness of their local shopping district.

In 1963, Jane Gilman and Dawne Goodwin started the *Larchmont Chronicle* to alert residents to the impending threat of the proposed Beverly Hills freeway that would imperil village life. Gilman recalled that there were 23 businesses on Larchmont at the time. The *Larchmont Chronicle* gave the community a voice as well as a canvas to tell its stories. Both were very active in civic affairs and contributed to the improvement and preservation of the community. Their images are reproduced in this book.

Larchmont continues to change. There are boutique stores, retail pop-ups testing the tastes of affluent customers, and many more restaurants. Most of the old buildings remain, though some of the historic facades are gone. The ethos of Larchmont, envisioned by La Bonte, runs deep. There is a core of old-timers, like Chevalier's Books and the Landis Department Store. Picket Fences and Flicka have been around over 20 years. Personalized service is still a hallmark, attracting new owners who want to run the kind of business that belongs on Larchmont Boulevard.

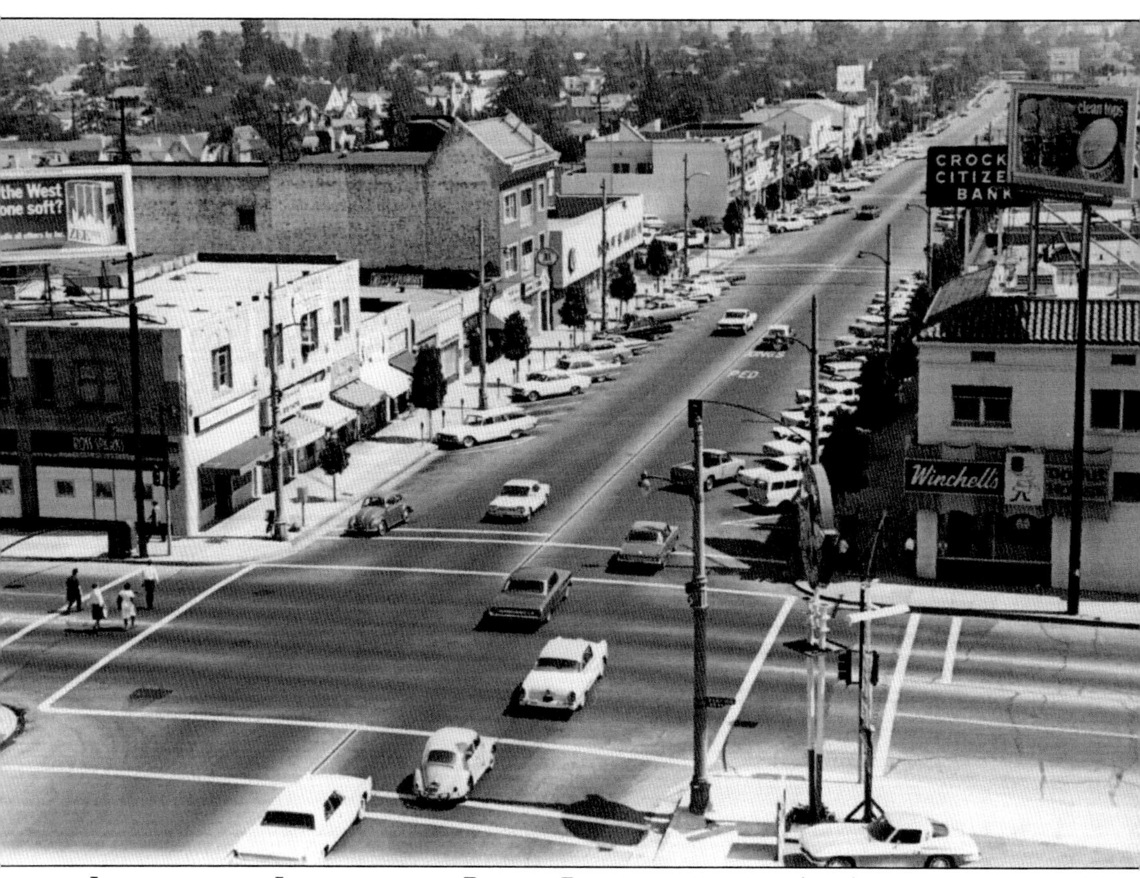

Intersection of Larchmont and Beverly Boulevards, 1964. This photograph could have been taken from the newly built Larchmont Medical Building that towered over the neighborhood. (Courtesy of Marc Wanamaker at Bison Archives.)

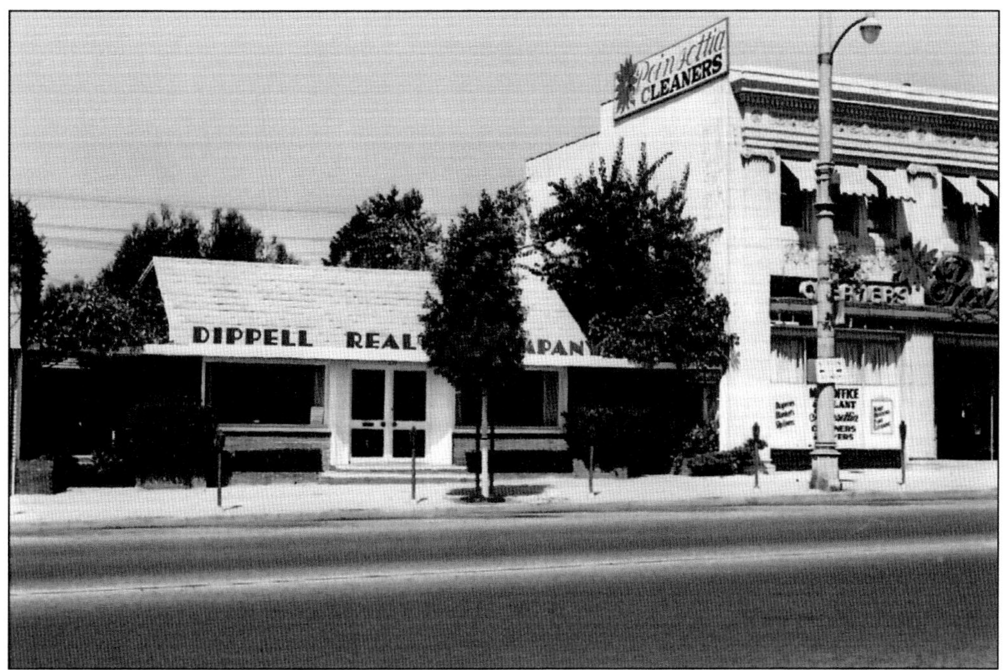

Dippell Realty and Poinsettia Cleaners at 107 and 113 North Larchmont. Albert Dippell and his sons Cutler and Howard were mainstays on the boulevard; so was Poinsettia Cleaners, established in 1923, whose longtime customers could have their laundry delivered right to their closets.

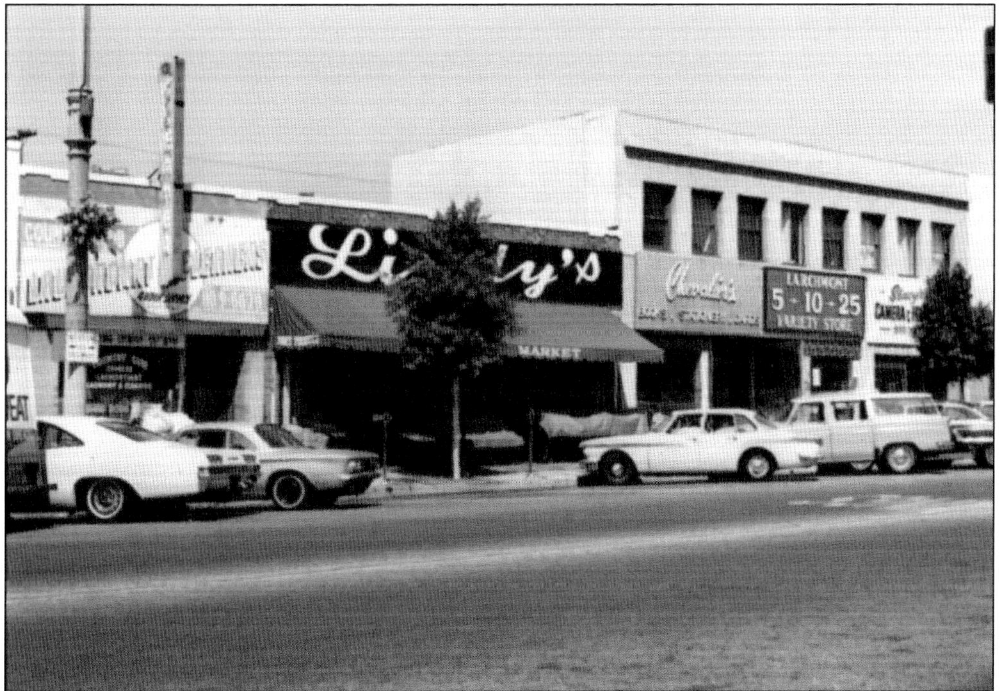

Lindy's Meats at 235 North Larchmont, c. 1956. This street view of the west side of Larchmont Boulevard includes Lindy's Meats and Country Club Chinese Laundry.

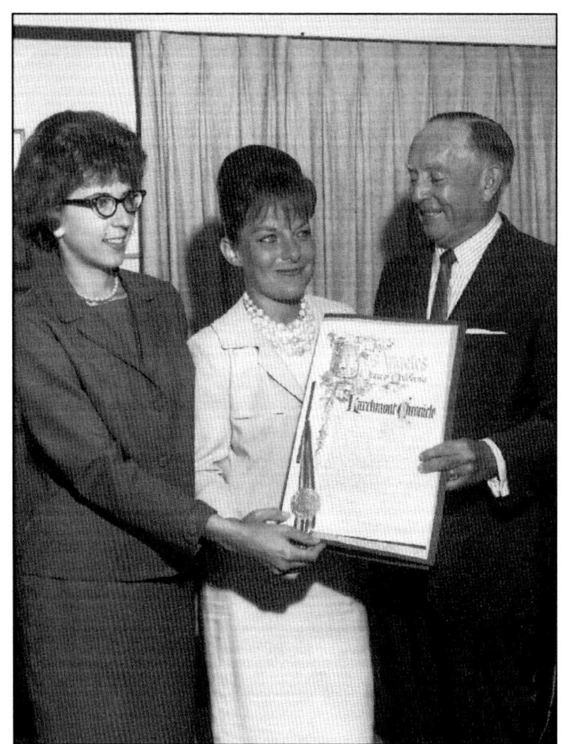

LOS ANGELES CITY COUNCILMAN HAROLD HENRY WITH *LARCHMONT CHRONICLE* COPUBLISHERS JANE GILMAN (LEFT) AND DAWNE GOODWIN. Goodwin and Gilman accept a resolution from Councilman Henry, congratulating them on a successful first year of operation. The *Larchmont Chronicle* celebrated its first anniversary on September 19, 1964, and was cited for its contribution to the community.

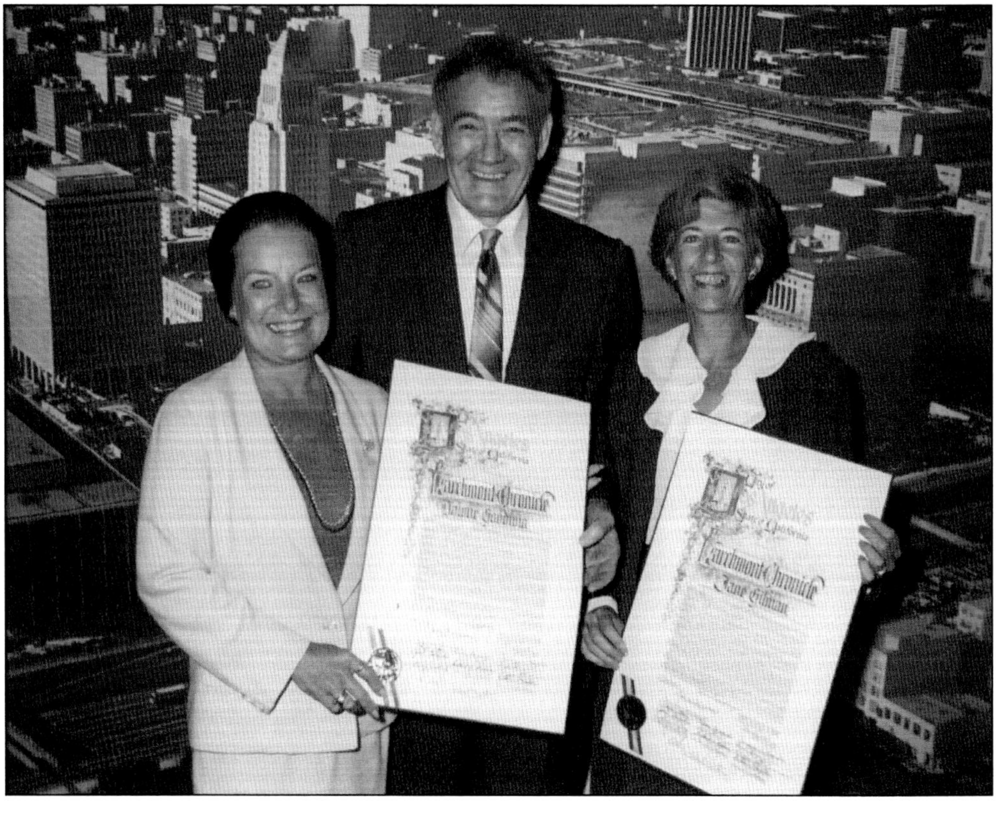

LOS ANGELES CITY COUNCILMAN JOHN FERRARO WITH *LARCHMONT CHRONICLE* COPUBLISHERS JANE GILMAN AND DAWNE GOODWIN. Councilman John Ferraro commends Goodwin and Gilman for their service to the community with a proclamation. Ferraro was the longest-serving Los Angeles City Council member in the history of the city. He served 35 years, from 1966 until his death in 2001 and was the president of the council for 14 of them.

LARCHMONT CHRONICLE PUBLISHERS WITH SERVICE STATION OWNER. The Chevron gasoline and service station was located in the center of Larchmont and was used for community events like the Larchmont Family Art Show, featured in the following photographs. It was sponsored by the Larchmont Boulevard Association, whose events helped reinforce the strong sense of community and village feel of the street.

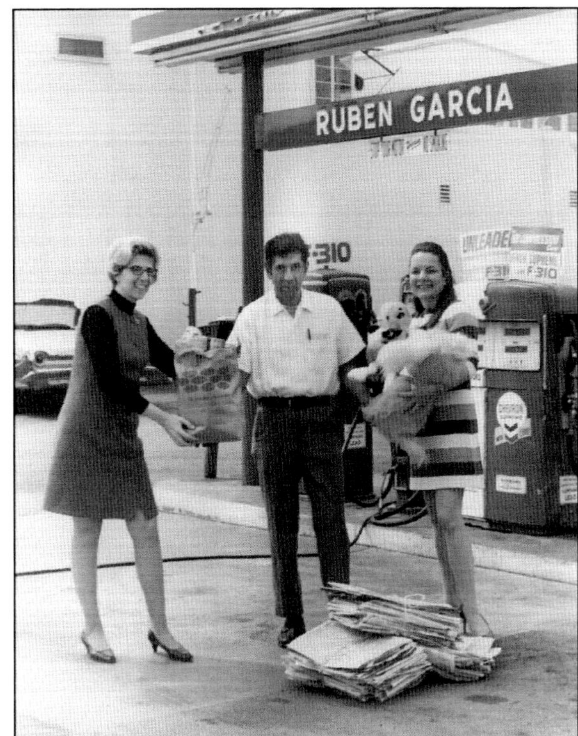

LARCHMONT FAMILY ART SHOW. An annual event, the Larchmont Family Art Show attracts families from all over the community.

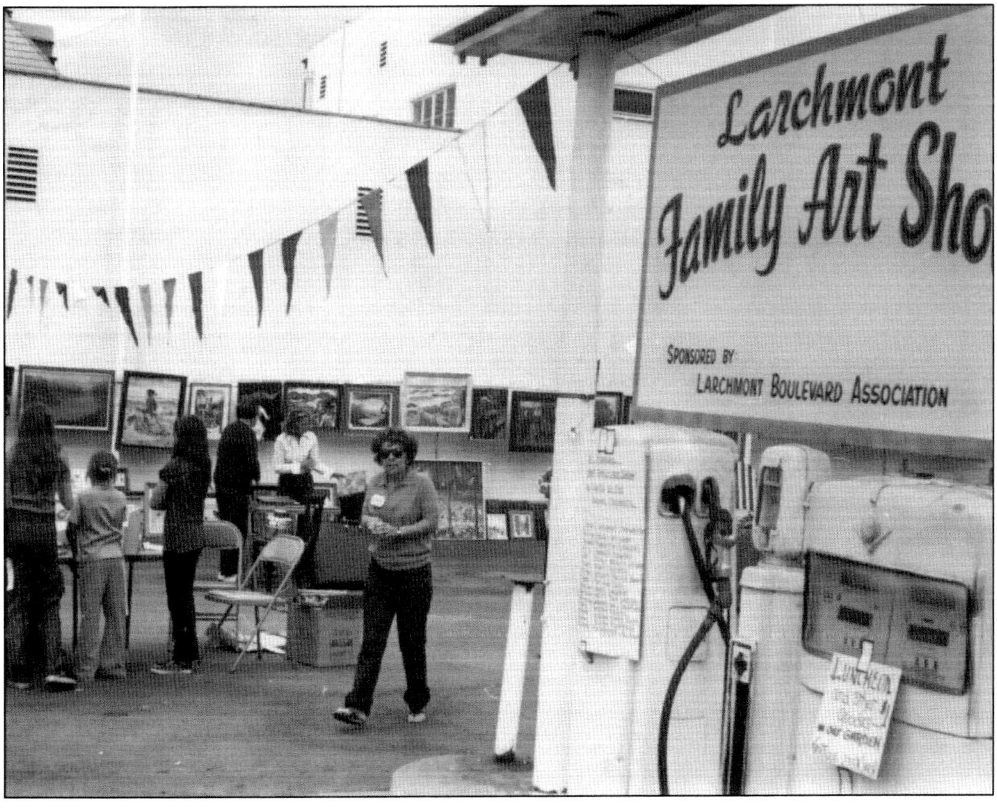

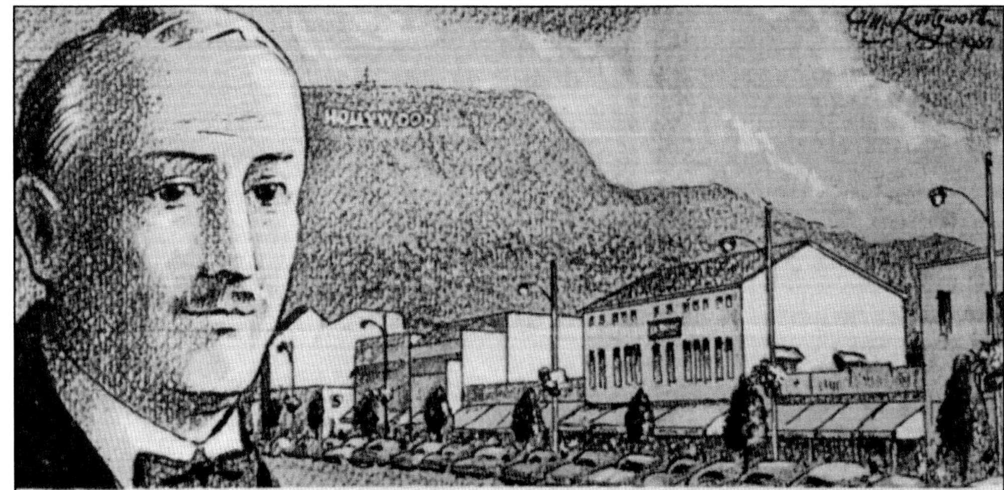

LOCAL HISTORIAN AND ARTIST DR. HARRY MUIR KURTZWORTH. Dr. H.M. Kurtzworth, a resident, served as the *Larchmont Chronicle*'s historian, writing articles about important residents and their homes for the newspaper. Kurtzworth's body of work was extensive and included this feature on founder Julius La Bonte and other important early civic pioneers. An accomplished artist, Kurtzworth designed the logo for the 1932 Los Angeles Olympics. He also served as the director of the Los Angeles Art Association.

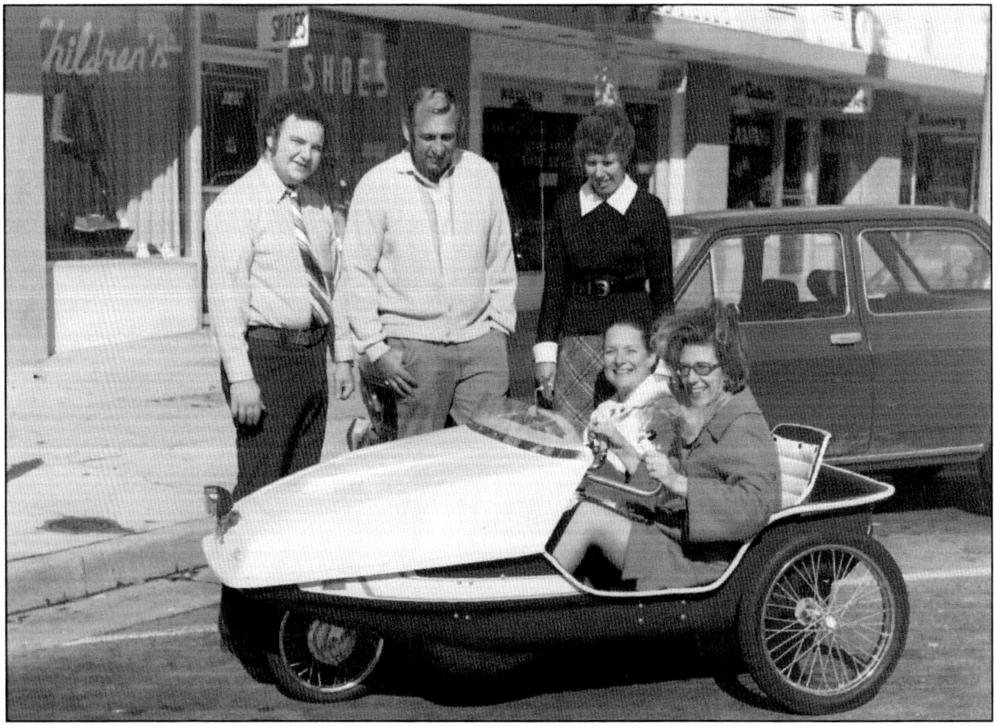

***LARCHMONT CHRONICLE* PUBLISHERS IN THE NEWS.** Copublishers Goodwin and Gilman were very active in the community as well as huge advocates for all the best aspects of the community. In this photograph, they are test-parking a three-wheeled vehicle in front of 139 North Larchmont Boulevard.

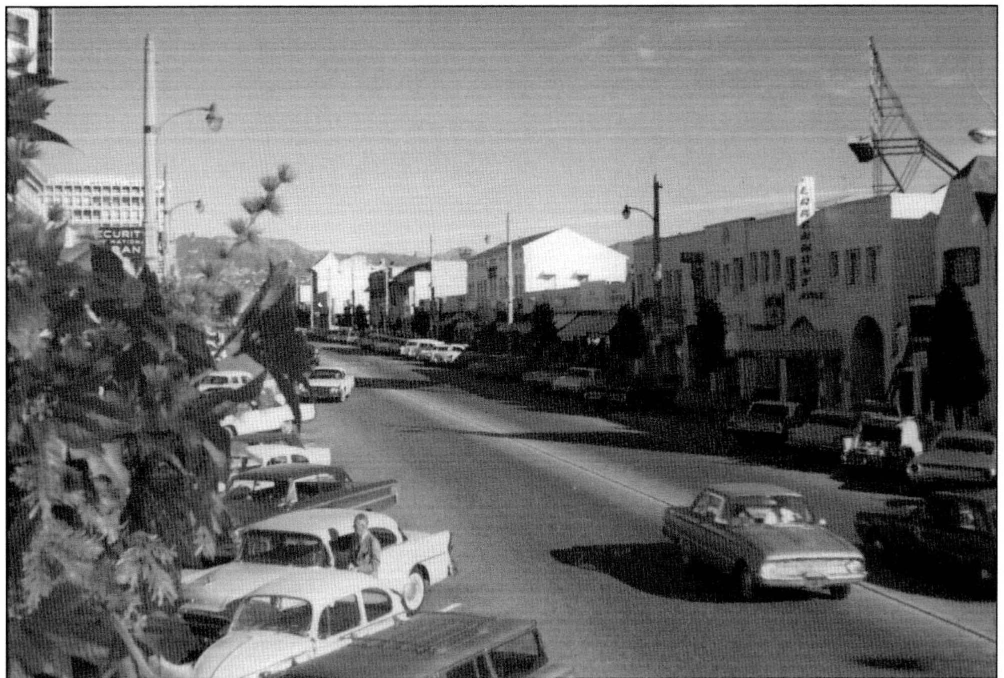

Street View from the Second Floor of 113 North Larchmont, c. 1960. This view is looking northeast from the second floor, with poinsettia Christmas decorations on the light posts. Larchmont Hall can be seen on the east side of the street.

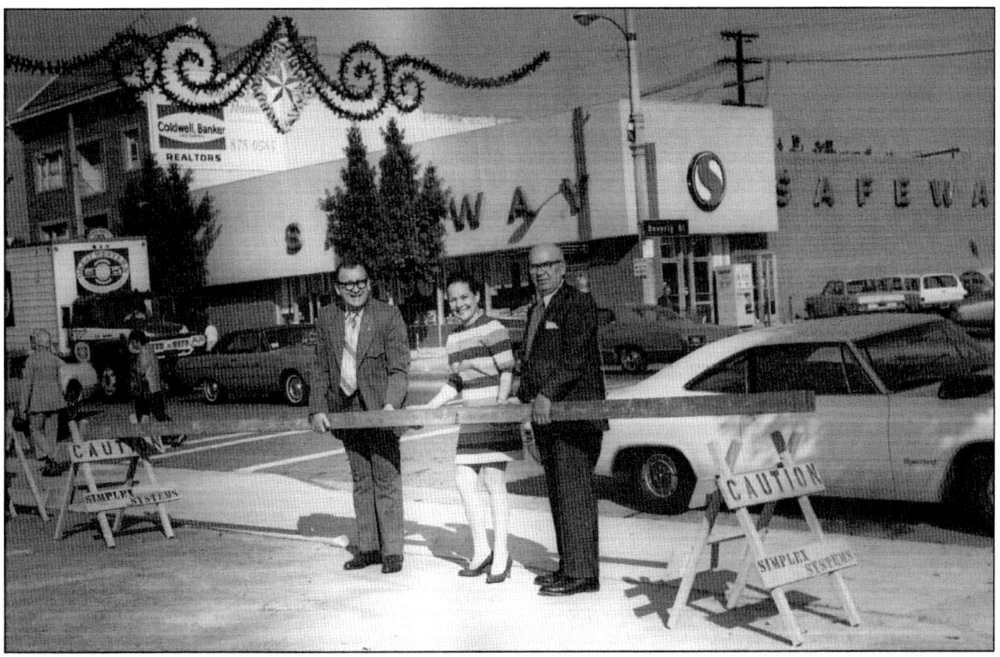

Opening of City Parking Lot, 1972. *Larchmont Chronicle* copublisher Dawne Goodwin helps city officials remove the barriers for a new parking lot on Larchmont, formerly the site of a gas station. The City of Los Angeles developed the 36-space lot to provide more parking for shops and businesses on Larchmont.

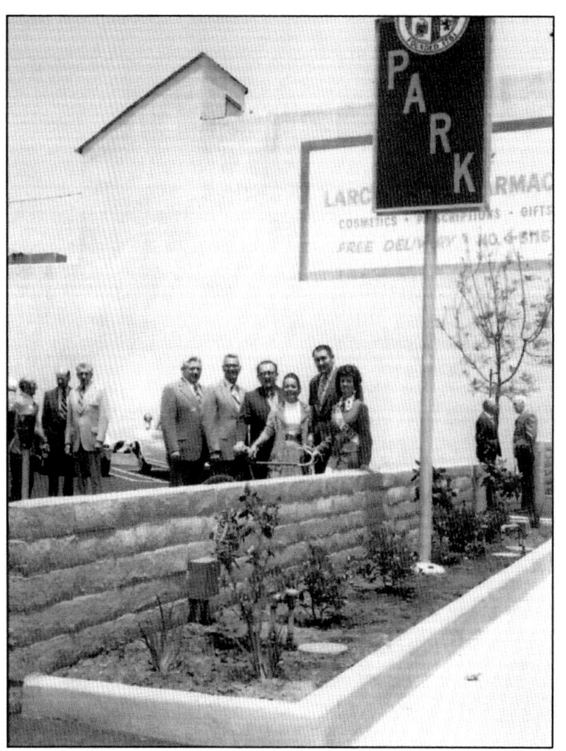

CIVIC LEADERS GATHER AT NEW PARKING LOT. Councilman John Ferraro and others are pictured at the official opening of the 36-space parking lot. Landscaping helps beautify this new City of Los Angeles parking lot, which provided much-needed parking for Larchmont.

CELEBRATING THE INSTALLATION OF NEW HEADS ON LARCHMONT BOULEVARD PARKING METERS. *Larchmont Chronicle* copublisher Jane Gilman, Councilman John Ferraro, and others check out the new parking meters on Larchmont. This photograph was taken in front of Bank of America at 100 North Larchmont Boulevard. By changing the heads, the city increased revenue by 50 percent, charging a penny for 6 minutes (instead of 12), a nickel for 30 minutes, and a dime for an hour.

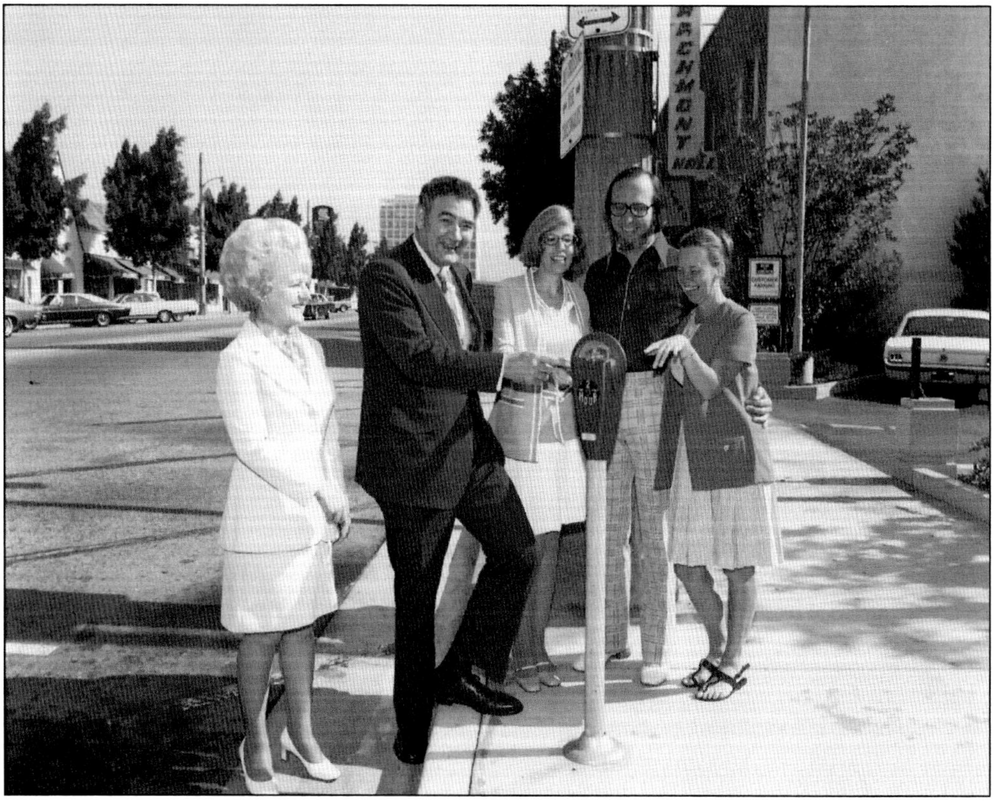

Decorating the Larchmont Boulevard Trees. Larchmont Boulevard Association president Dr. Tim Gogan (right) decorates a street tree for Christmas. Holiday decorations are a tradition on Larchmont.

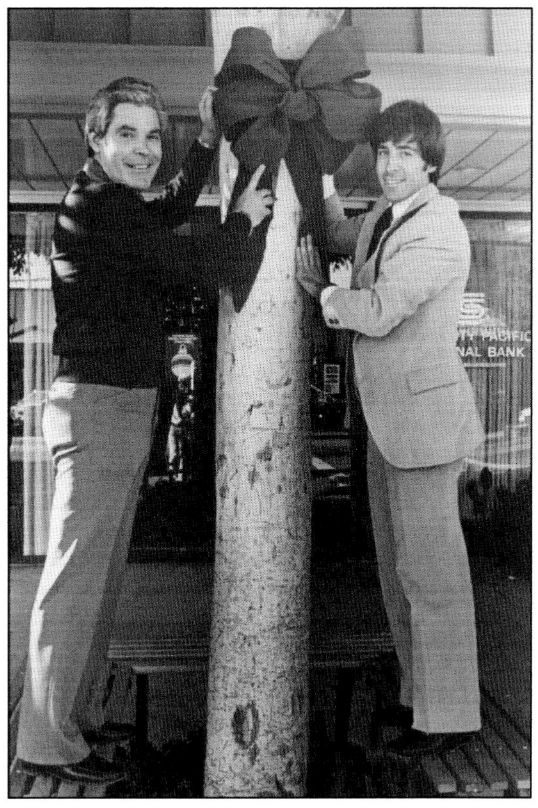

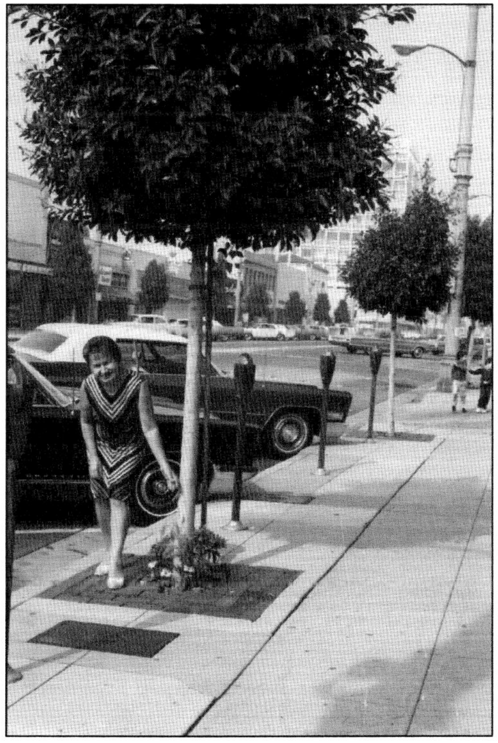

Watering the Trees. The responsibility for keeping the street trees alive fell (and still falls) to the shopkeepers and business owners on Larchmont Boulevard. The trees continue to be part of the charm of the street and a constant challenge to maintain.

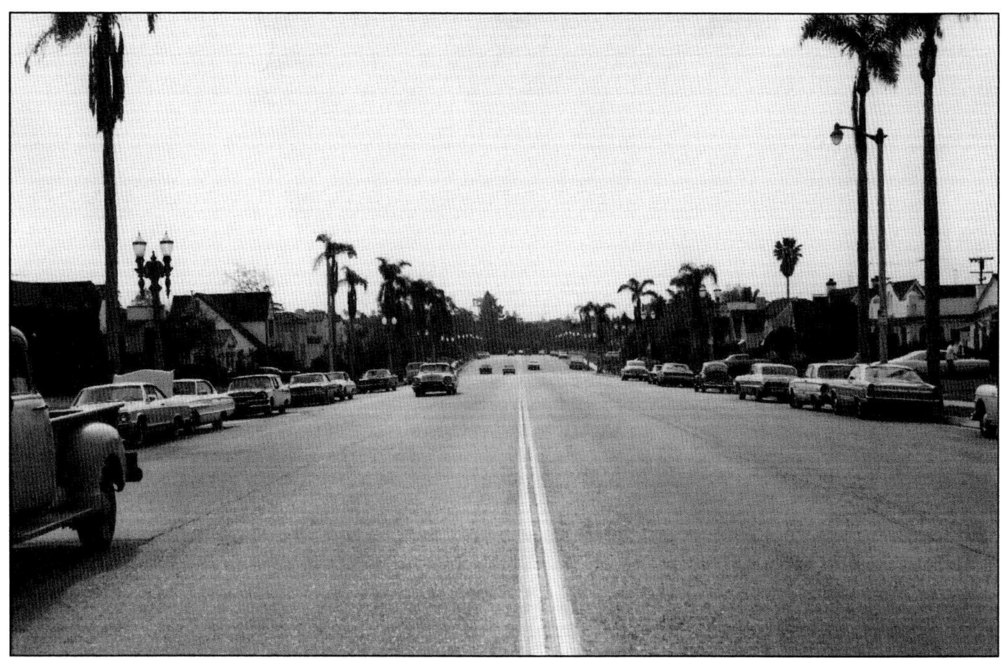

View of Larchmont Looking South toward Third Street, c. 1960. After the removal of the railway tracks, the street was very wide. In later years, residents would push for the installation of a landscaped median. (Courtesy of Marc Wanamaker at Bison Archives.)

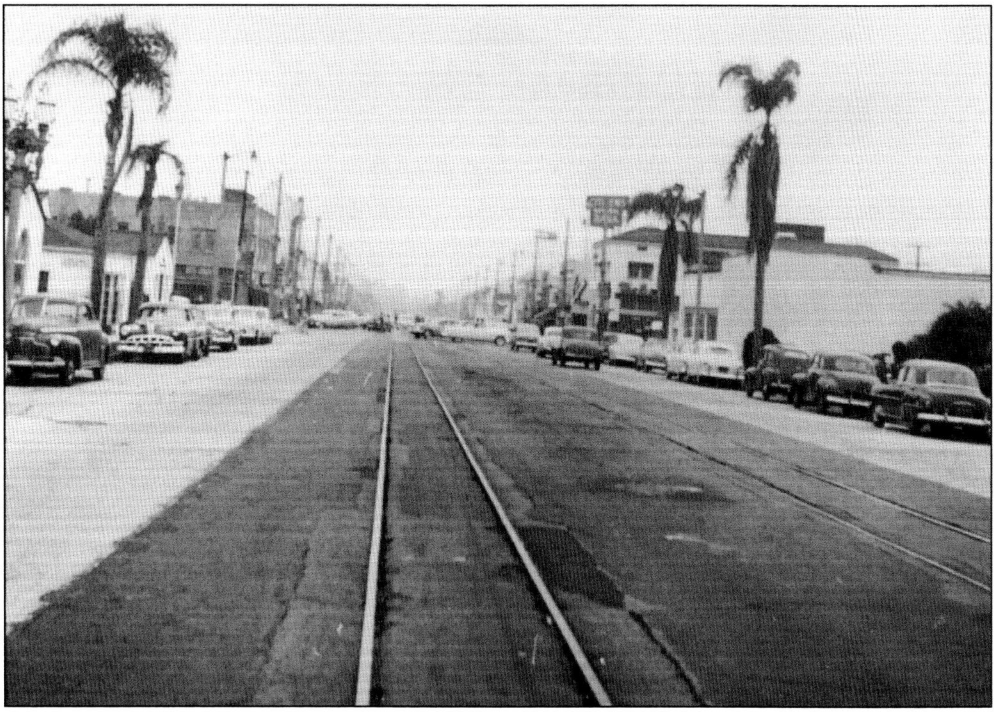

View of Larchmont Looking South from Upper Larchmont, c. 1950. Railway tracks can be seen in the street, but the rail poles and lines have been removed. Upper Larchmont had more residential buildings even though it was zoned for commercial use in the 1930s.

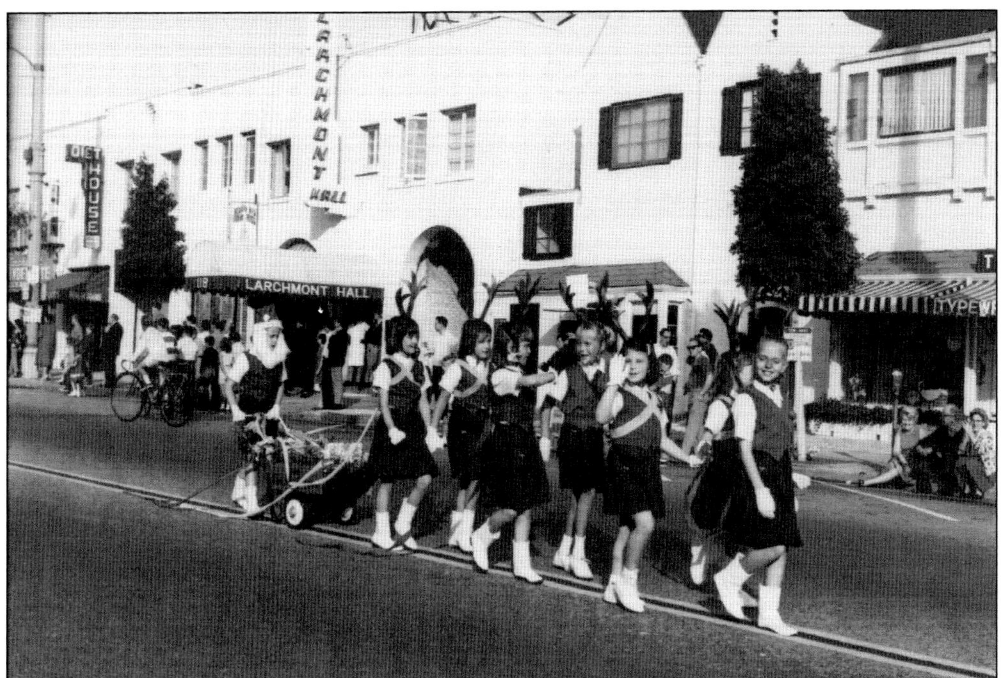

Santa and Her Reindeer at Larchmont Holiday Parade. Family-friendly events, like the holiday parade, were part of Larchmont's unique charm that knitted the community together and gave everyone a sense of belonging. In the background is Larchmont Hall, which served as gathering place for the local civic groups. The typewriter store was eventually torn down in 1973 when the Bank of America was built along with a 16-space parking lot.

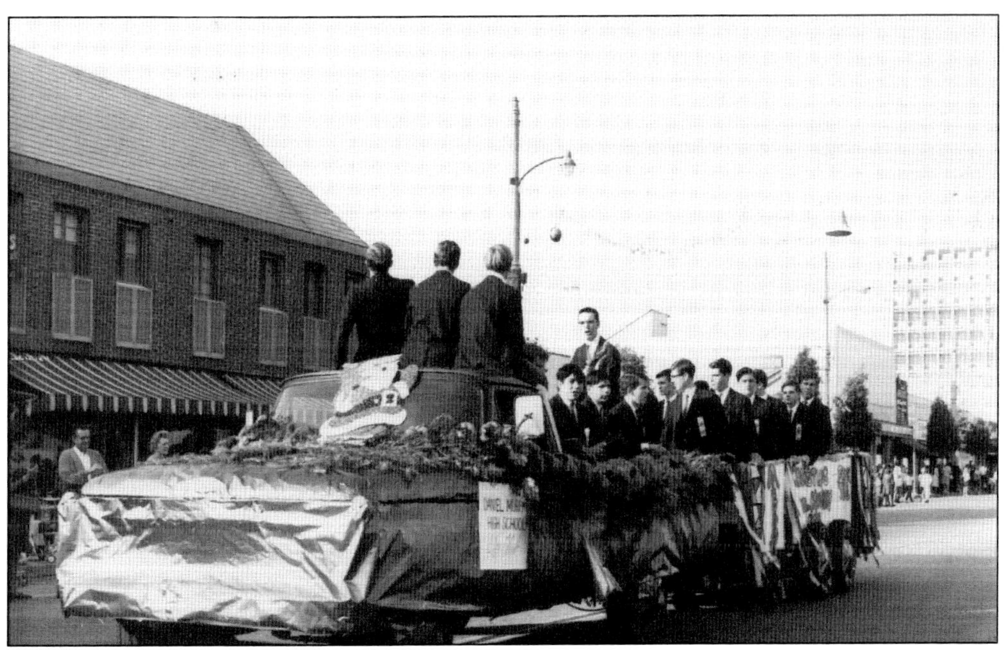

Daniel Murphy High School Glee Club, c. 1960. Students of Daniel Murphy High School, a Catholic all-boys school, ride past Landis Department Store in the Larchmont holiday parade.

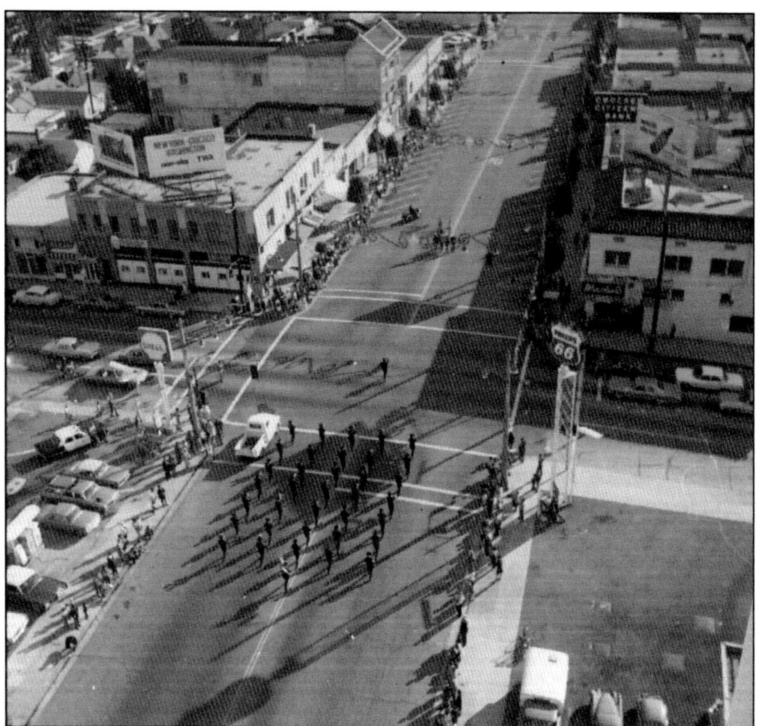

Aerial View of Parade at Beverly and Larchmont Boulevards. A marching band approaches the intersection of Larchmont and Beverly Boulevards heading south on Larchmont. Gas stations on both corners can be seen in the photograph.

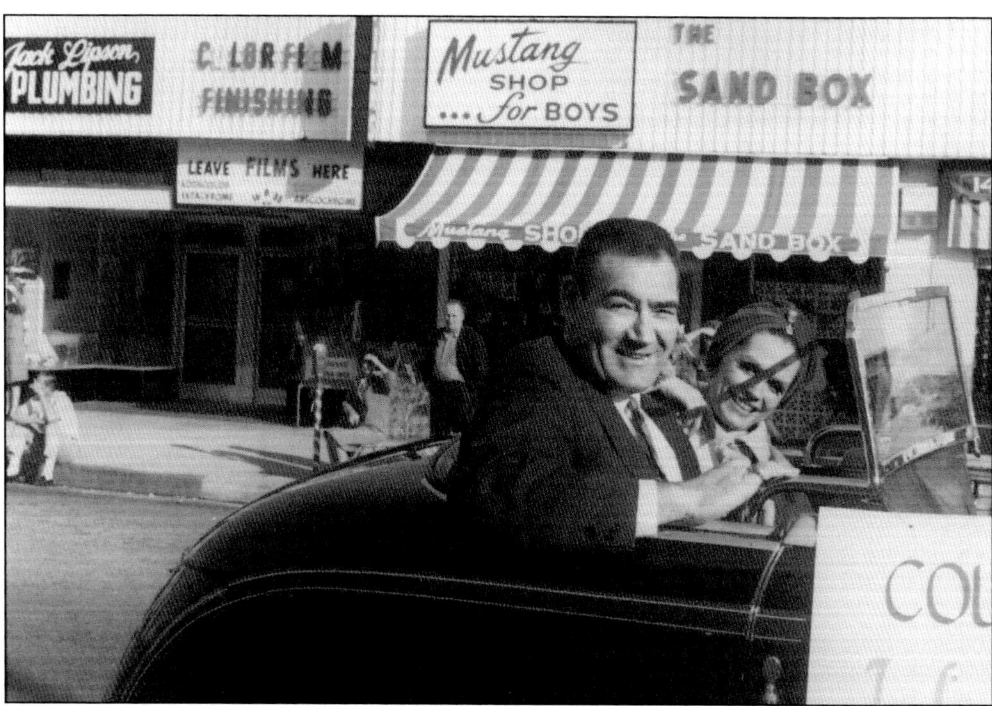

The Ferraros in the Larchmont Parade. Councilman John Ferraro and his wife, Julie Marie Luckey, ride past stores at 126–148 North Larchmont. In the background is Jack Lipson Plumbing, whose owner married La Bonte's daughter Charlotte.

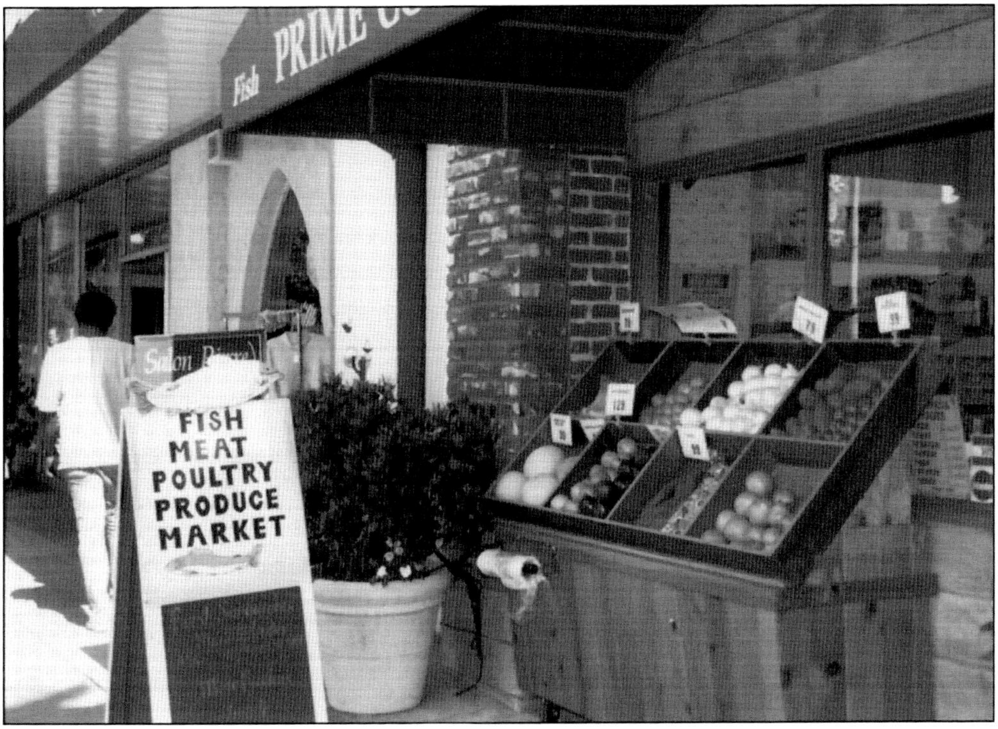

Phil's Poultry and Fish at 124 North Larchmont, c. 1987. Shopping on Larchmont was like visiting old friends. A great deal of the charm of the street is derived from the shop owners, who went to great lengths to get to know their customers and provide personalized service. Even though the types of stores have changed—the grocery stores on the street have been replaced by clothing stores or coffee shops—the same sense of community continues, and it is quite likely that people will see others they know on any given day shopping on Larchmont.

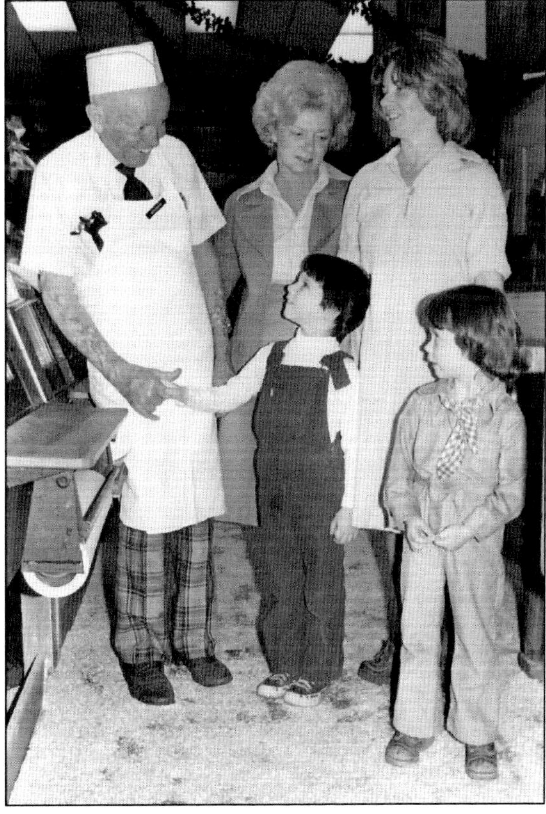

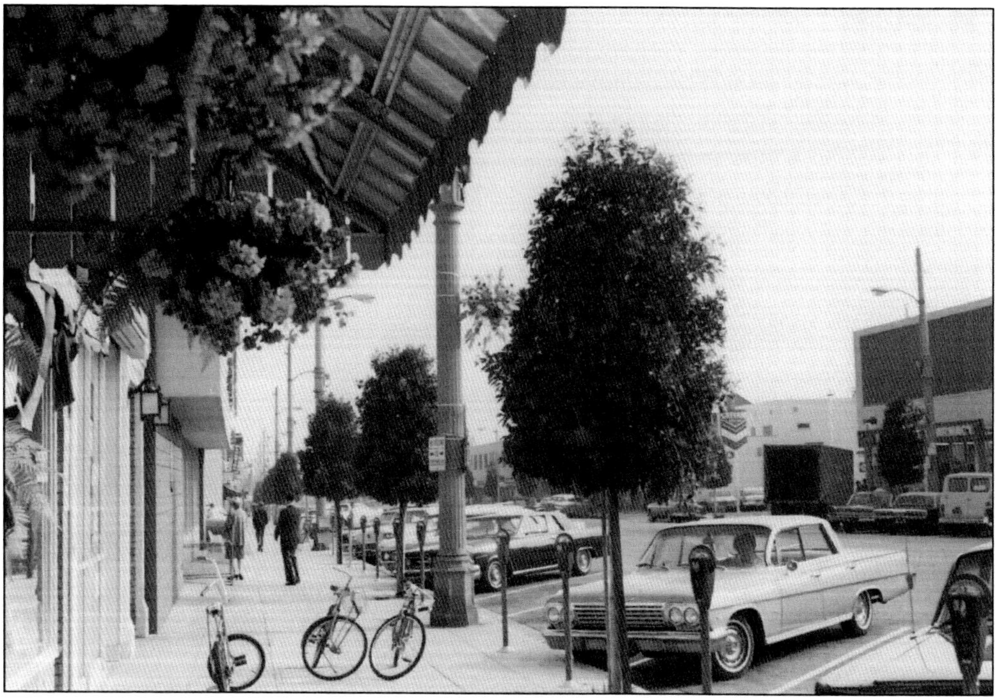

Street View Looking South from 230 North Larchmont. Hanging plants and awnings added to the village feel of Larchmont. The Chevron gas station is on the other side of the street, next door to the Larchmont Beverly Pharmacy.

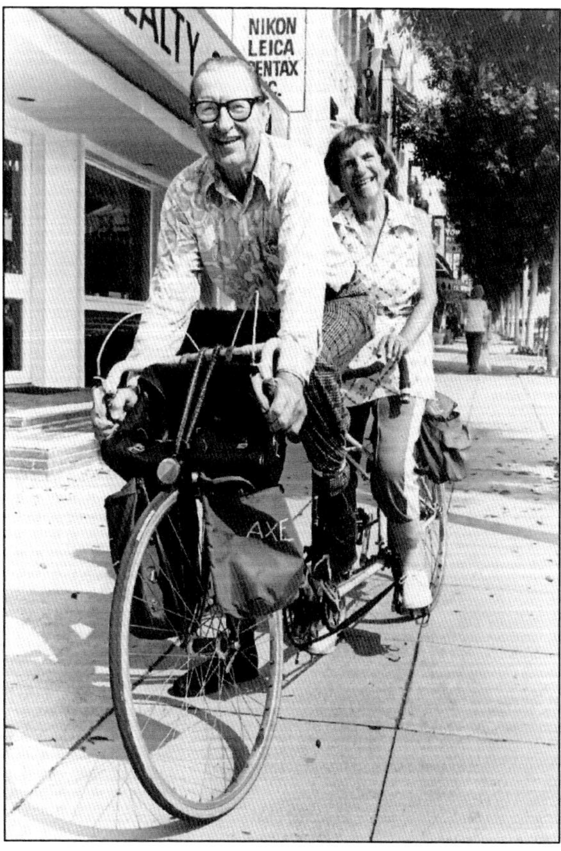

Enjoying a Bicycle Built for Two. Bicycling is a great way to run errands on Larchmont Boulevard. This couple is shown in front of 107 North Larchmont, heading south.

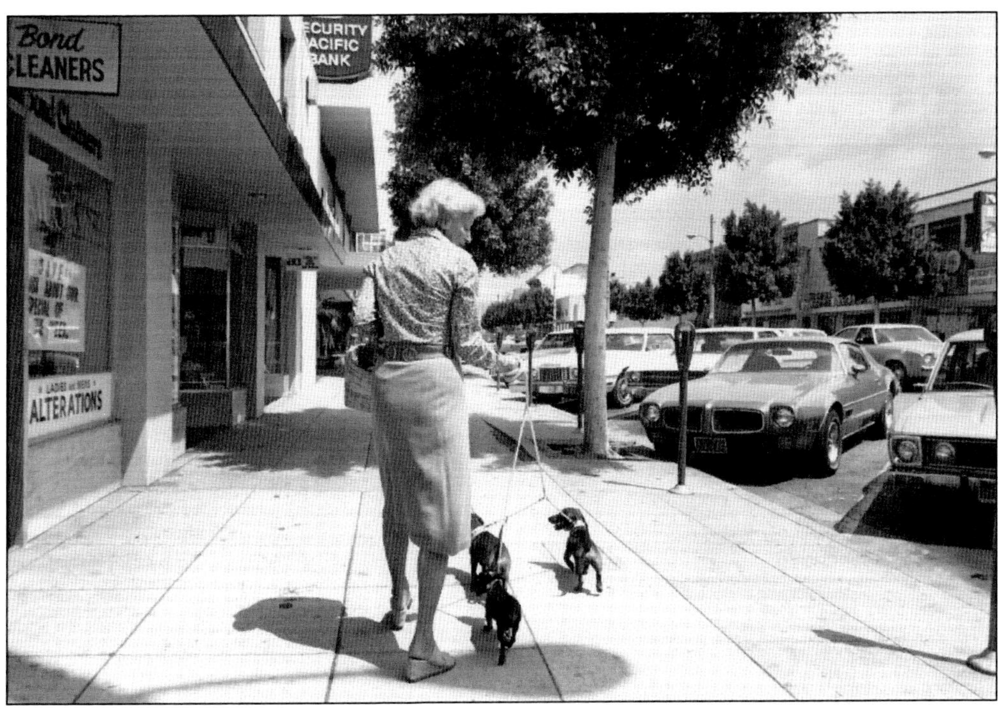

Dog Walking at 141 North Larchmont. Dogs have always felt at home shopping on Larchmont. Many shops have water dishes outside for pets on hot summer days.

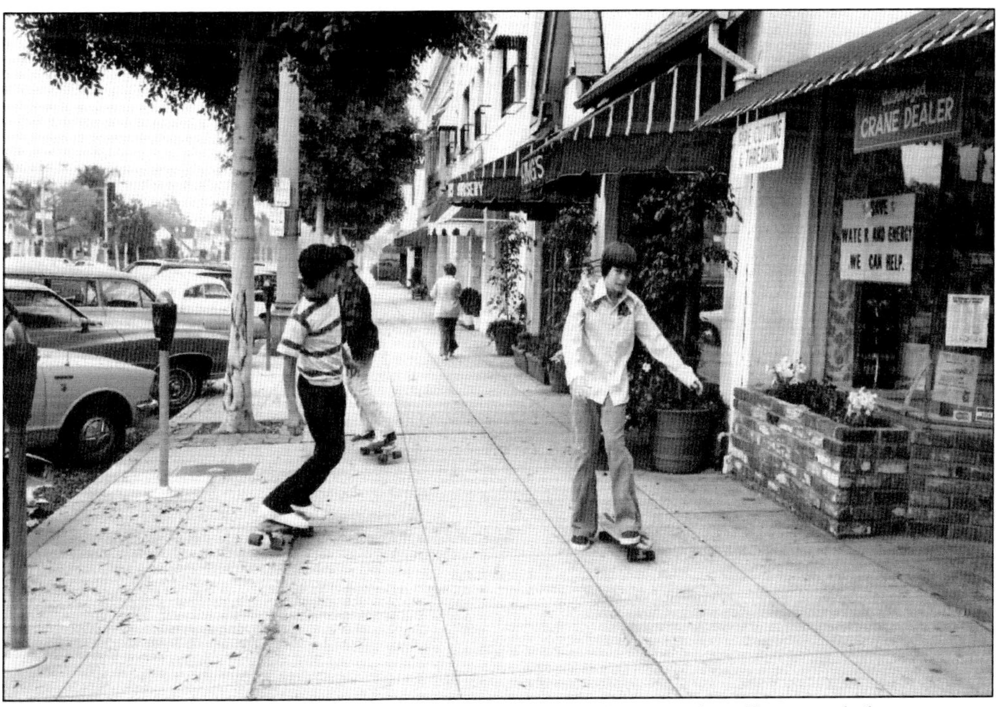

Skateboarders at 121 North Larchmont, c. 1988. Empty sidewalks provided a tempting place for skateboarders.

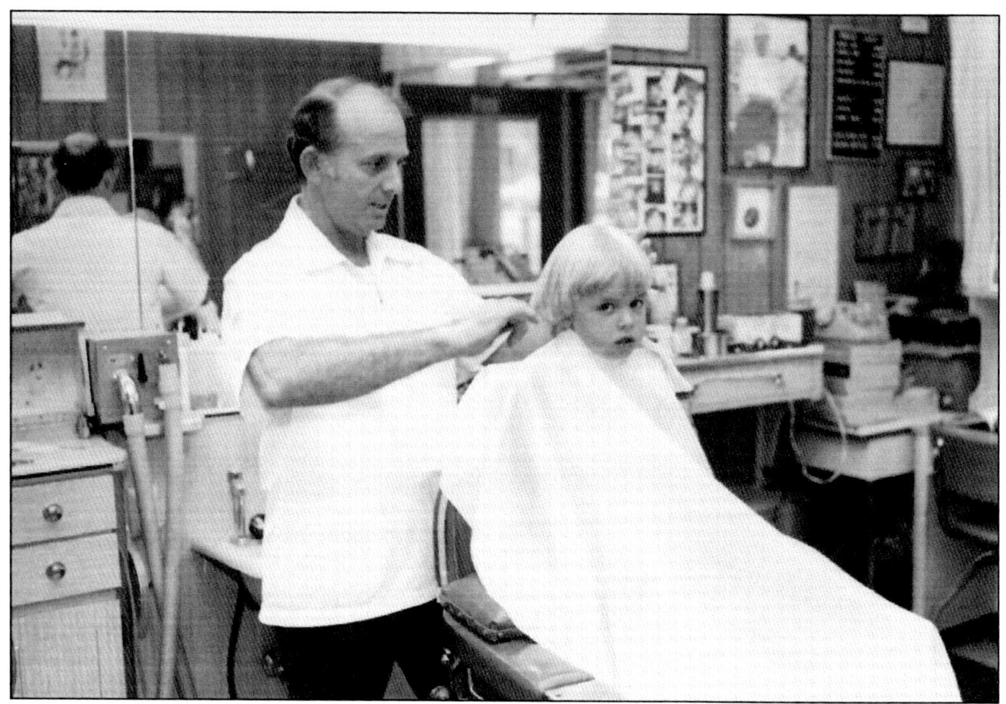

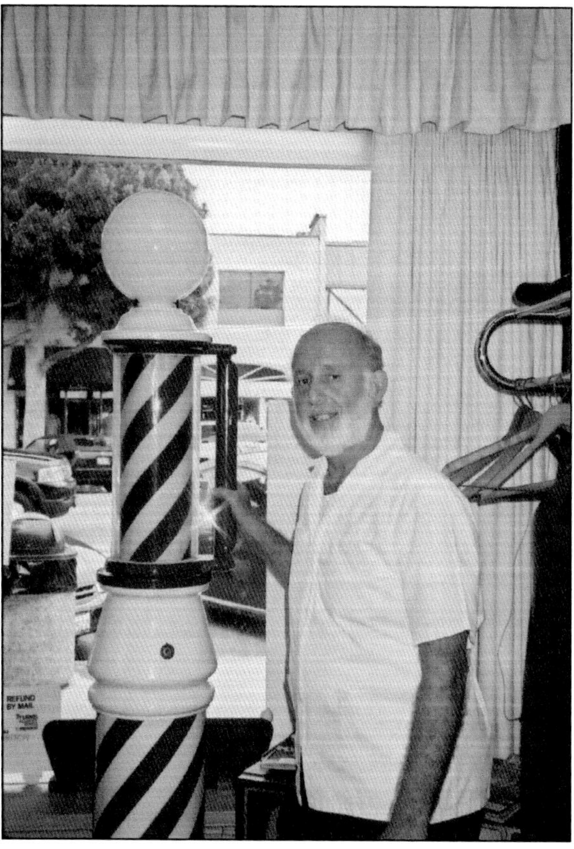

Jerry the Barber at 142 1/2 North Larchmont. Jerry Cottone started working at his father's barbershop on Larchmont in 1957 as a teenager and stayed for over 50 years. Jerry and his father ran the shop for 70-plus years. If ever there was an example of a family business passing from one generation to the next, it is the barbershop; generations of neighbors have been customers. Neighbors mourned the closure of the shop when Jerry retired in 2014 due to ill health. Fortunately, George Hilario (Jorge) and his nephew Cesar bought the business and have kept the shop much the same as it was when Jerry was there. Jerry passed away in April 2015 at 76 years old.

G.B. Harb and Son, c. 1980. George Harb and family are pictured in front of Harb's fine men's clothing store at 158 North Larchmont. Harb opened the shop on Larchmont Boulevard in the 1970s and moved the store downtown in 1990.

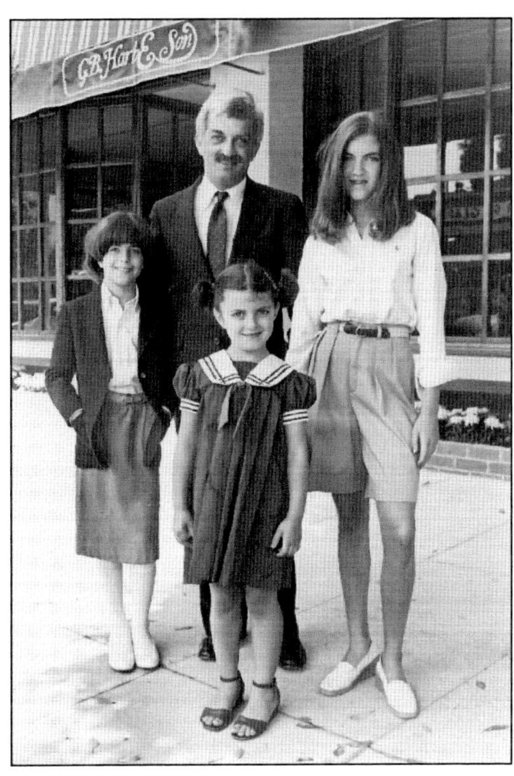

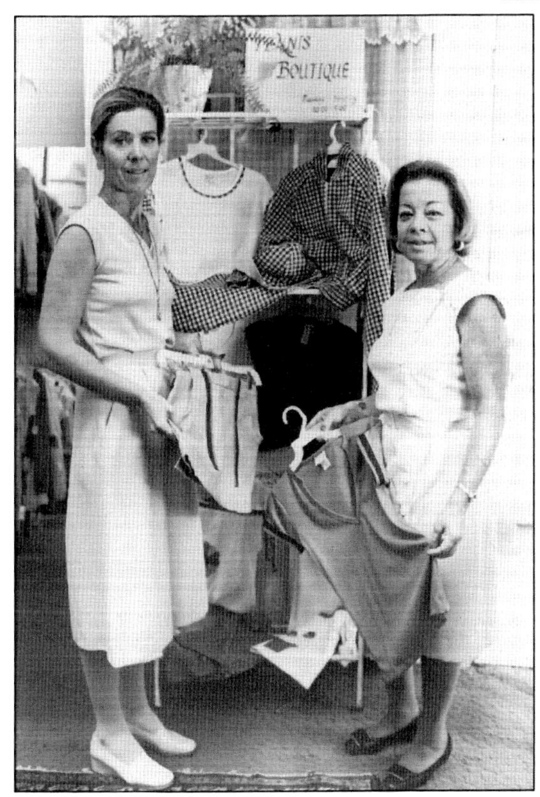

Tennis Boutique at 142 North Larchmont, c. 1987. Pictured is a tennis boutique for the Los Angeles Tennis Club crowd and other tennis-playing residents.

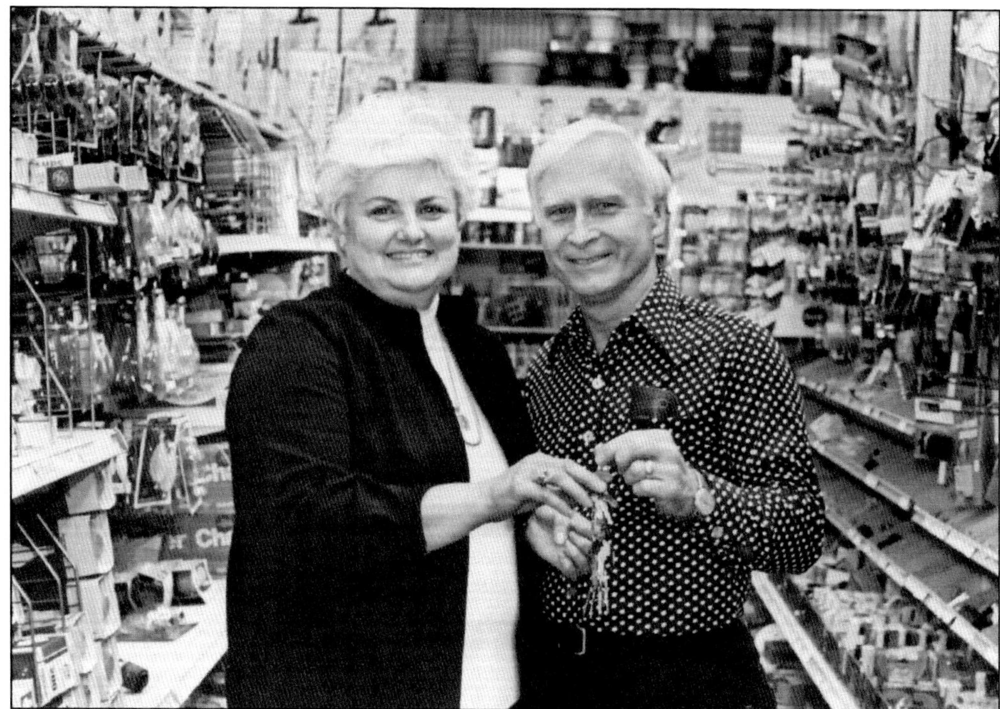

LARCHMONT HARDWARE AT 152 NORTH LARCHMONT. Established in 1926, Larchmont Hardware was one of the most popular stores on the boulevard. The store carried every kind of screw, bolt, tool, or home-repair accessory needed by residents. Owner Russ Wilson acquired the store in 1982 from the original owner's family. When the hardware store closed in 2008, residents were in an uproar because the building was bought by a developer who tripled the store's rent. Years later, locals still miss the store.

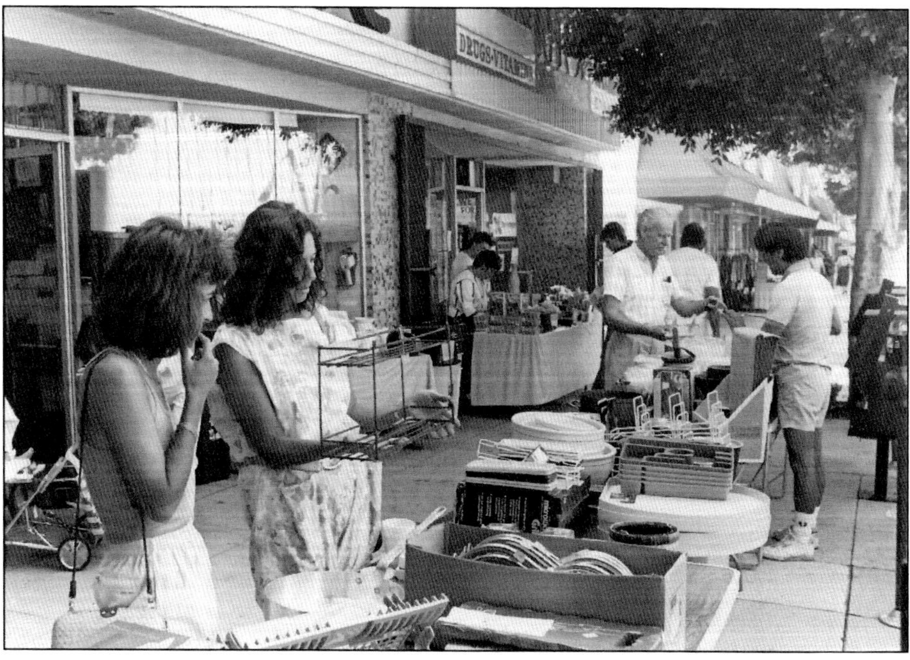

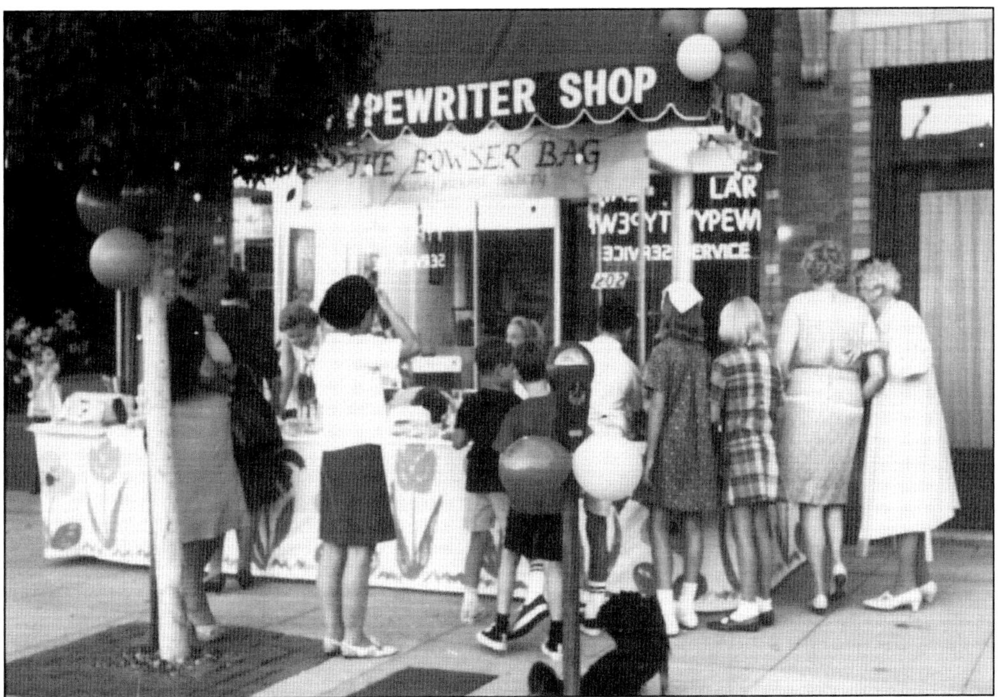

Larchmont Typewriter Shop at 202 North Larchmont, c. 1973. Pictured is a holiday sidewalk sale at the Larchmont Typewriter Shop. The shop moved from 110 North Larchmont, where it was located in 1960 according to the Los Angeles telephone directory.

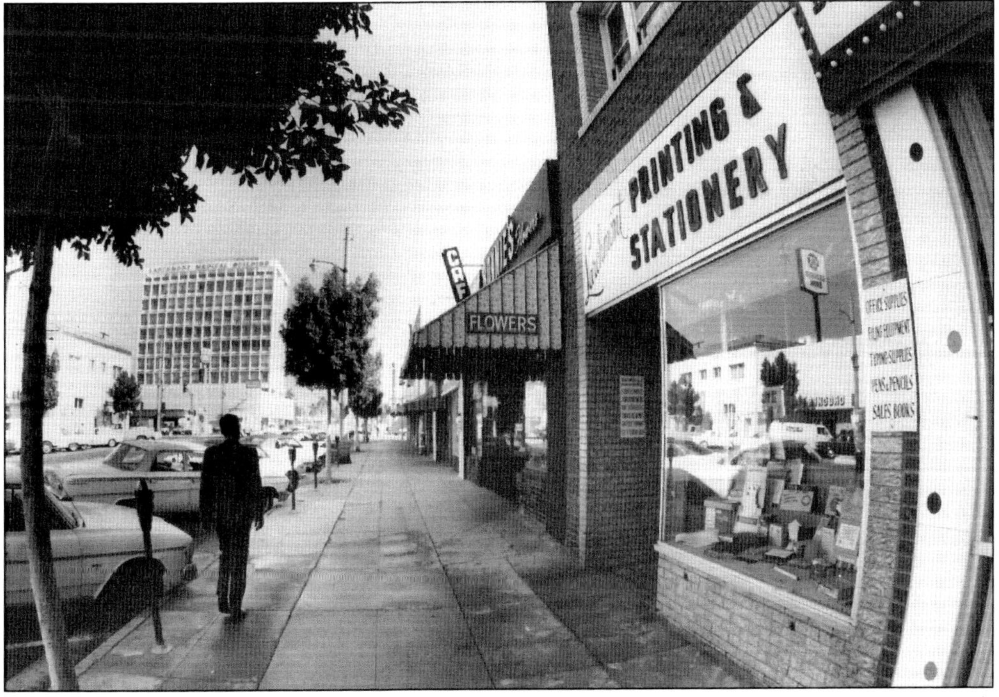

Street View Taken with Fish-Eye Lens at 232 North Larchmont, c. 1973. This photograph was taken on the east side of the street looking north.

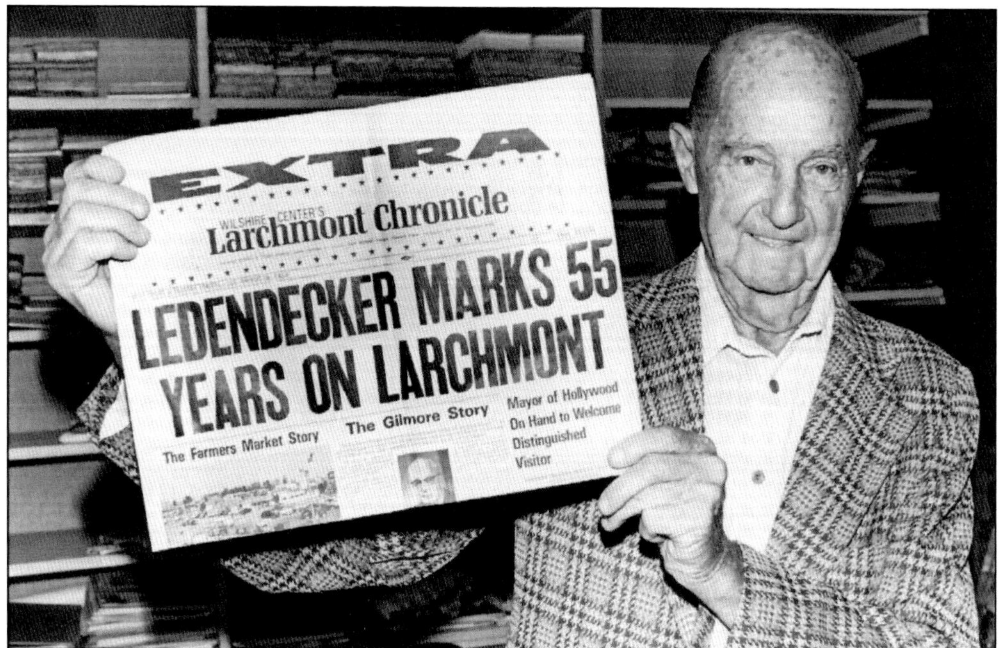

William Ledendecker of Wilshire Studios Upholstery. Wilshire Studios upholstery company had been on Larchmont since 1929, though it moved from 108 North Larchmont to 103 North Larchmont. Owner William Ledendecker holds up an edition of the *Larchmont Chronicle*, marking 55 years of doing business on Larchmont Boulevard.

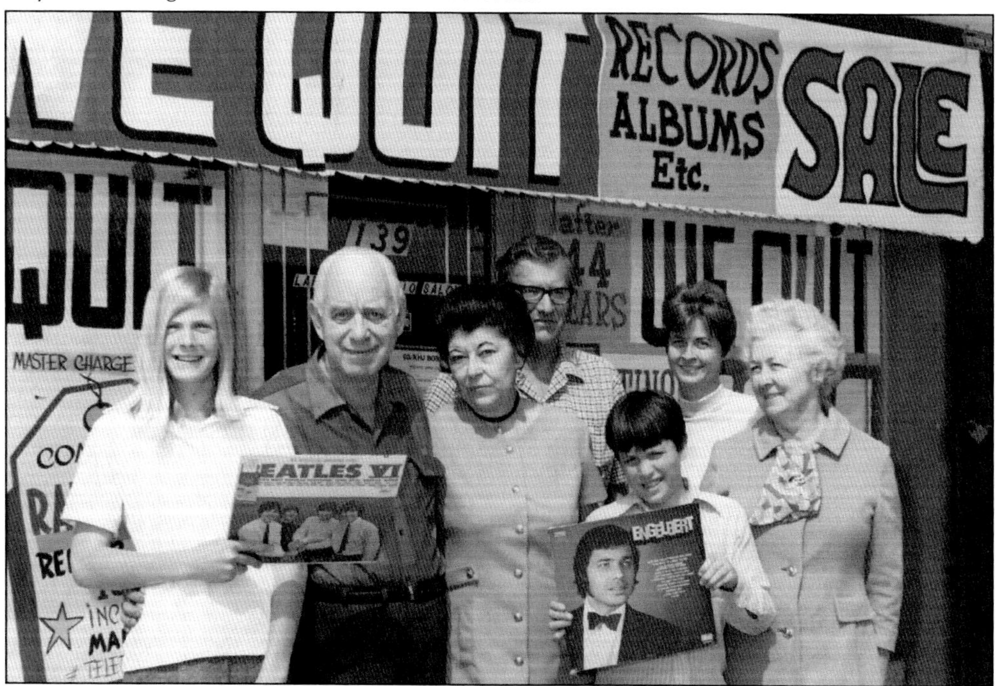

Larchmont Radio Salon at 139 North Larchmont, c. 1970. Larchmont Radio Salon, owned by Ross "Stratt" Stratton, was a favorite shop for teenagers. Locals recall private listening booths, where kids would hang out until chased out by Stratton.

Haas and Company Hair Design Celebrates 10th Anniversary at 136 North Larchmont. In 1987, David Haas and Carmen Wall celebrated 10 years of David Haas Hair Design and over 20 years of business on Larchmont. Wall is the former co-owner of Larchmont Beauty, which became Haas and Company in 1977.

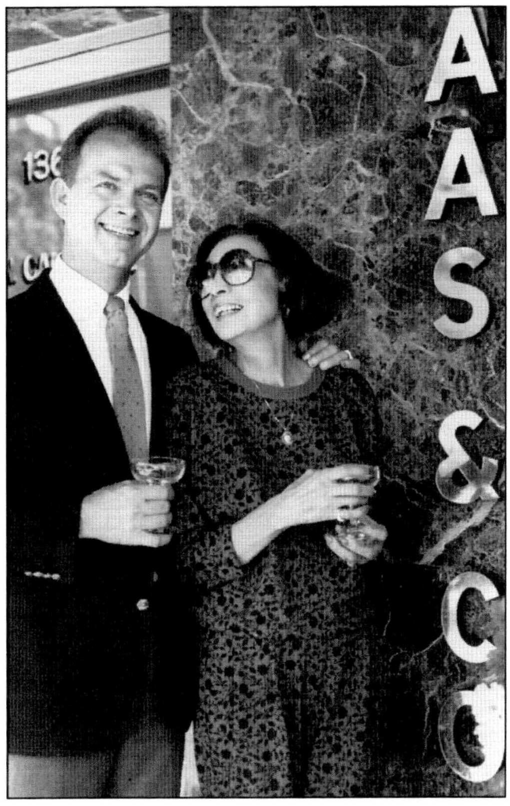

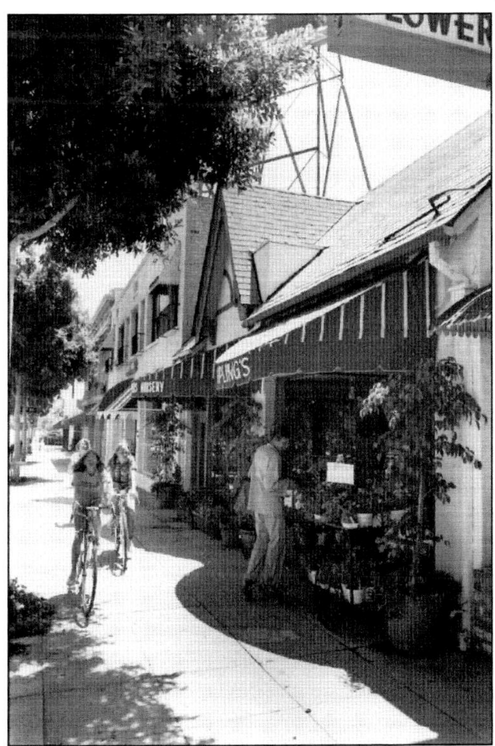

Kipling's Flowers at 121 1/2 North Larchmont. Beautifully decorated storefronts, like that of Kipling's Flowers, invited shoppers to stroll the boulevard. It also contributed to the small village feeling.

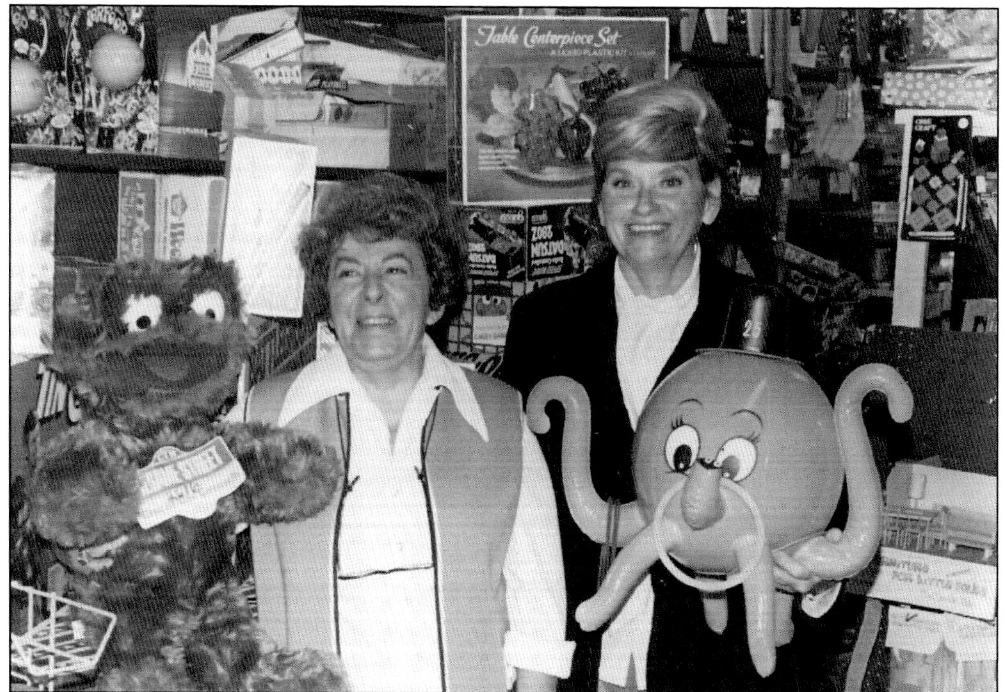

Toy Store Owners. No shopping boulevard would be complete without a great toy store. Larchmont had many though the years; when one store would close, another would open. Typically, they were jam-packed with toys, balls, games, and stuffed animals to the delight of young shoppers who never wanted to leave.

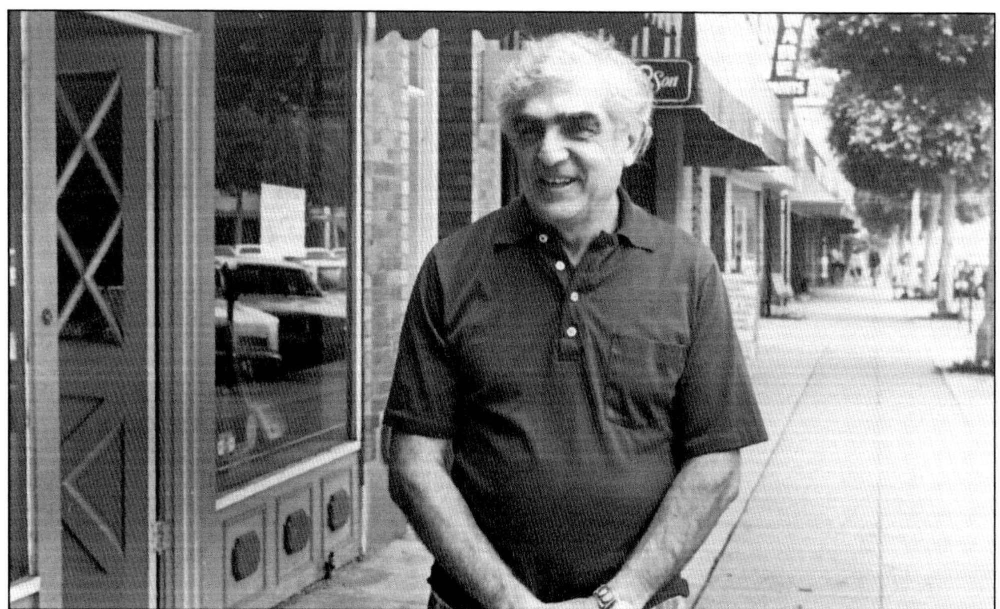

Shopkeepers on Larchmont. The shopkeepers are the heart and soul of Larchmont. At the founding of the street, virtually all were small business owners who worked in the stores and got to know all their customers by name. George Harb raised his family in nearby Hancock Park and operated his fine men's clothing store, G.H. Harb and Sons, on Larchmont for 20 years.

Ground-Breaking for Parking Garage and New Retail Shops at 226 North Larchmont. In 1985, with the assistance of city councilman John Ferraro, developer Ron Simms won the support of the neighborhood and the city to build a 145-space parking garage and 6,000 square feet of new retail shops. The 10,000-square-foot space, formerly the Safeway grocery store, was also remodeled.

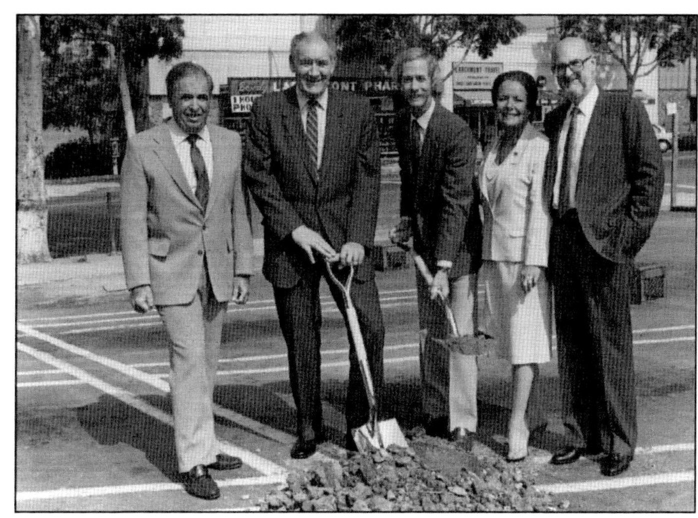

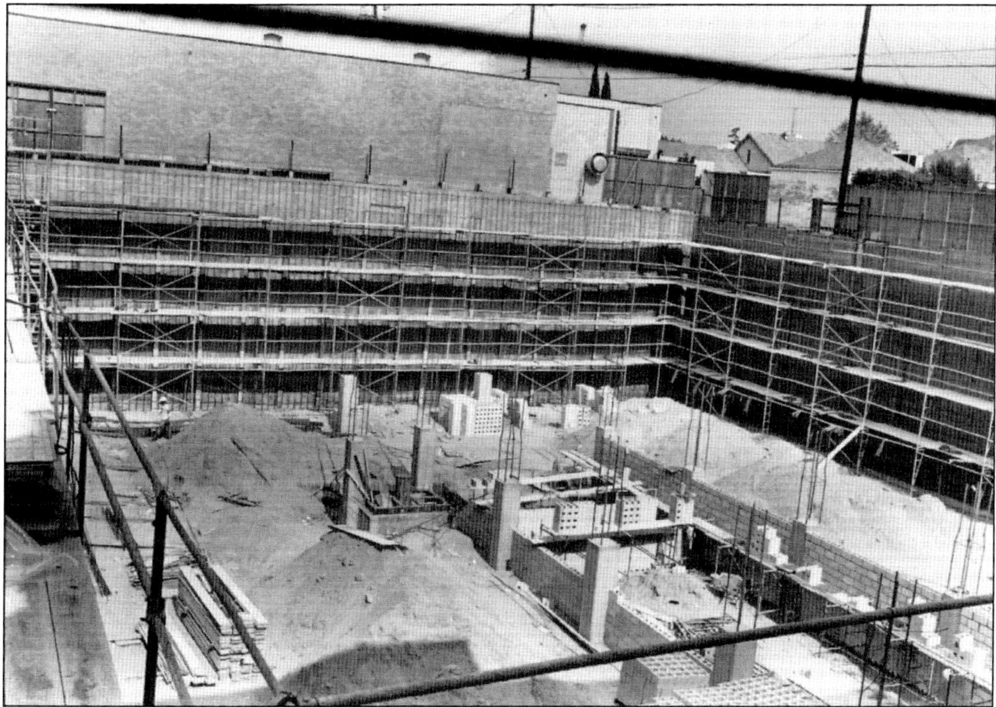

New Parking Garage under Construction at 226 North Larchmont, 1985. Motivated by a lack of parking on Larchmont, business leaders supported the project, and the city agreed to lease the garage for 24 years, with the option to purchase for $1 at the end of the 24-year lease and pay up to $2.75 million to build the parking structure. Parking revenues from Larchmont and citywide parking funds were used to pay for the project. In return, Simms was supported for his application for lower interest rate state bond financing. He also got first right of refusal to develop the 36-space parking lot across the street if the city decided to develop the property.

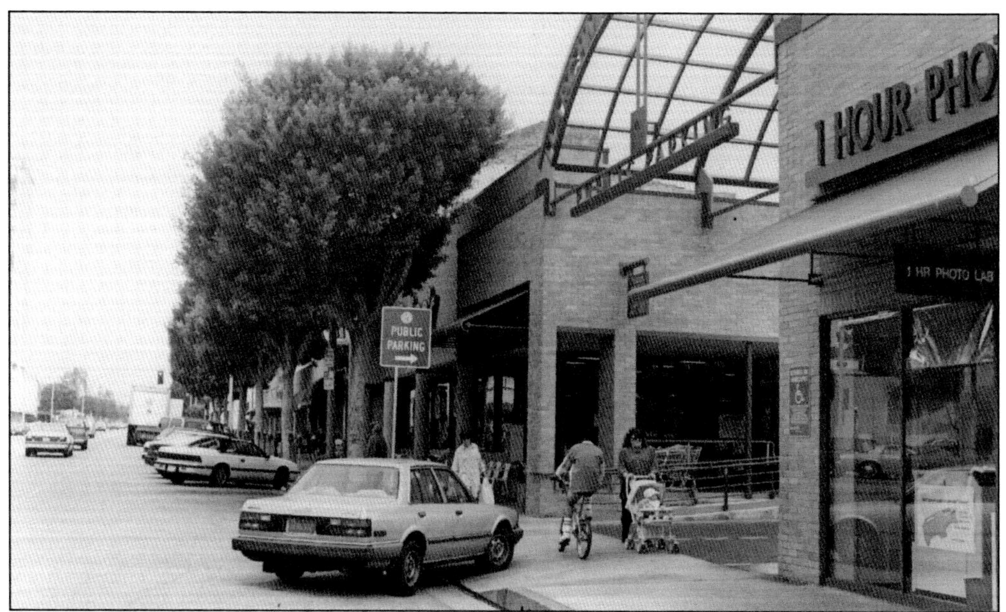

NEW PARKING GARAGE AT 226 NORTH LARCHMONT. The new parking lot added 256 public parking spaces on Larchmont. Parking had been a problem on the street for many years as the popularity of Larchmont grew.

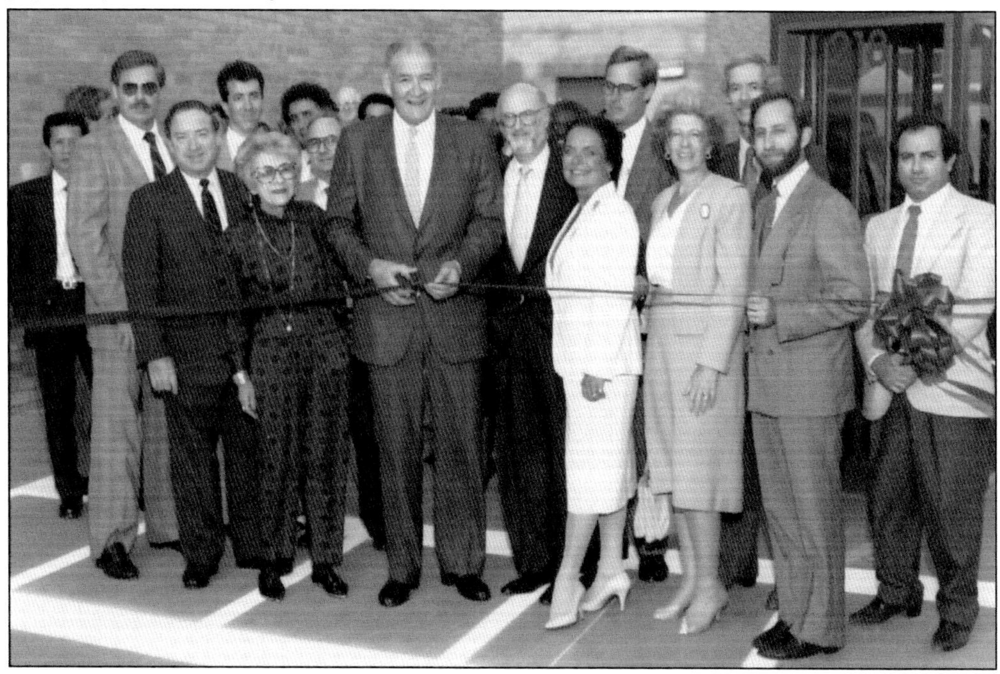

RIBBON-CUTTING FOR NEW PARKING GARAGE AND RETAIL STORES AT 226 NORTH LARCHMONT. Larchmont leaders, including *Larchmont Chronicle* copublishers Jane Gilman and Dawne Goodwin, join Councilman John Ferraro (center) and developer Ron Simms (right) for the ribbon-cutting ceremony for the new parking garage and retail stores. While enthusiastic about the much-needed parking, Larchmont shopkeepers regretted the loss of the Safeway grocery store, foot traffic, and convenience for the neighborhood.

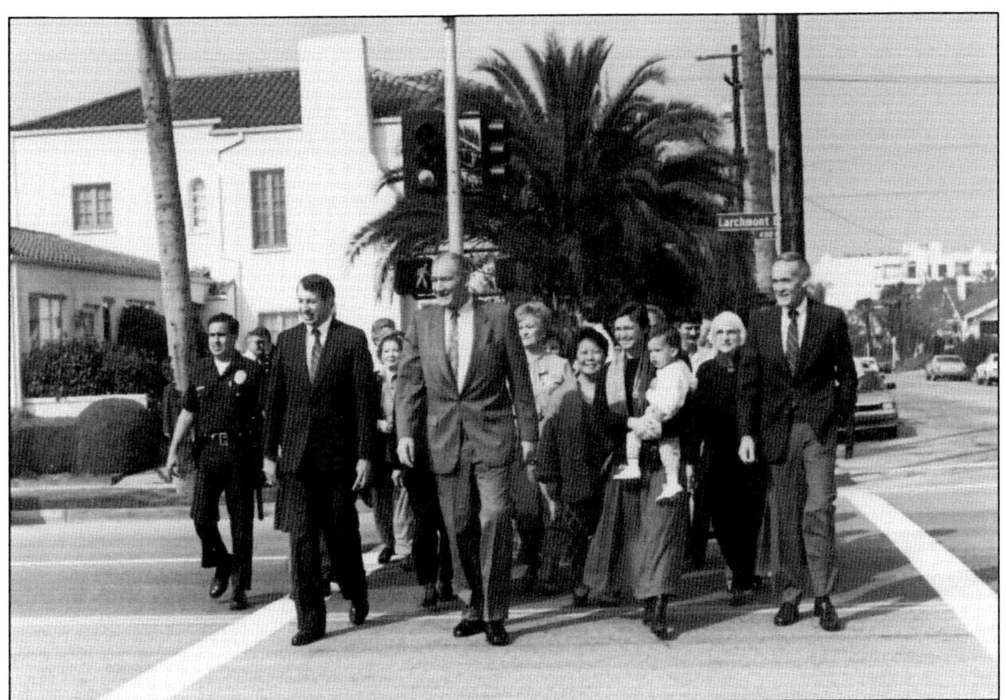

COUNCILMAN JOHN FERRARO AND LARCHMONT CONSTITUENTS. It has been said that the city of Los Angeles operates as 13 small cities, giving all the power to each city councilman. No city councilman was more effective for his district than John Ferraro, who represented Larchmont for 35 years until his death in 2001. Residents and business owners understood the importance of spending time with the councilman (shown here in the center crossing the street on upper Larchmont).

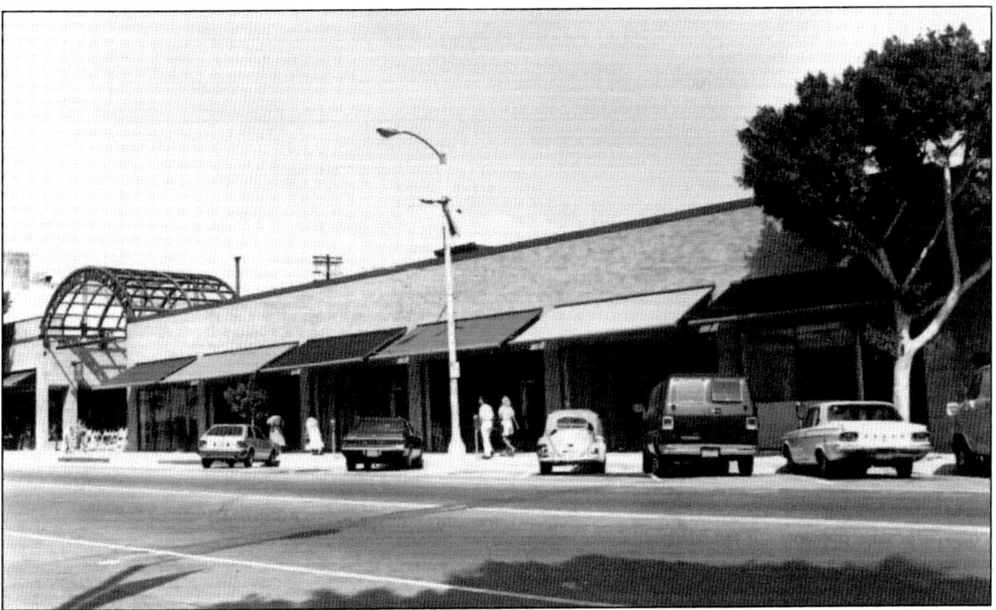

STREET VIEW OF NEW RETAIL DEVELOPMENT, 1986. This is a view from across the street of the new retail shops. It was taken shortly after construction was completed but before all of the retail spaces were leased.

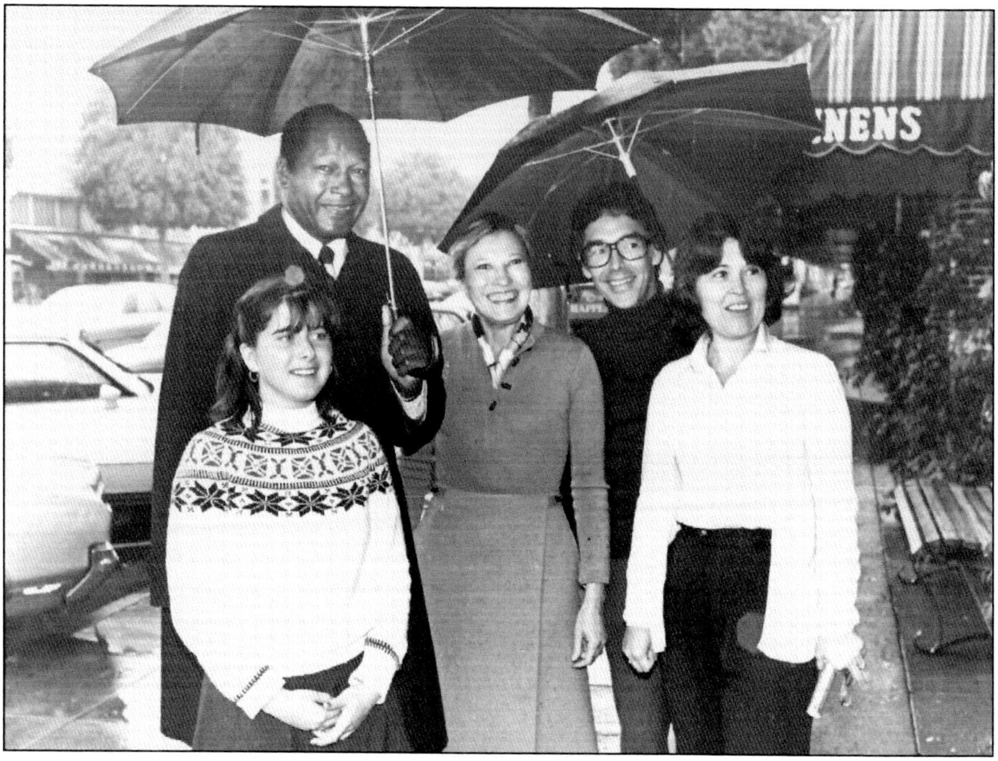

Mayor Tom Bradley on Larchmont. Larchmont is fortunate to be surrounded by some of the nicest homes in the city of Los Angeles as well as the official residence of the mayor. Getty House, named after J. Paul Getty (whose oil company donated it to the city in 1975), is just a few blocks away from Larchmont on Irving and Sixth Streets. Mayor Tom Bradley was the first mayoral resident at Getty House.

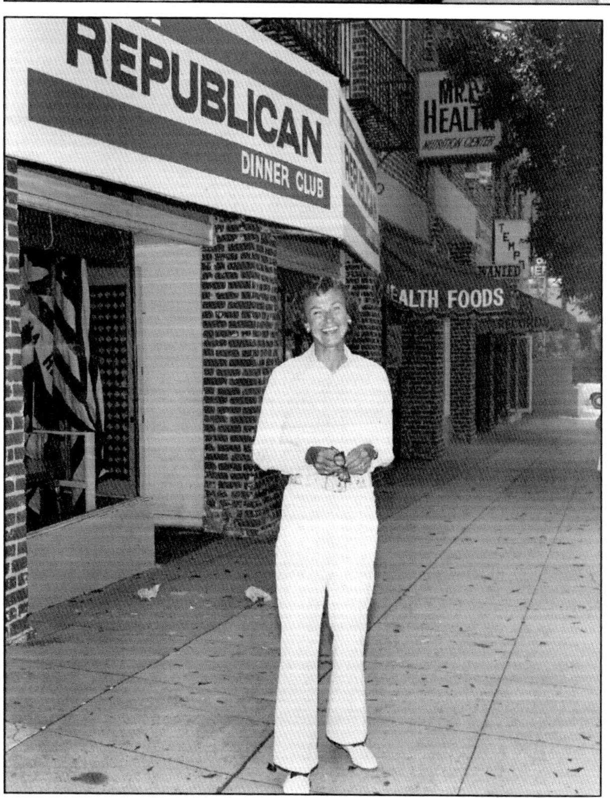

Republican Dinner Club at 215 North Larchmont. The Southern California's Republican Women club had an office above the Beverly Larchmont Pharmacy. It was the headquarters for the club's 500-plus members.

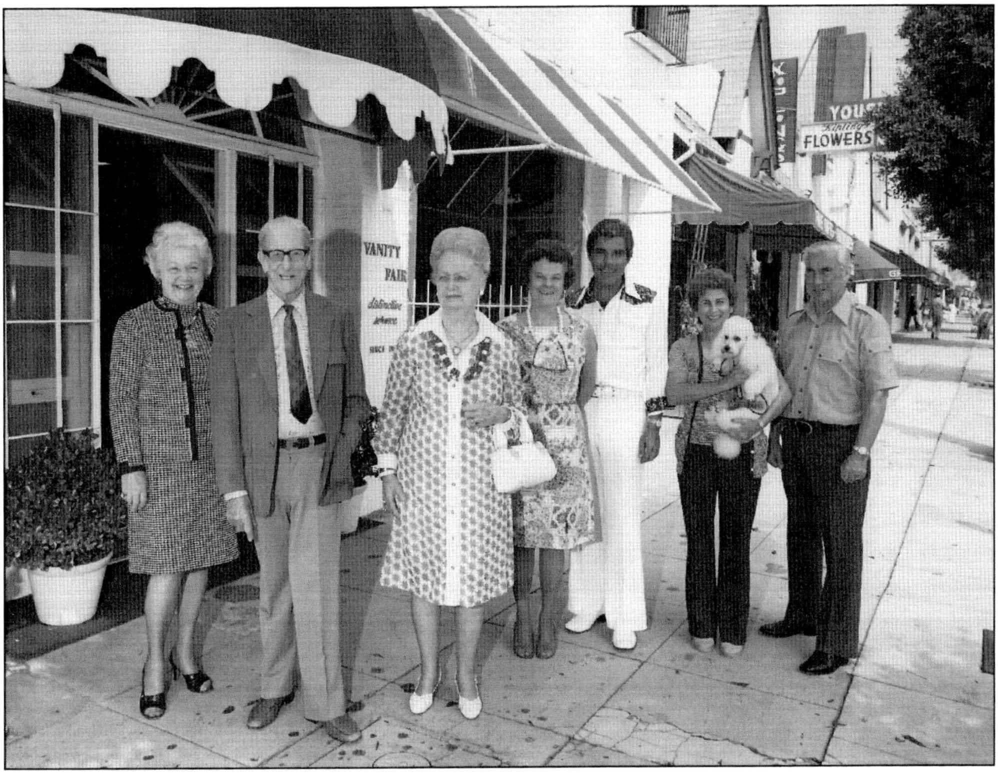

Vanity Fair at 119 North Larchmont, c. 1980. Before casual Fridays, everyone used to dress up to shop and go out to lunch, and Larchmont was no exception. Vanity Fair boasted distinctive personal service as well as fine clothing for women. This photograph shows a view of the west side of the street, looking north.

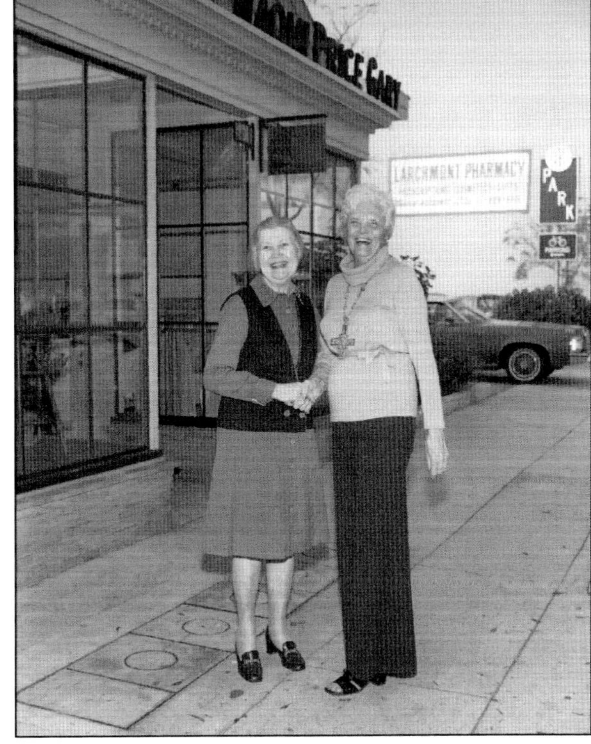

Naomi Price Gary (Left) at 205 North Larchmont. First and foremost, shopping on Larchmont was fun. Shopkeepers made sure that everyone felt welcome. Naomi Price Gary carried elegant clothes for stylish women.

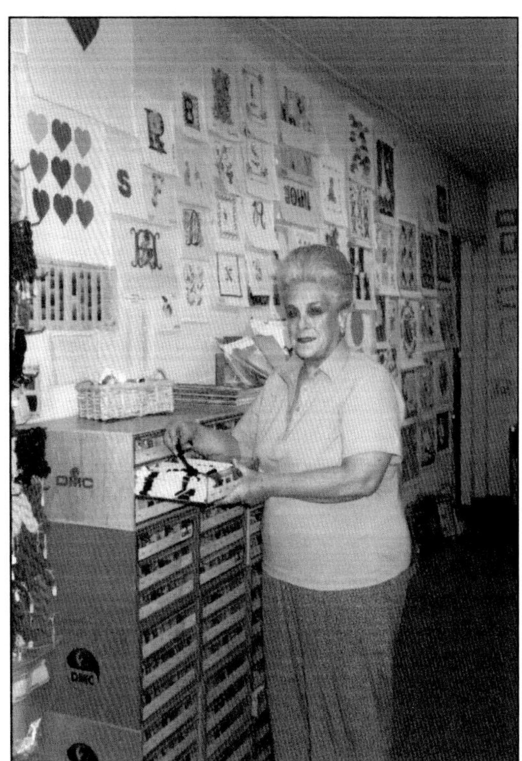

NATALIE'S NEEDLEPOINT AT 144 NORTH LARCHMONT. A well-stocked needlepoint shop is rare these days, but Larchmont had one of the best until Natalie Howard retired and closed the store in the mid-1990s.

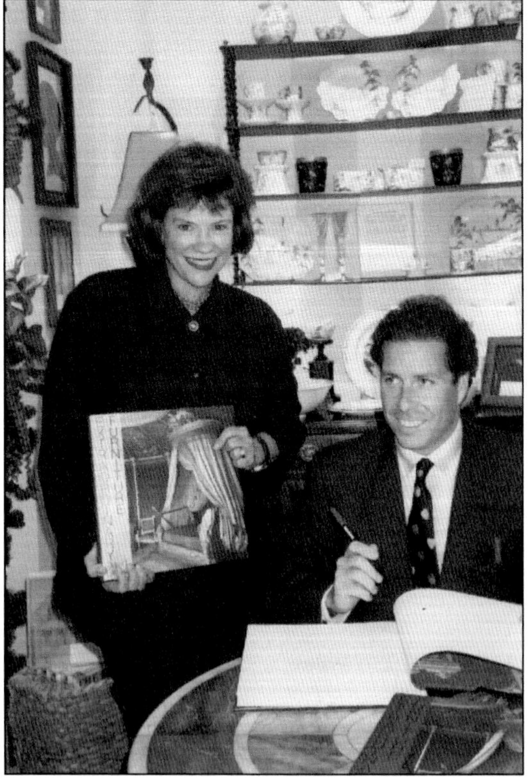

HOLLYHOCK AT 214 NORTH LARCHMONT, C. 2000. A book signing with Hollyhock owner Suzanne Rheinstein showcases Viscount Linley, who was an English furniture maker, chairman of auction house Christie's UK, and the son of Princess Margaret. Tastemaker Rheinstein's light and airy store with tropical peach and green colored walls stocked elegant antiques as well as fanciful home accessories.

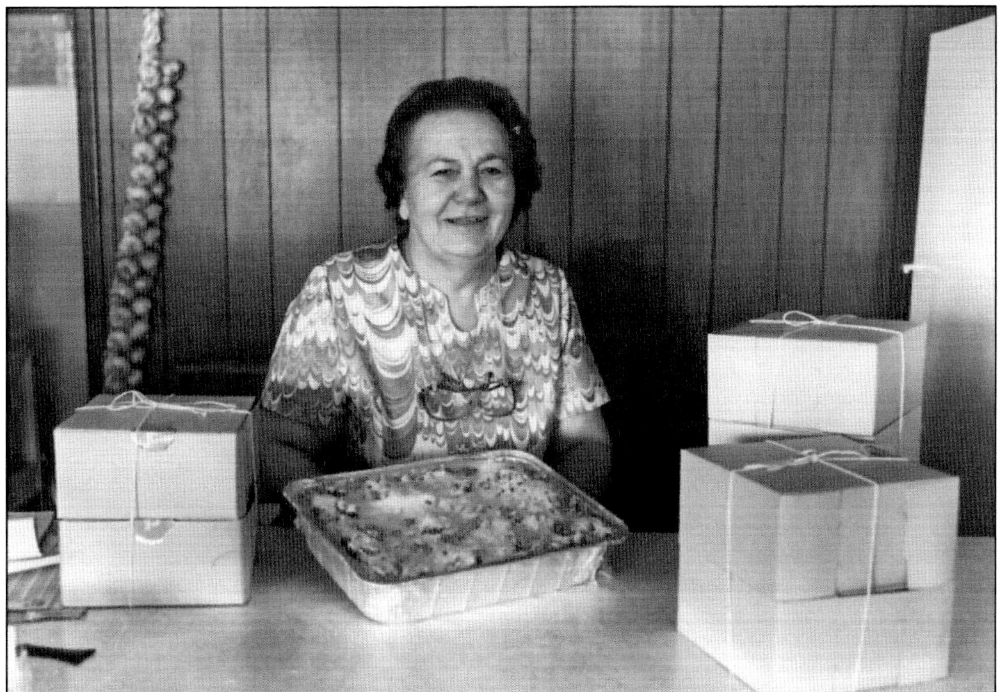

Paone Catering and Van de Kamp Bakery Shop at 225 1/2 North Larchmont. Van de Kamp Bakery Shop opened in 1926 on Larchmont, yet the family-owned business started in 1915 at Spring and Second Streets. Ted Van de Kamp became involved with the Larchmont store, which closed briefly for a remodel in 1963 when the ceiling was lowered and an ice cream freezer was added. Paone Catering moved from 112 North Larchmont into the space around 1973, offering authentic Italian cuisine. Then, Sonia and Ermanno Tolot opened Girasole Cucina Italiana around 1993. Steve and Joanna Vernetti, part of another family-owned venture, reopened as Vernetti in 2015 after a complete renovation and expansion of the space.

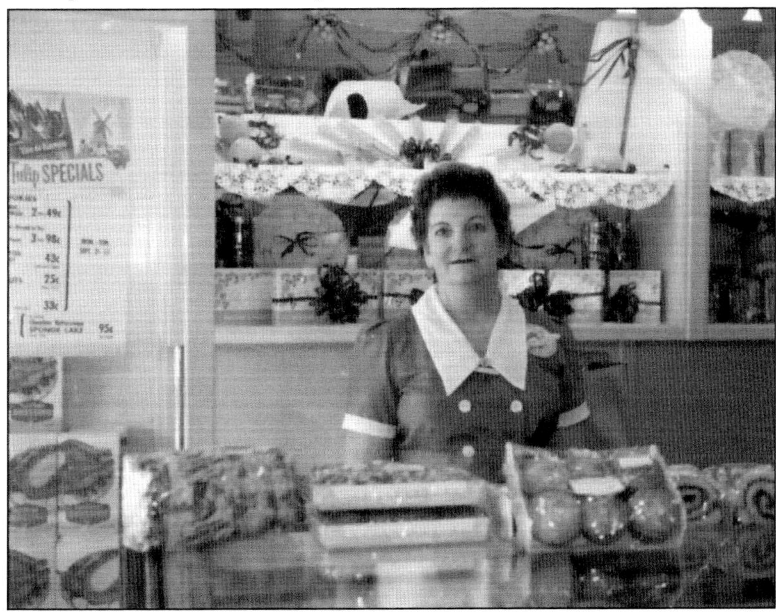

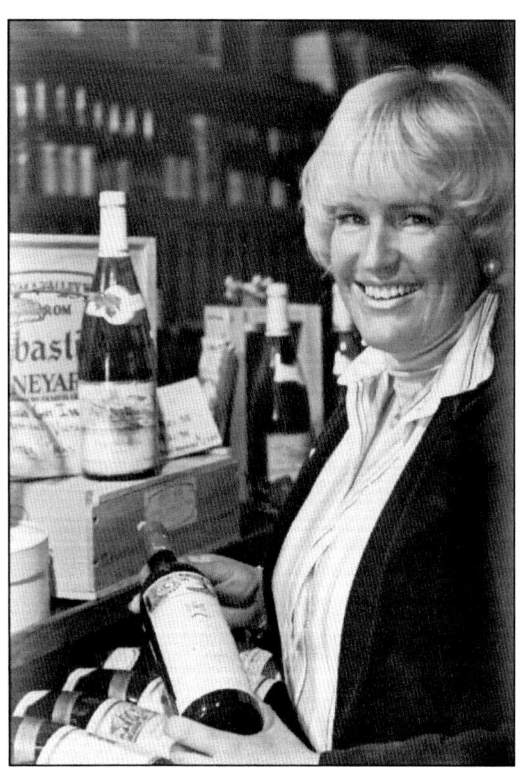

The Wine Shop at 223 North Larchmont, c. 1973. Opened in the 1970s, the narrow space was crowded with wine and spirits along with gourmet foods, including trout smoked by the owner. In 1995, John Boccato and Geoffrey B. Senior—noted wine authority and former manager of the wine and spirits departments at Jurgensen's in Pasadena—took over the business, now called the Larchmont Village Wine and Cheese Shop. Boccato's son Sergio and Simon Cocks now run the shop, offering a personalized selection. The shop is also known around the city for its sandwiches.

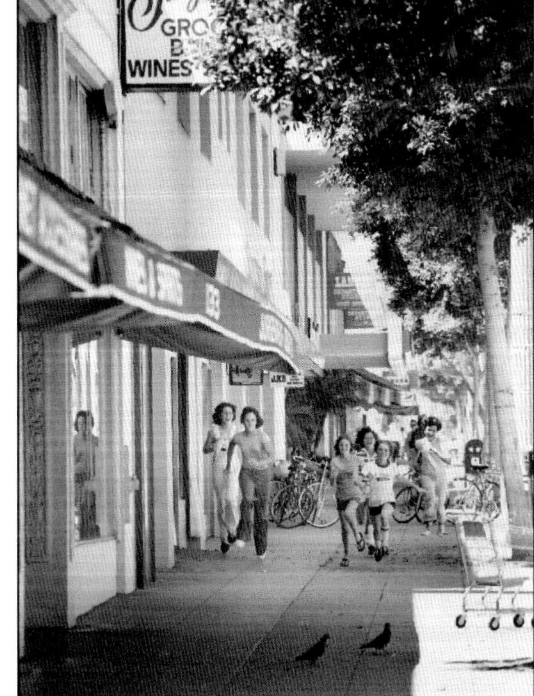

Jurgensen's Grocery Store at 133 North Larchmont. Kids and bicycles, a common scene on Larchmont, are pictured from the west side of the street, looking north. Landis Department Store can be seen in the background.

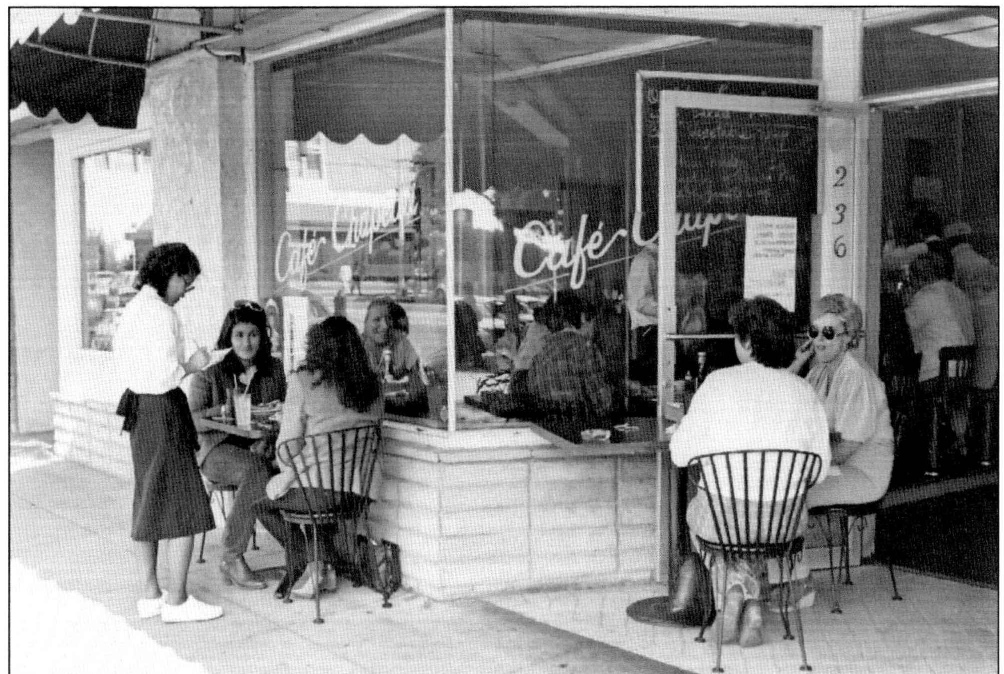

Café Chapeau at 236 North Larchmont, c. 1987. Café Chapeau coffee shop and restaurant offered residents a casual diner experience. Its predecessors include a long list of tenants. Most recent are Windsor Village Coffee Shop, Homer's in 1961, and Harlan House in 1956. In 1942, Chatham Lewis Confections had a candy store, and in 1939 Lois Brain had a secondhand clothing store. Hershel and Sara Gerson had a clothing-cleaners shop in 1926. The earliest listing in the Los Angeles telephone directory is for Snyder and Son Tailors in 1923.

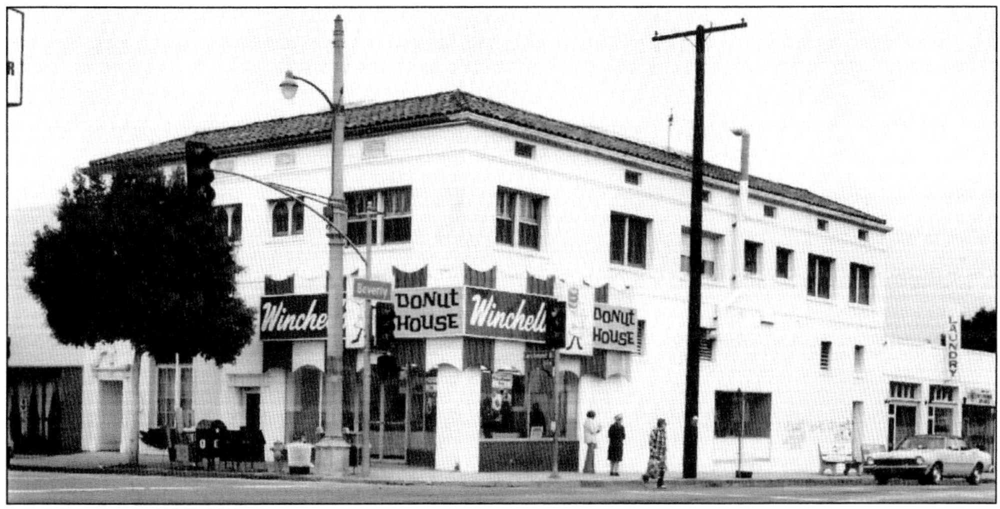

Winchell's Donut House at 251 North Larchmont, c. 1963. The building at the corner of Larchmont and Beverly Boulevards housed various businesses over the years, with retail shops on the bottom and apartments and later offices on the second floor. In 1923, the Windsor Square Pharmacy occupied the retail corner. In 1932, Samuel P. Snow Drugs took over the space, followed by the Owl Drug Company in 1936. In 1951, Bill Schulhoff opened the Beverly Larchmont Drug Company and stayed there until he moved down the street in 1960.

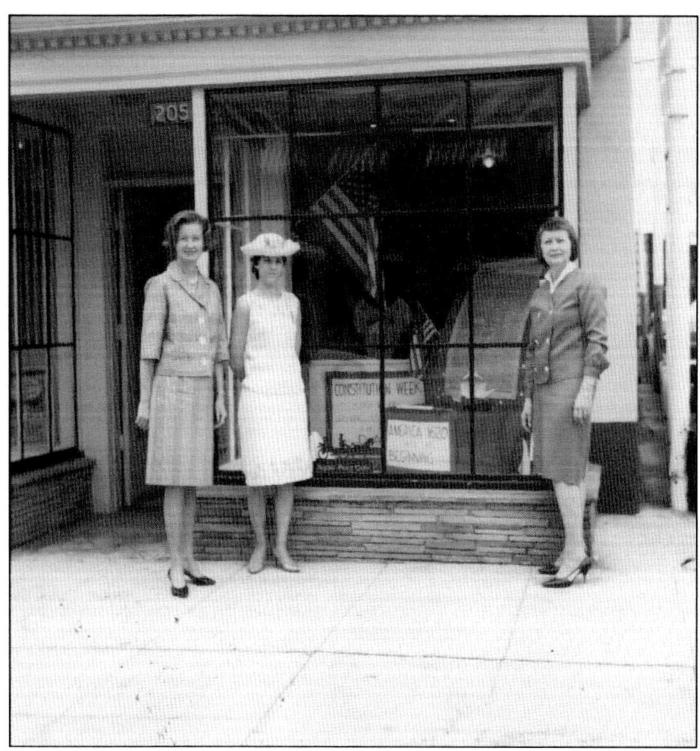

Naomi Price Gary Celebrates Constitution Week. Naomi Gary (right) dedicated the window space of her clothing store at 205 North Larchmont to the celebration of Constitution Week.

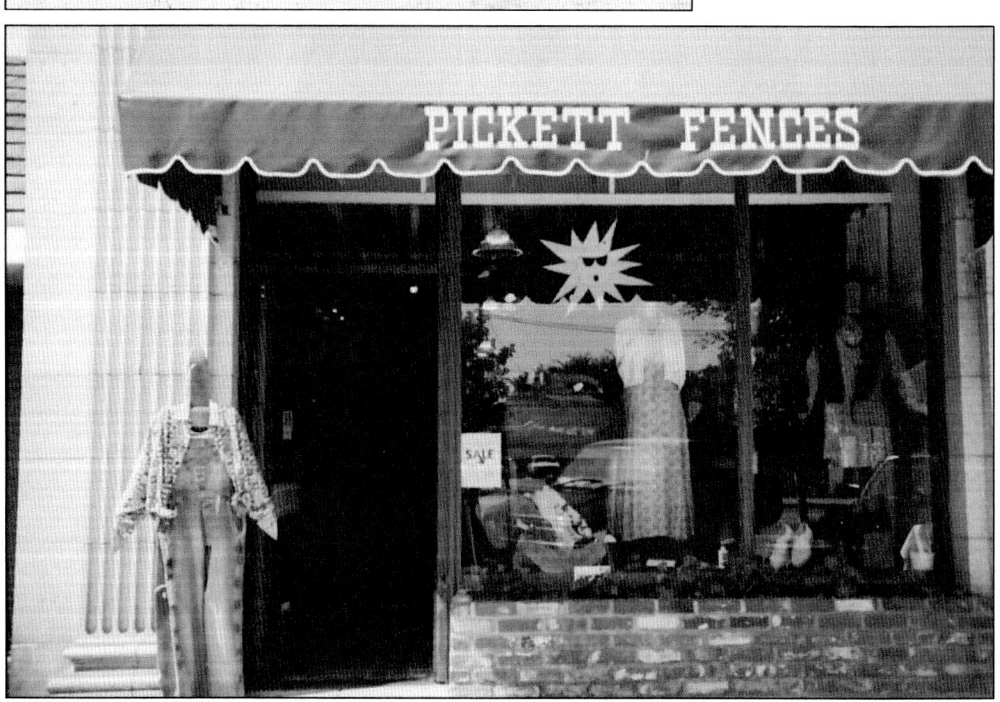

Picket Fences at 111 North Larchmont, 1994. Joane Hennenberger and her husband, Wiley Pickett, opened their clothing boutique in 1994, offering personal service and quality clothing for men and women. Hennenberger became very active on Larchmont Boulevard and served as president of the Larchmont Boulevard Association in the tradition of earlier Larchmont merchants.

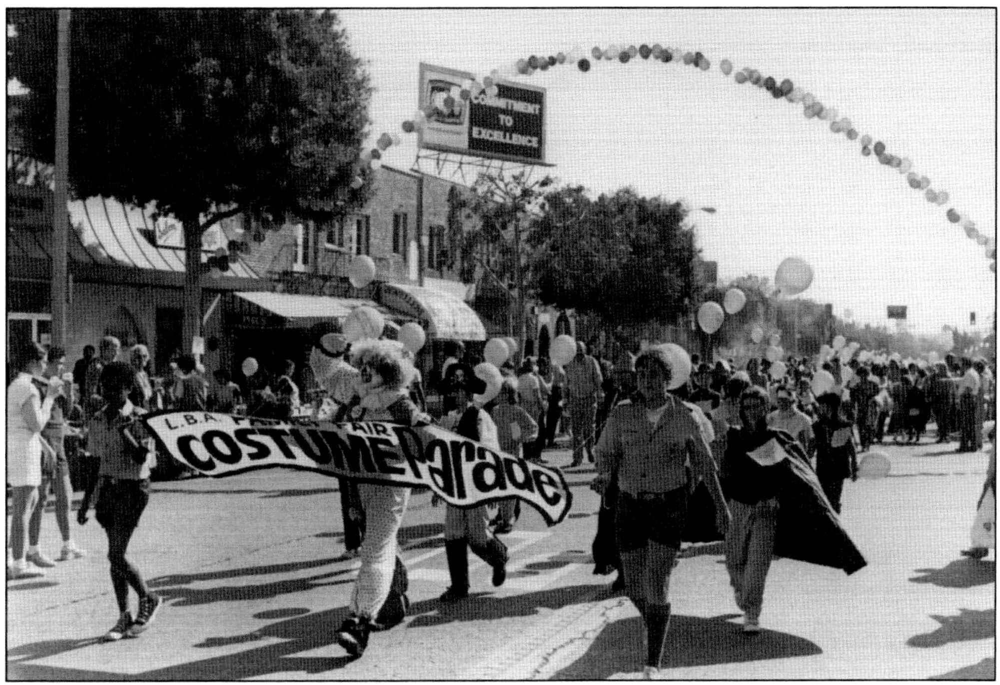

LARCHMONT FAMILY FAIR. The Larchmont Fair, just before Halloween, is an annual tradition that draws thousands of near-locals and residents to the street. Sponsored by the Larchmont Boulevard Association, the fair—with its annual Halloween parade—is a must-attend for kids of all ages.

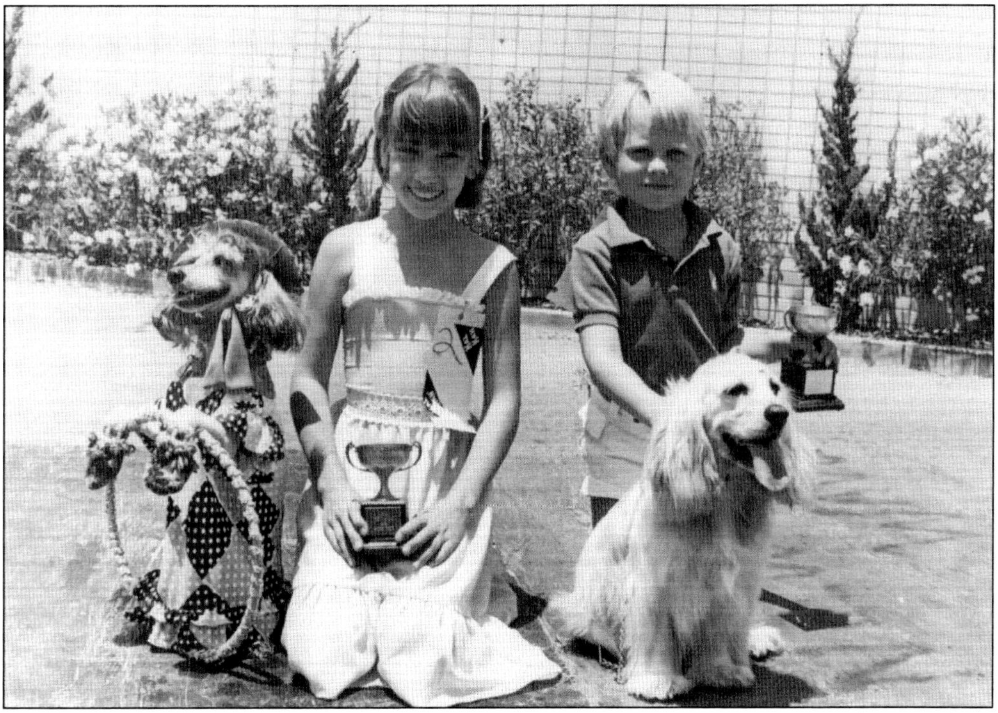

LARCHMONT PET SHOW, 1981. Pictured are Best Pet Award winners from the formerly held Larchmont Pet Show. The show was sponsored by the Larchmont Boulevard Association.

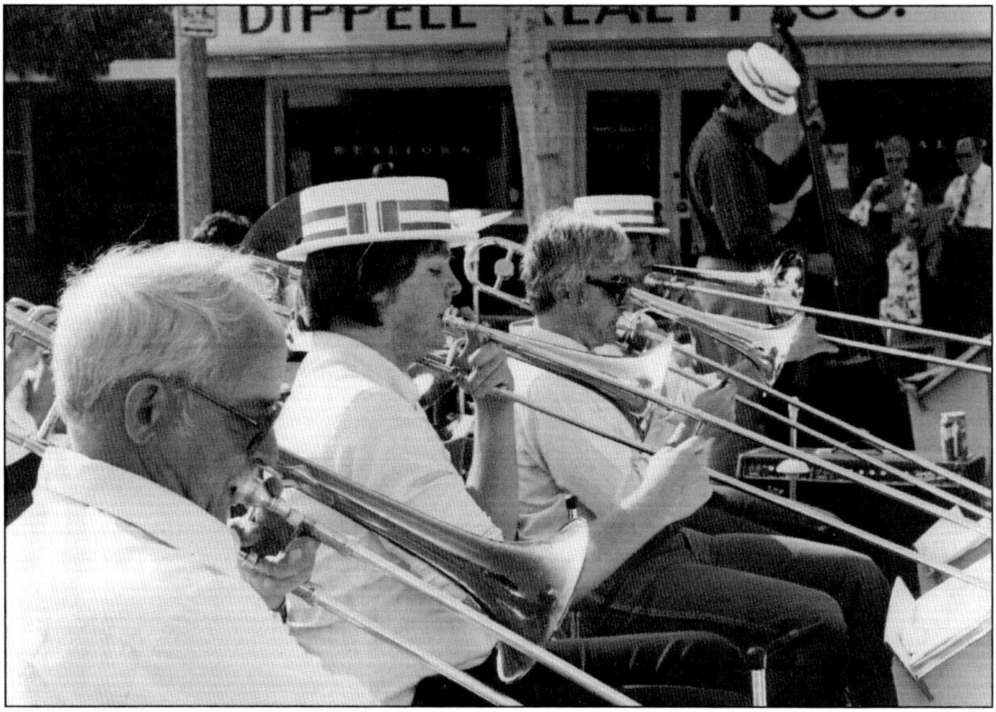

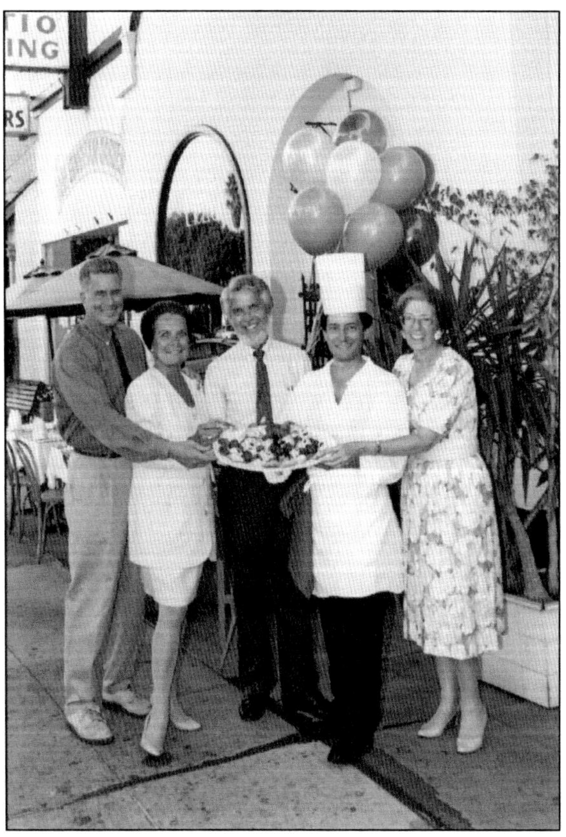

Taste of Larchmont. Started in 1992 as a fundraiser for Hope-Net (a social-service organization addressing homelessness and hunger) to celebrate the 30th anniversary of the *Larchmont Chronicle*, the Taste of Larchmont is another annual family-friendly tradition that brings the community together. The event features live music and food from Larchmont restaurants. Local celebrities attend to support the cause and the Larchmont community. Pictured from left to right are television personality Huell Howser, *Larchmont Chronicle* copublisher Dawne Goodwin, Larry Hixon, chef Thomas Houndalas of Le Petit Greek Restaurant at 127 North Larchmont, and *Larchmont Chronicle* copublisher Jane Gilman.

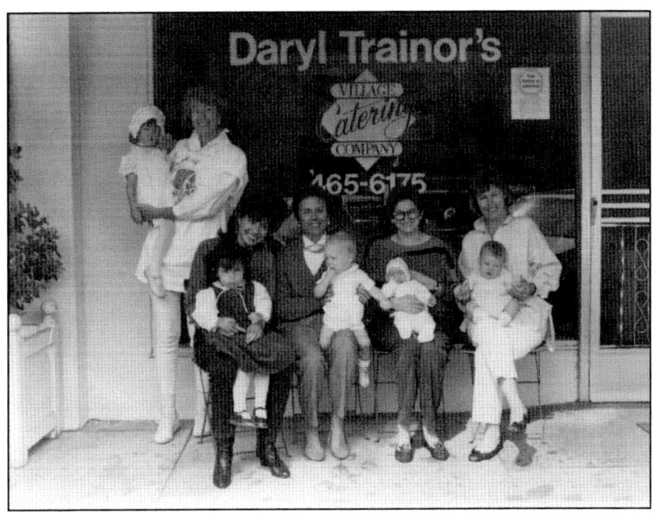

Village Catering at 139 1/2 North Larchmont. Village Catering was founded in 1976 and purchased by Daryl Trainor in 1982. Trainor (now Trainor-Twerdahl) was very active in civic affairs of Larchmont and served as an officer of the Larchmont Boulevard Association. She is shown here (standing) with friends and customers holding their children in a photograph that ran in the *Larchmont Chronicle* honoring moms on Mother's Day.

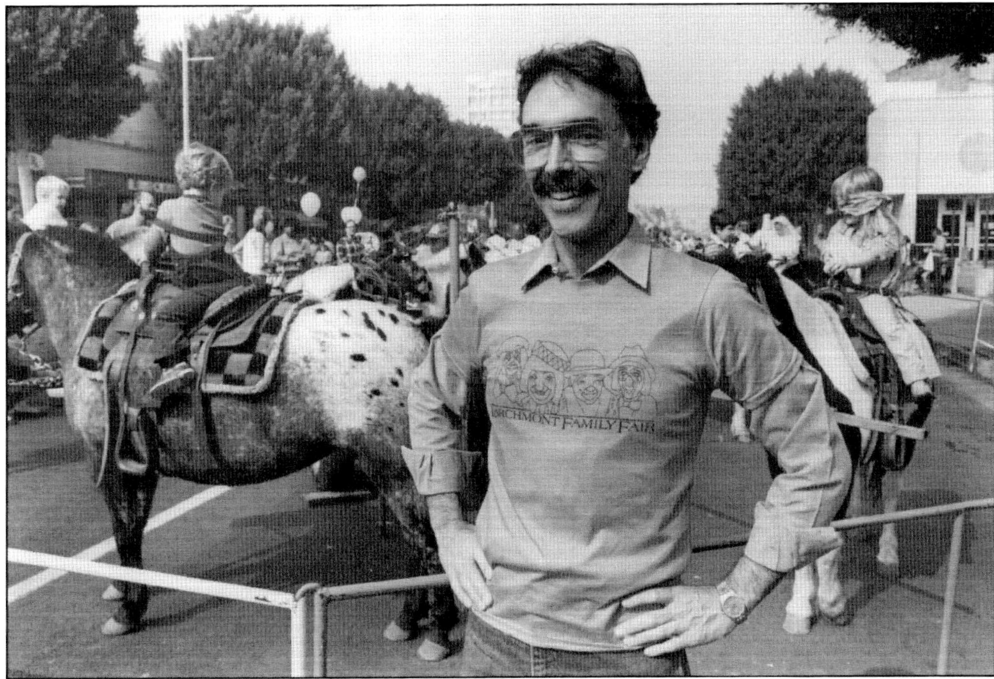

Paul Thompson, Owner of Paul Thompson Jewelers at 122 1/2 North Larchmont. A master gemologist, Paul Thompson was a pillar of the Larchmont community. In 1980, Thompson opened an elegant jewelry and gift store that sold fine stationery and antiques. He was also very committed to Larchmont and served as president of the Larchmont Boulevard Association.

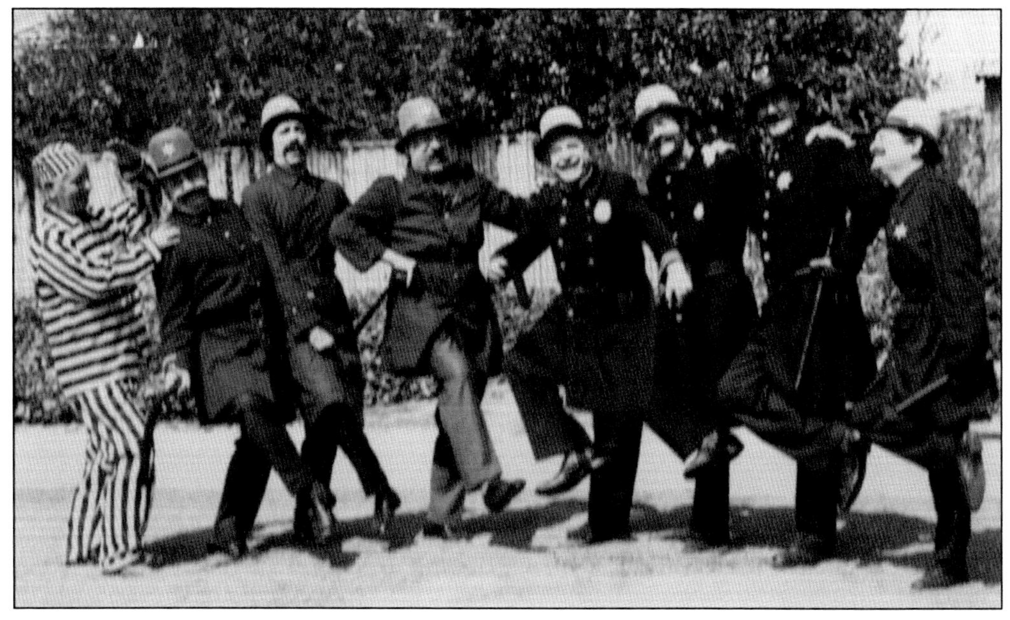

Keystone Kops on Larchmont. Eddie LeVeque, one of the original Keystone Kops, lived in the neighborhood and would often participate in local events on the boulevard, including the 50th anniversary of Larchmont in 1971.

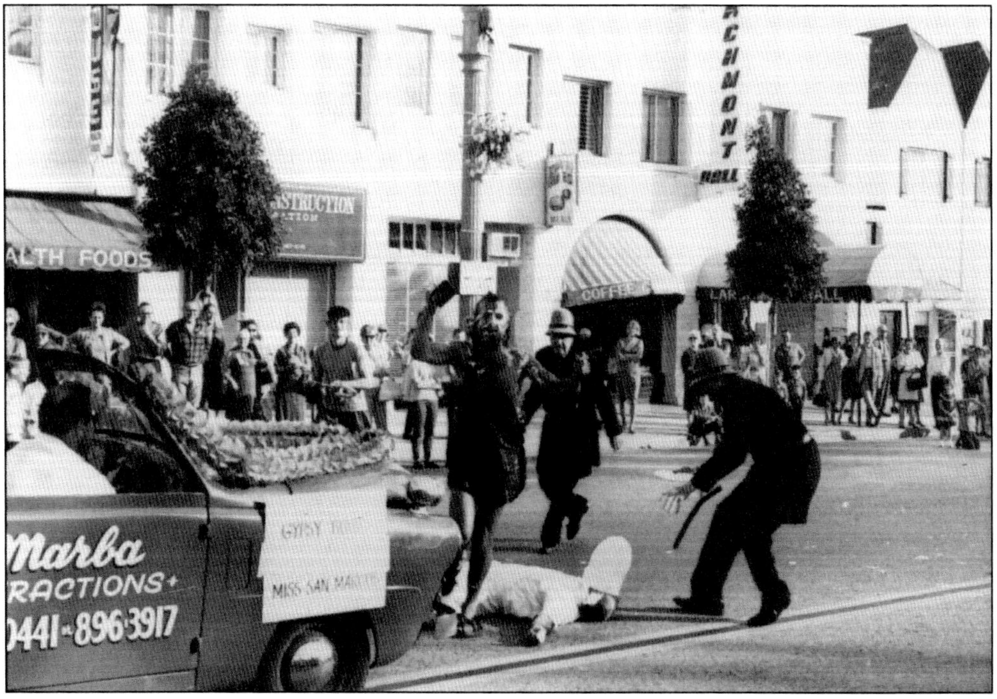

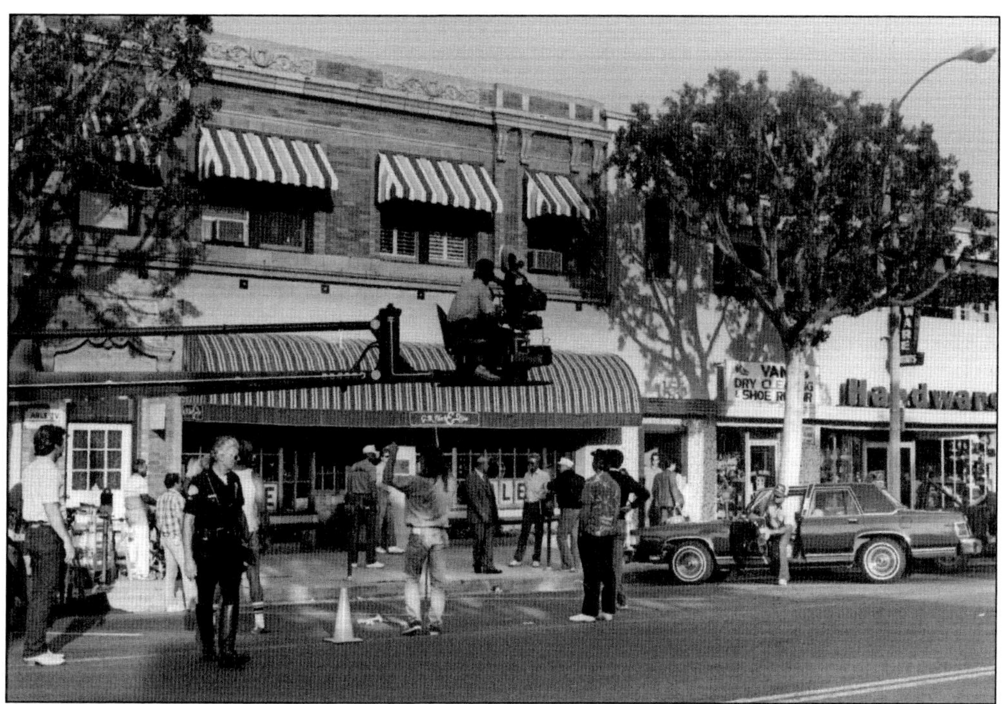

Larchmont as a Movie Location. Picturesque Larchmont was often a stand-in for the main street of a typical American small town.

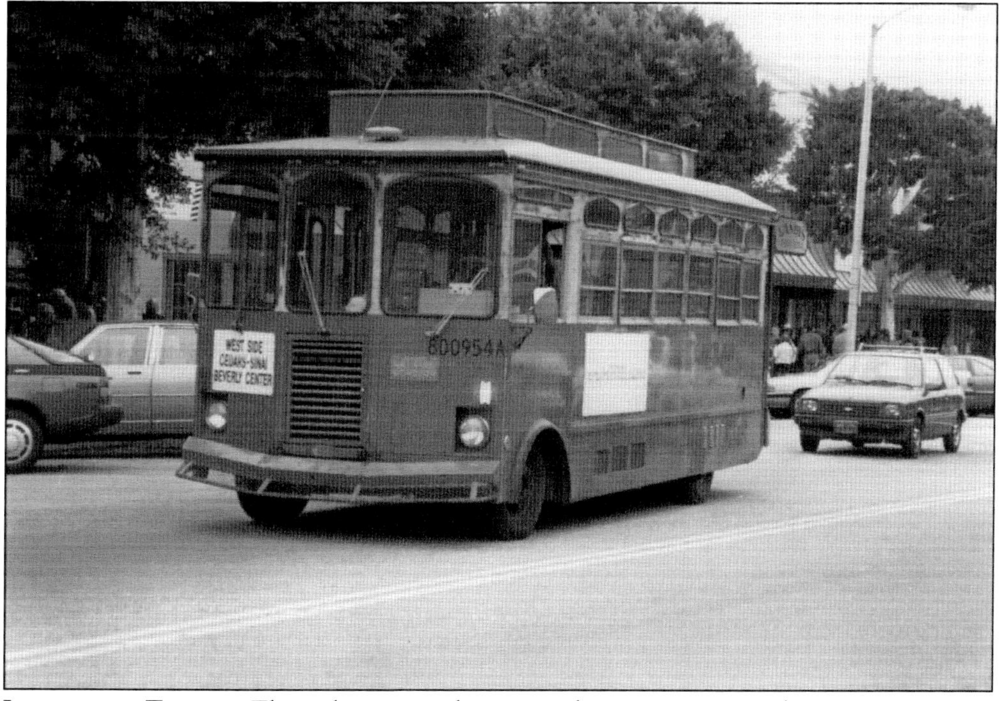

Larchmont Trolley. The railway car is long gone, but in 2006 councilman Tom LaBonge responded to community and business owner complaints about the lack of parking by funding a trolley bus to take shoppers up and down Larchmont during the holiday shopping season.

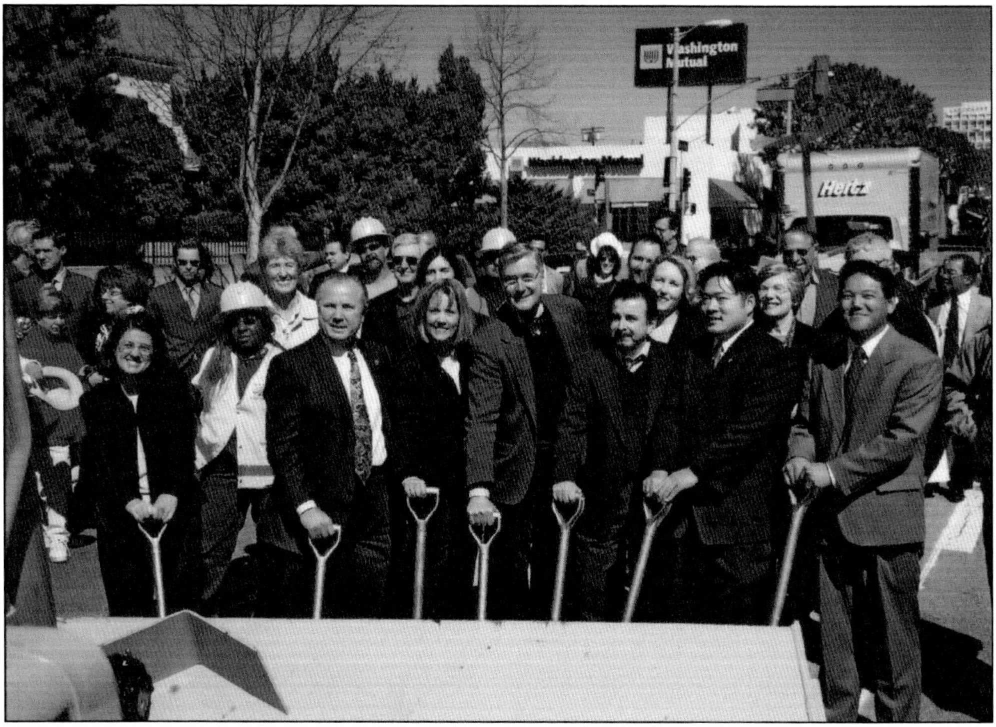

LARCHMONT MEDIAN, 2002. In 1998, residents initiated a project to create a landscaped median on Larchmont between First and Third Streets. Architect and Windsor Square resident Douglas Meyer and resident Linda McKnight, with assistance from residents Norman Murdoch and Carolyn Ramsay, developed the plan. With financial support from the Windsor Square Association and the City of Los Angeles Bureau of Street Services, the plan to create an entryway for Larchmont was completed in 2002. The plan called for the creation of an entry monument and the planting of 28 jacaranda trees. The project was initiated by neighbors in 1998 and completed in 2002. Funding was provided by generous donations from neighbors, local organizations, and a grant from the Metropolitan Transportation Authority.

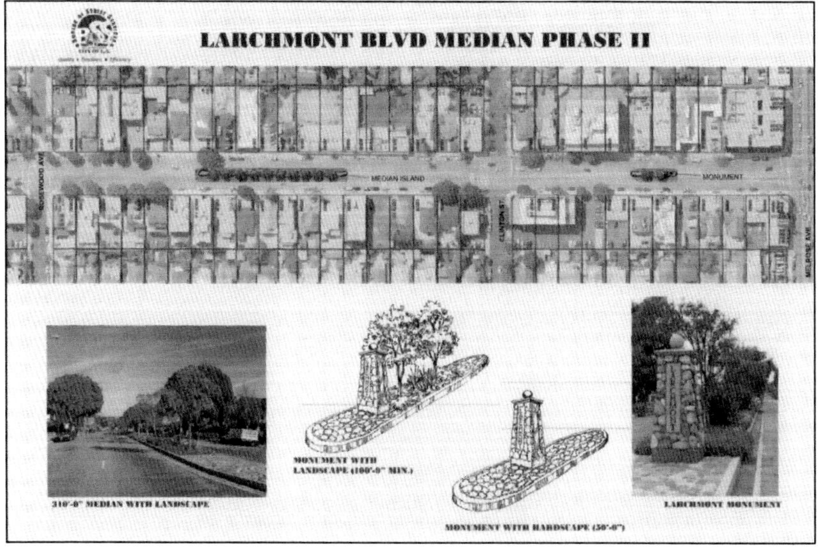

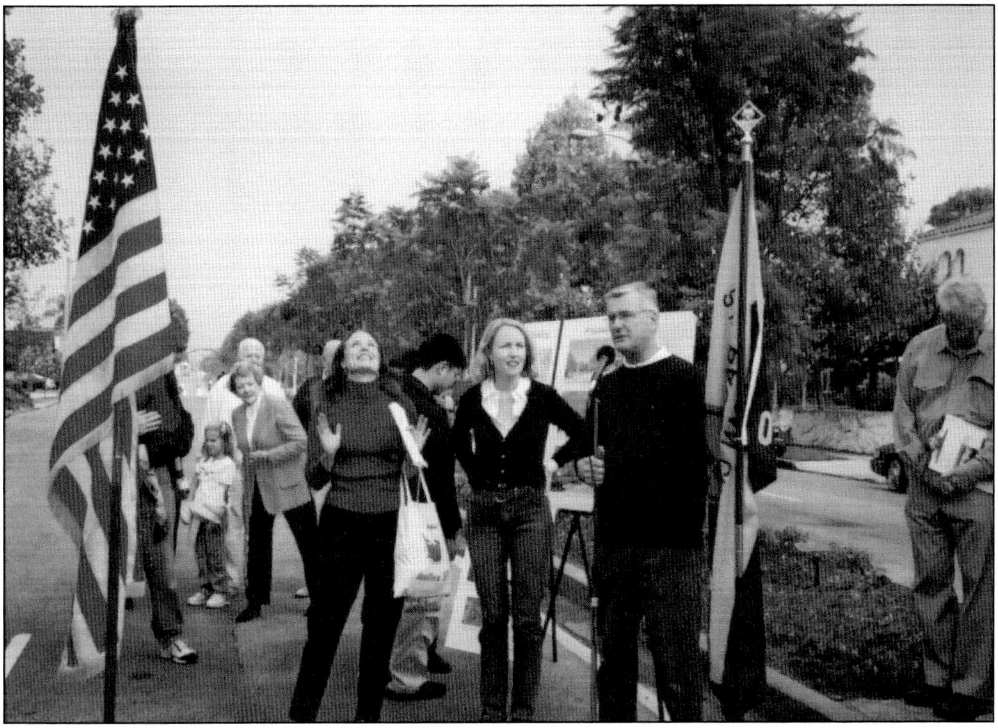

COMPLETING THE LARCHMONT MEDIAN, 2002. Linda McKnight (left), Carolyn Ramsay (center), and Doug Meyer—residents of Windsor Square and leaders of the median project—celebrate the completion.

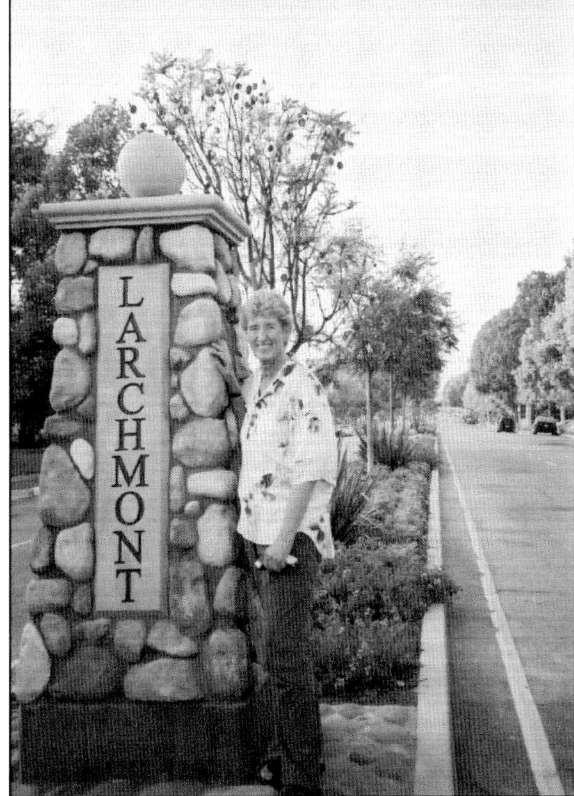

LANDSCAPE DESIGNER SANDY KENNEDY. Without the railway tracks, Larchmont Boulevard—between Third and First Streets, south of the commercial district—was very wide and the prime place for a landscaped median. Sandy Kennedy, active in the Windsor Square tree canopy project, lent her expertise to the Larchmont median project.

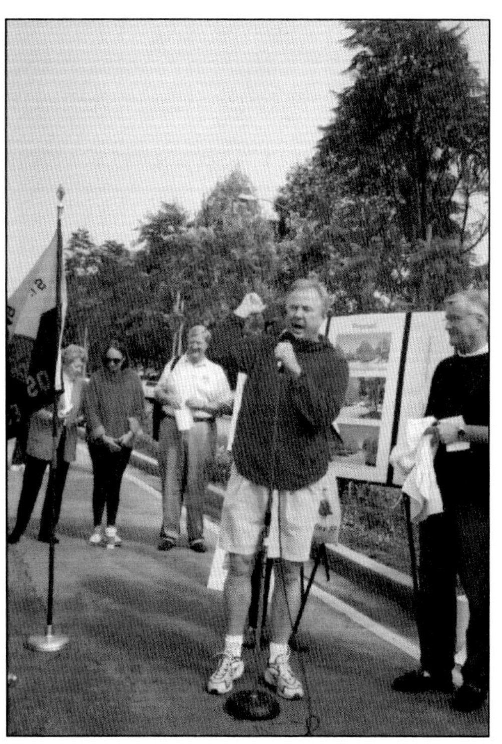

COUNCILMAN TOM LABONGE. LaBonge, who previously worked as a field deputy for Councilman Ferraro, served as councilman for Council District 4 for 14 years. During his almost 40 years in public service, LaBonge was hands-on and very active in the neighborhood.

GROUND-BREAKING OF MINI MEDIANS. The success of the median inspired another median in the commercial district. Councilman LaBonge and civic leaders break ground on new medians in the village.

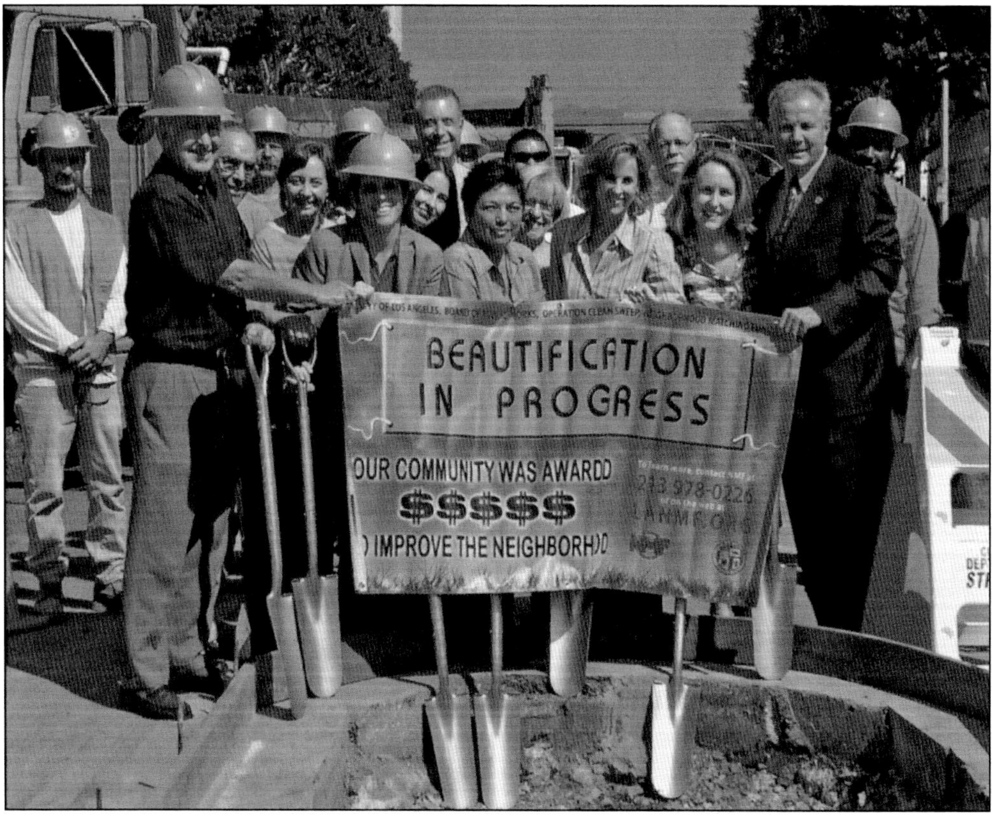

Four

Upper Larchmont

When the Los Angeles streetcar line traveled up Larchmont, it went all the way to Melrose Avenue to take bathers to the Hollywood Mineral Hot Springs, just east of Larchmont near Gower Street. Upper Larchmont was developed as part of the Larchmont Heights tract, now known as Larchmont Village. Most of the homes were built around the same time as nearby neighborhoods, though there was no single developer. According to the Larchmont Village Neighborhood Association, most of the homes were built by individuals to occupy or sell to the growing population of newcomers.

In time, the residential homes were converted to businesses, and upper Larchmont became an extension of Larchmont, though distinctly different. The intersection at Beverly and Larchmont serves as a kind of "four-corners," connecting upper Larchmont to the village. As a result, the corner and adjacent lots were the first to be converted into stores. In the 1980s, the corner gas station was converted into a drive-through hamburger stand. Across the street, the first and only high-rise on the road was built.

The charming bungalow homes now house offices, shops, and even a school—Page Private School—that opened in the 1930s. Specialty shops like Dawson's Books opened, taking advantage of the proximity to the village and more affordable space.

The eclectic nature of the street still exists, and now there are opportunities to live even closer than before. The Larchmoyne, built in 1929, still offers studio and bachelor apartments for those who want convenience and walkability, a very rare and valuable commodity in Los Angeles. As a result, upper Larchmont is a very desirable place to live, if people can find the space.

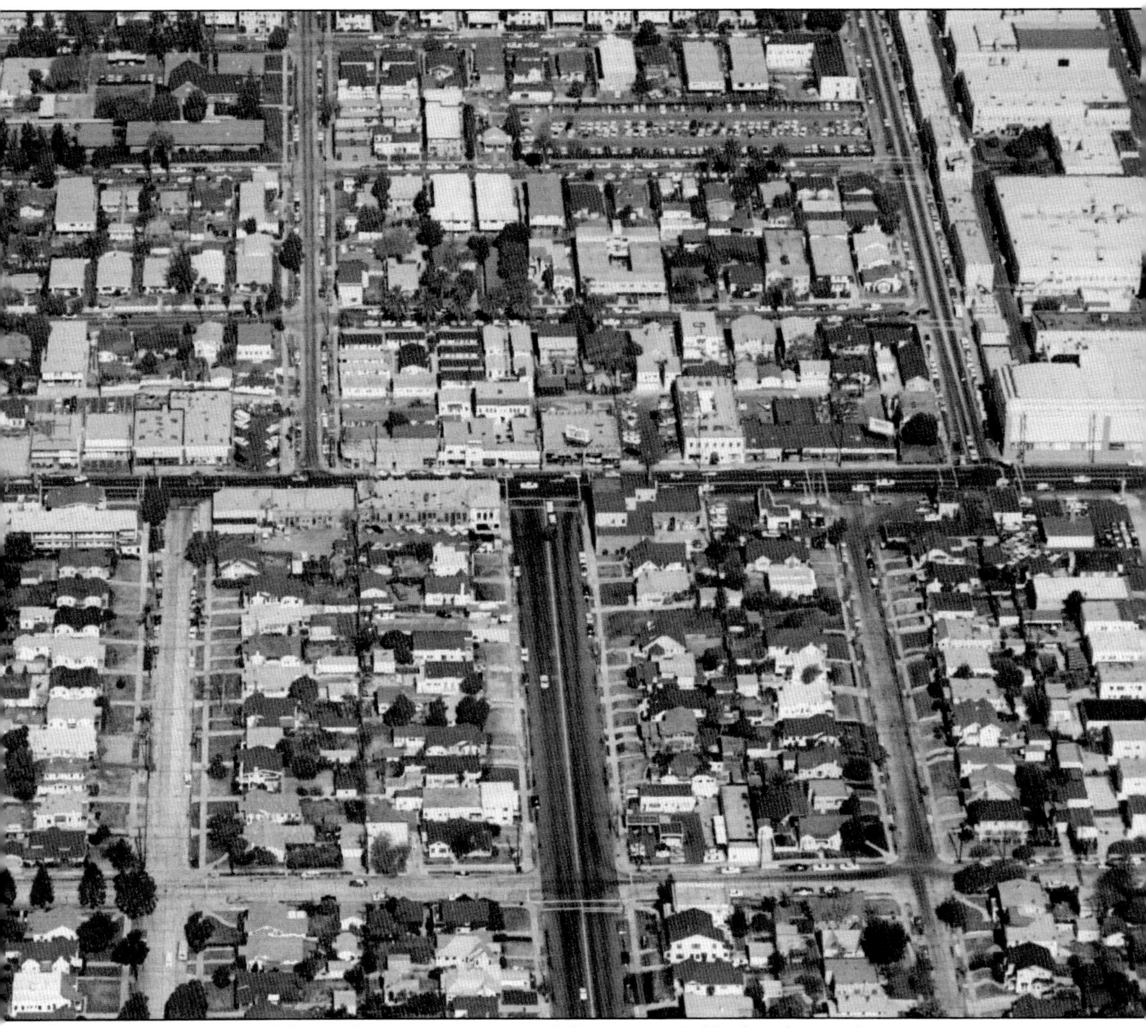

Aerial View of Upper Larchmont near Melrose, 1964. Larchmont's proximity to movie studios has drawn residents who work in the entertainment industry. Paramount Pictures is shown here.

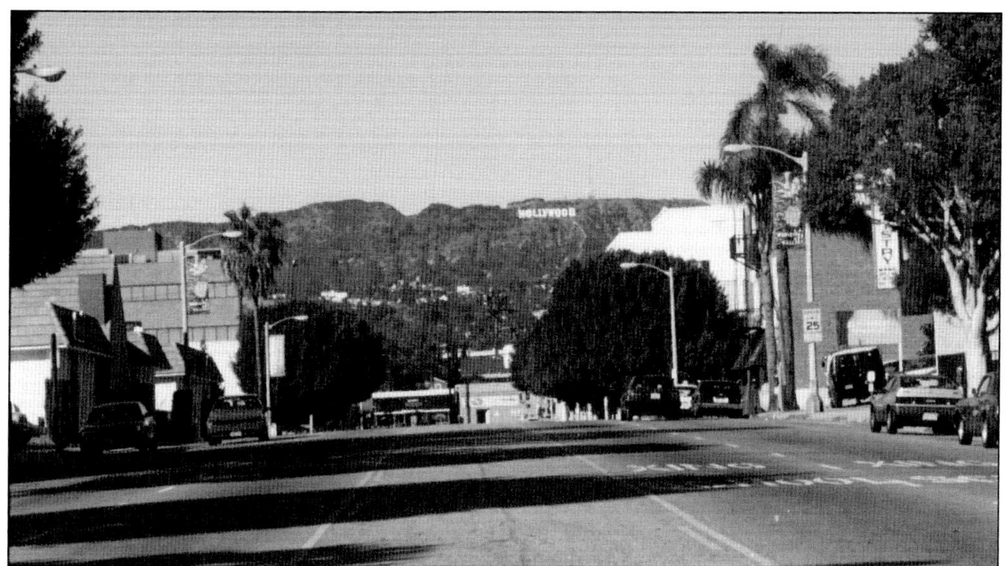

STREET VIEW OF LARCHMONT LOOKING NORTH, 1985. The Hollywood sign can clearly be seen from Larmont. At left is Page Private School. There is now a landscaped median on upper Larchmont Boulevard.

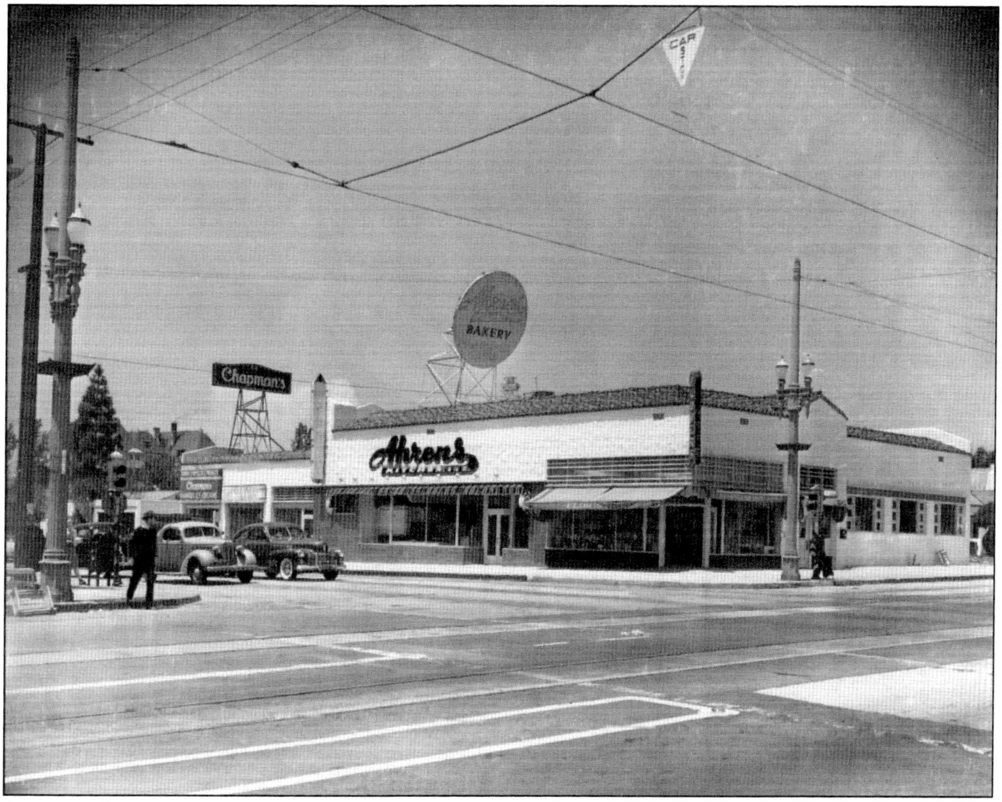

AHREN'S KITCHEN AND BAKERY, C. 1940. Ahren's Kitchen and Bakery, Champan Ice Cream, Beverly Cleaners, and Country Florist occupied the northwest corner of Larchmont and Beverly Boulevards.

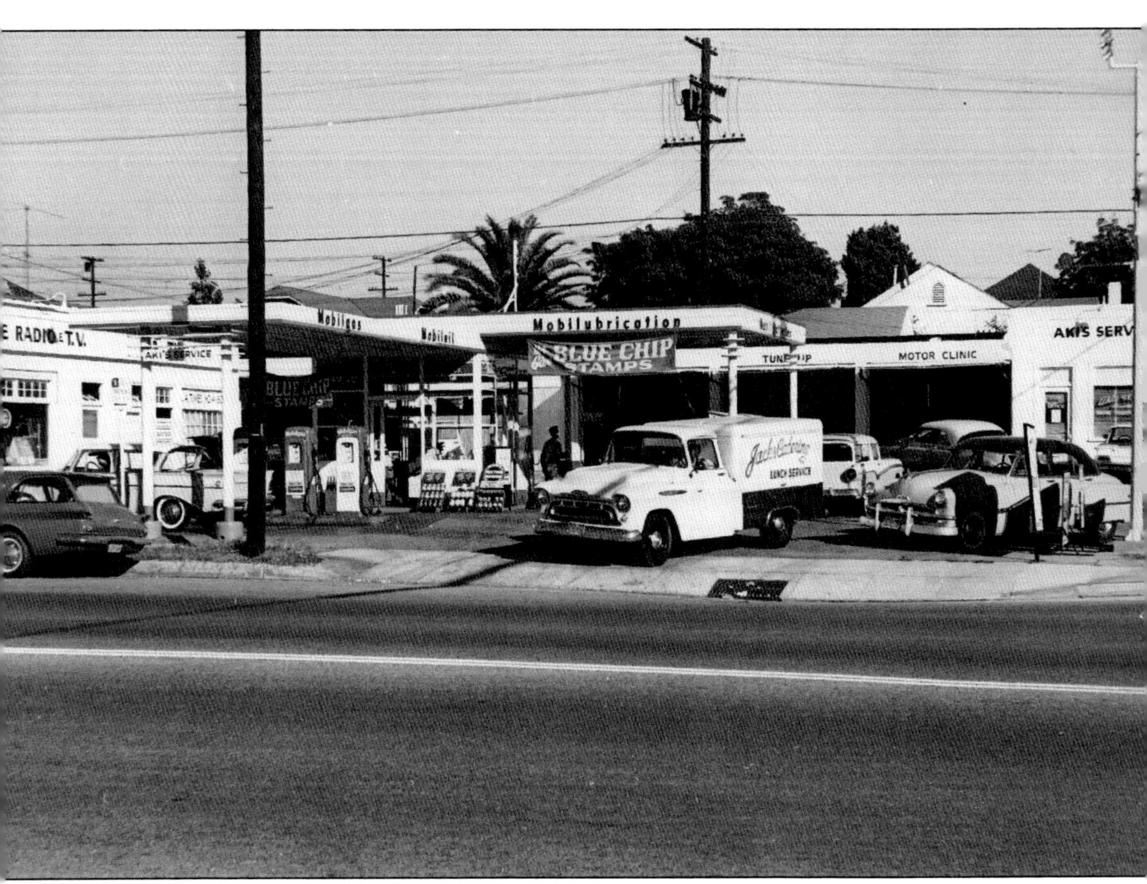

MOBIL SERVICE STATION AT 600 NORTH LARCHMONT, C. 1960. At the northeast corner of Clinton and Larchmont Boulevards, Aki's Service Station offered residents yet another place to fill up their tanks in the neighborhood. (Courtesy of Marc Wanamaker at Bison Archives.)

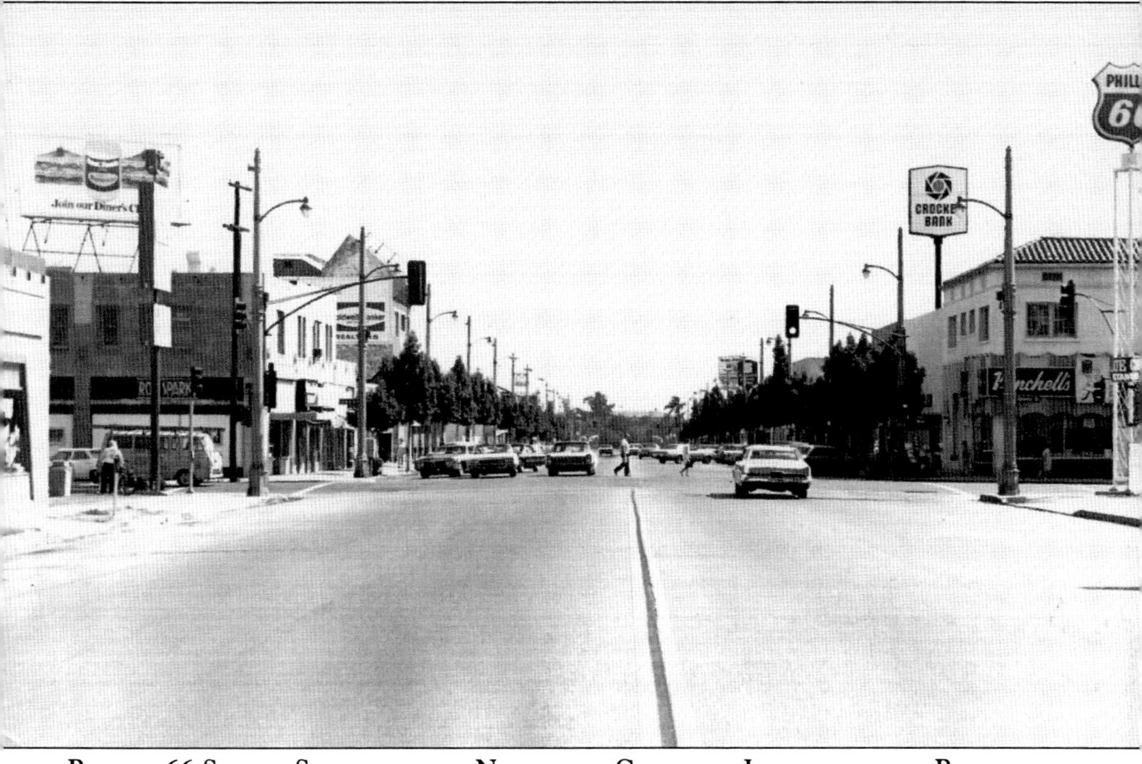

PHILLIPS 66 SERVICE STATION AT THE NORTHWEST CORNER OF LARCHMONT AND BEVERLY, C. 1970. At one time there were half a dozen gas stations along Larchmont. Real estate values and gasoline prices have risen dramatically over the years. The buildings on the south side of Beverly Boulevard remain the same, but the gas stations on the north side have been replaced by Ritz Cleaners on the east side of the street and a Chipotle restaurant on the west side at 301 North Larchmont, which started as a real estate office when it was built in 1921. The next year, Julius LaBonte and Charles Ramson took over and enlarged the space and built a garage in the rear. In 1926, the new owners converted the space to a flower shop, where it remained a retail space. In 1996, Koo Koo Roo restaurant moved in and did business until 2003, when the space became the said Chipotle Mexican Grill.

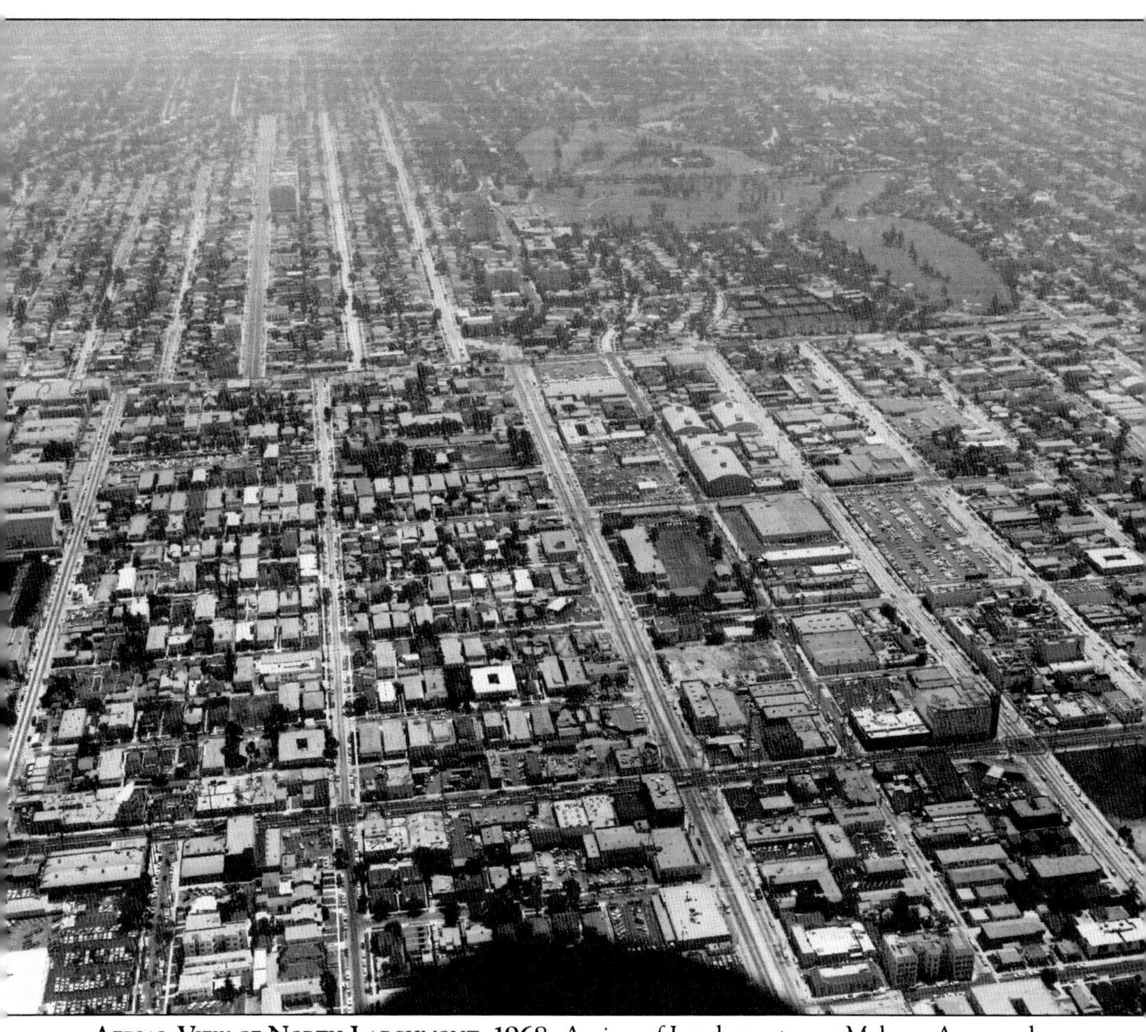

Aerial View of North Larchmont, 1968. A view of Larchmont near Melrose Avenue shows the shift from residential bungalows to commercial use and small apartment buildings.

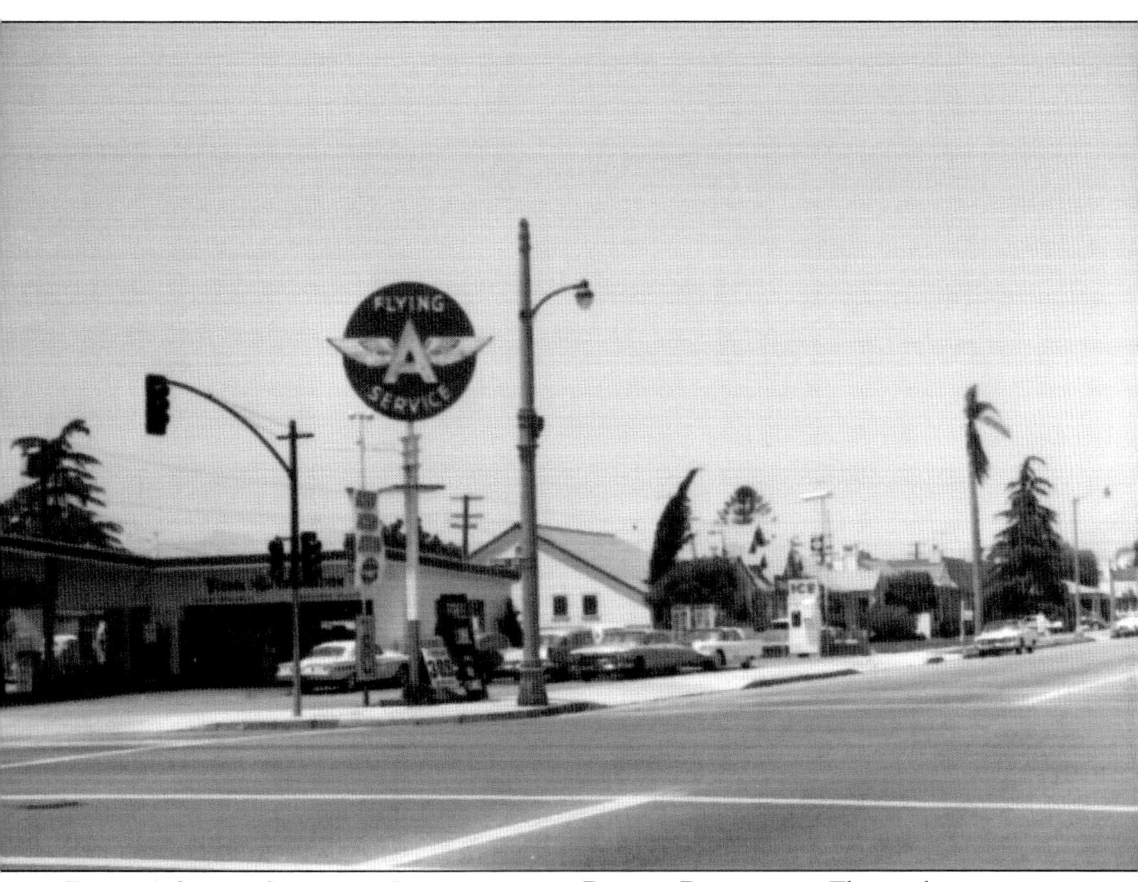

Flying A Service Station at Larchmont and Beverly Boulevards. The northwest corner of Larchmont and Beverly Boulevards became a very prominent intersection and featured two service stations on each corner. Along the West Coast, Flying A stations were rebranded as Phillips 66 in the early 1960s, when Phillips Petroleum purchased the western network of Tidewater Associated Oil Company.

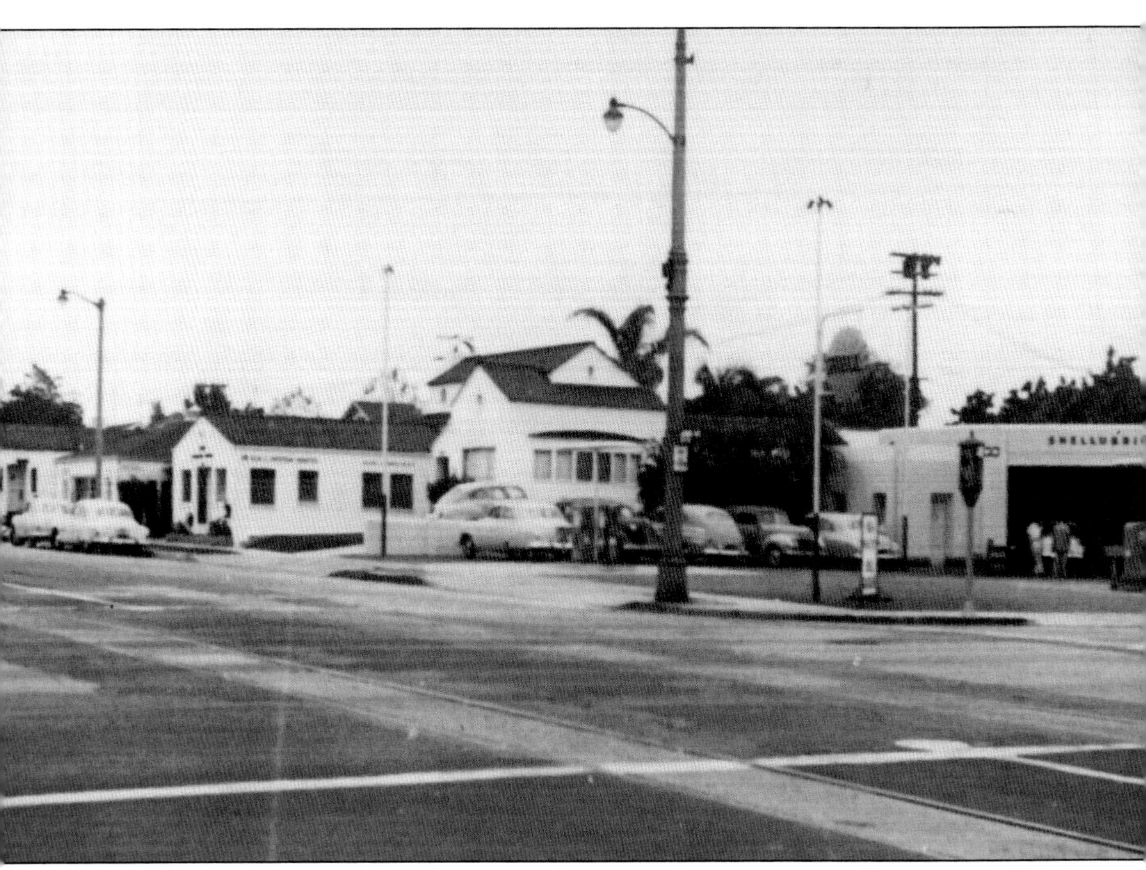

Shell Service Station at the Northeast Corner of Larchmont and Beverly, c. 1950. A gas station stood at 306 North Larchmont until sometime in the late 1960s. The earliest building permit for the address is for construction of a large pole sign in 1969, possibly to advertise Baker's Burgers, a drive-through restaurant. In 1994, a permit was issued to convert the addition to a photograph-processing driver-through. Currently it houses the tailoring workshop of Ritz Cleaners, owned and operated by Raj Patel and his family since 1969.

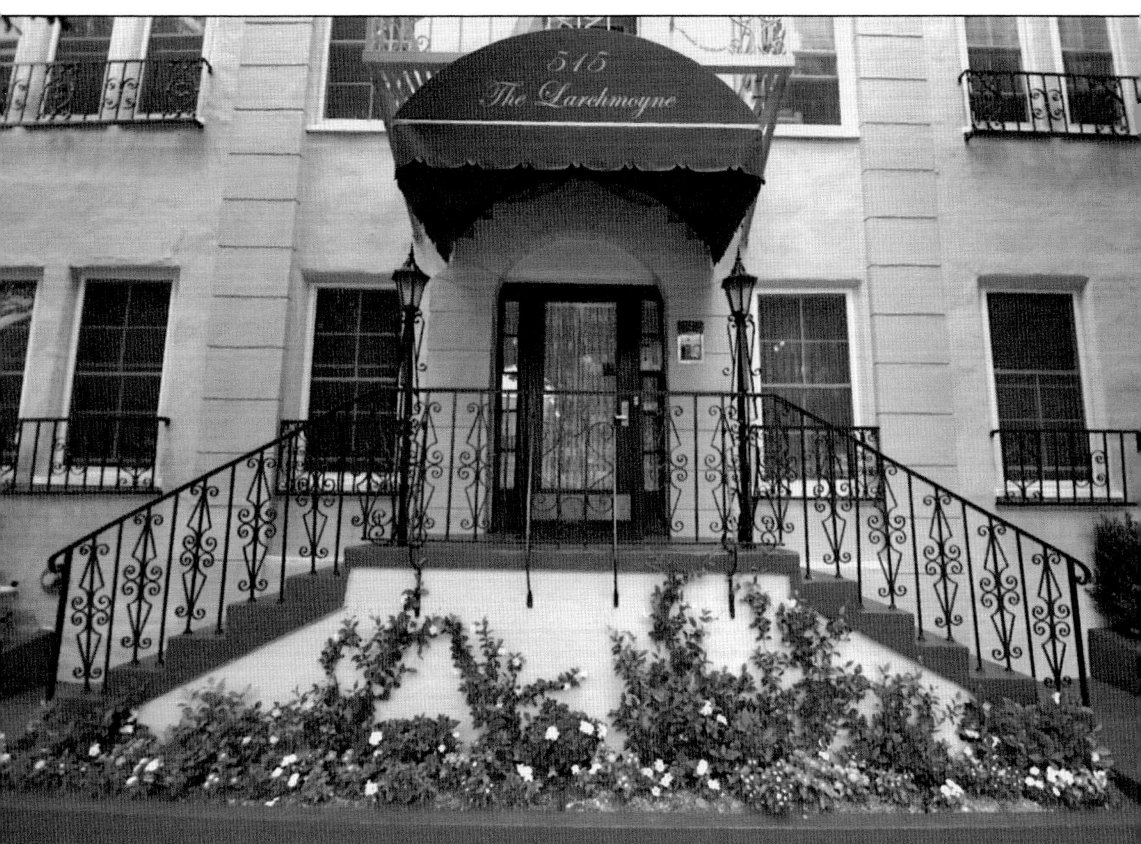

THE LARCHMOYNE AT 515 NORTH LARCHMONT. When the Larchmoyne opened in 1929, it was advertised as "ultra-modern and luxuriously furnished," with an Art Deco–style building featuring touches of Spanish Colonial Revival. The Larchmoyne apartment building was home to a mixture of blue-collar and white-collar residents, some of whom worked for nearby motion picture studios. Lovingly maintained, the building's current 24 apartments are never without tenants, who exude the ambiance of the building and the charm of upper Larchmont.

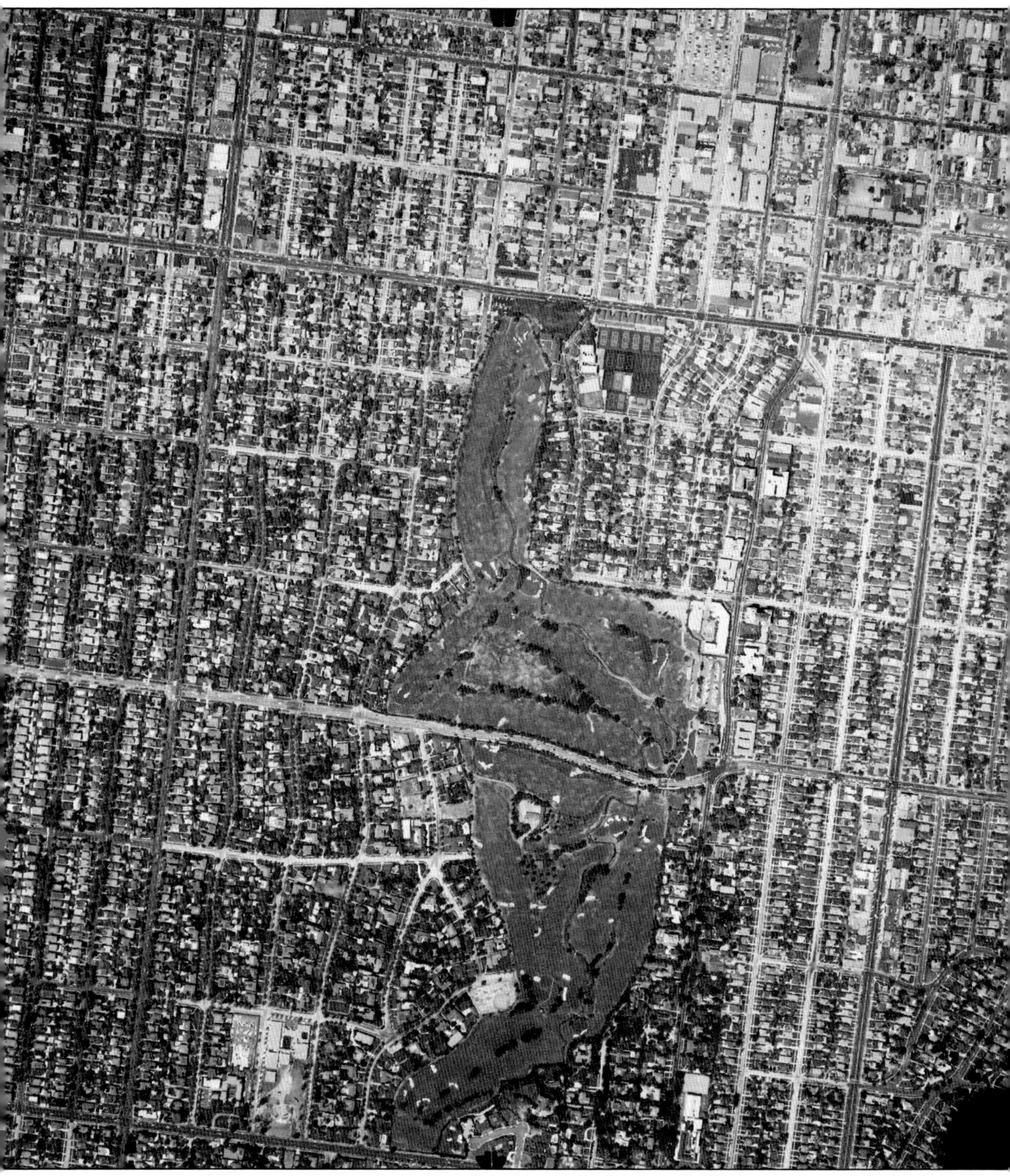

Aerial View of Larchmont Area, 1961. The density of the neighborhood can be seen in this shot. More and more residents were enjoying Larchmont in the 1960s.

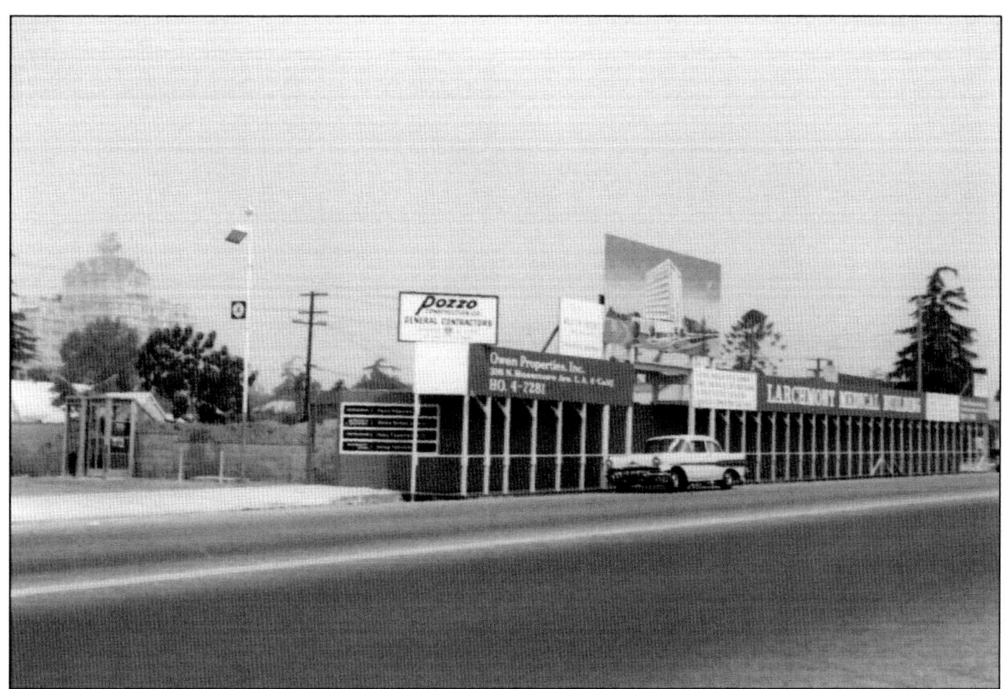

VIEW OF NORTH LARCHMONT FROM THE WEST SIDE OF THE STREET. Construction fences show the proposed Larchmont Medical Building in the early stages of construction. At the time, the building was welcomed in the area, though it would dominate the Larchmont skyline. The elegant El Royale apartment building can be seen in the distance.

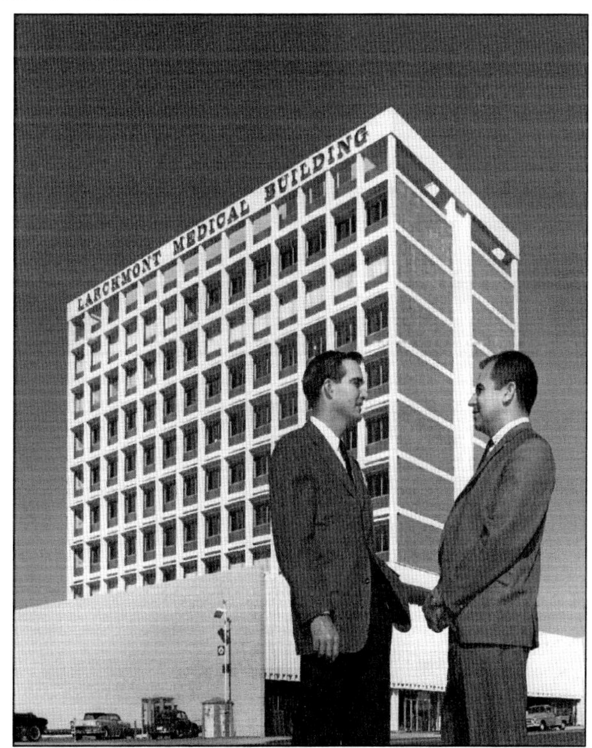

LARCHMONT MEDICAL BUILDING, 1964. Completed in 1964, the Larchmont Medical Building was developed by Owen Properties, Inc. and located at 316 North Rossmore Avenue. Welton Becket and Associates were the architects and engineers of the 10-story building, constructed for $1.5 million. Becket's other work includes the Capitol Records Building, Beverly Hilton Hotel, Pan Pacific Auditorium (destroyed by a fire), the Equitable Building, Cinerama Dome, and a host of buildings on the UCLA campus.

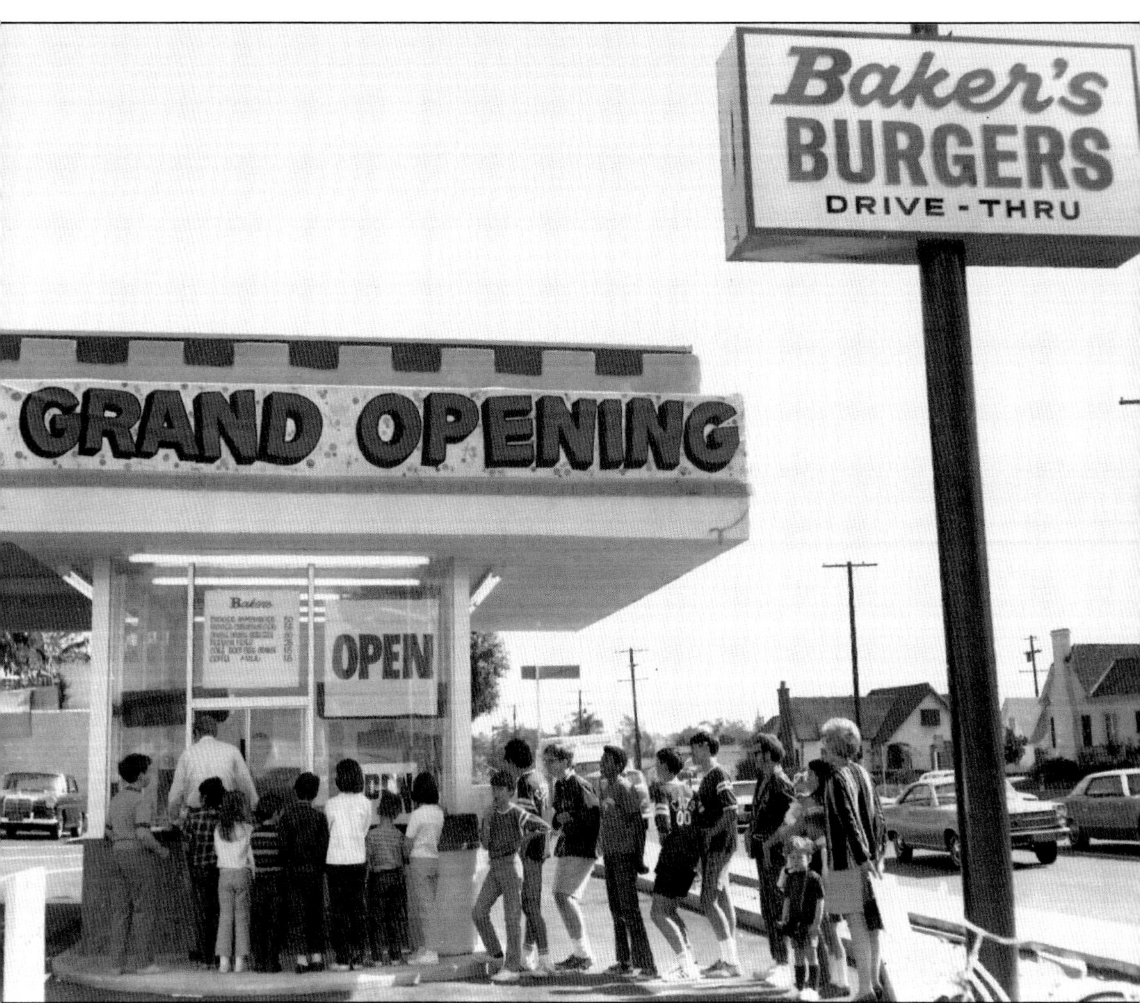

BAKER'S BURGERS AT 306 NORTH LARCHMONT, C. 1970. Now the Ritz Cleaners, this small drive-through commercial space was home to a number of different businesses. There were many of these buildings constructed to offer convenience to drivers.

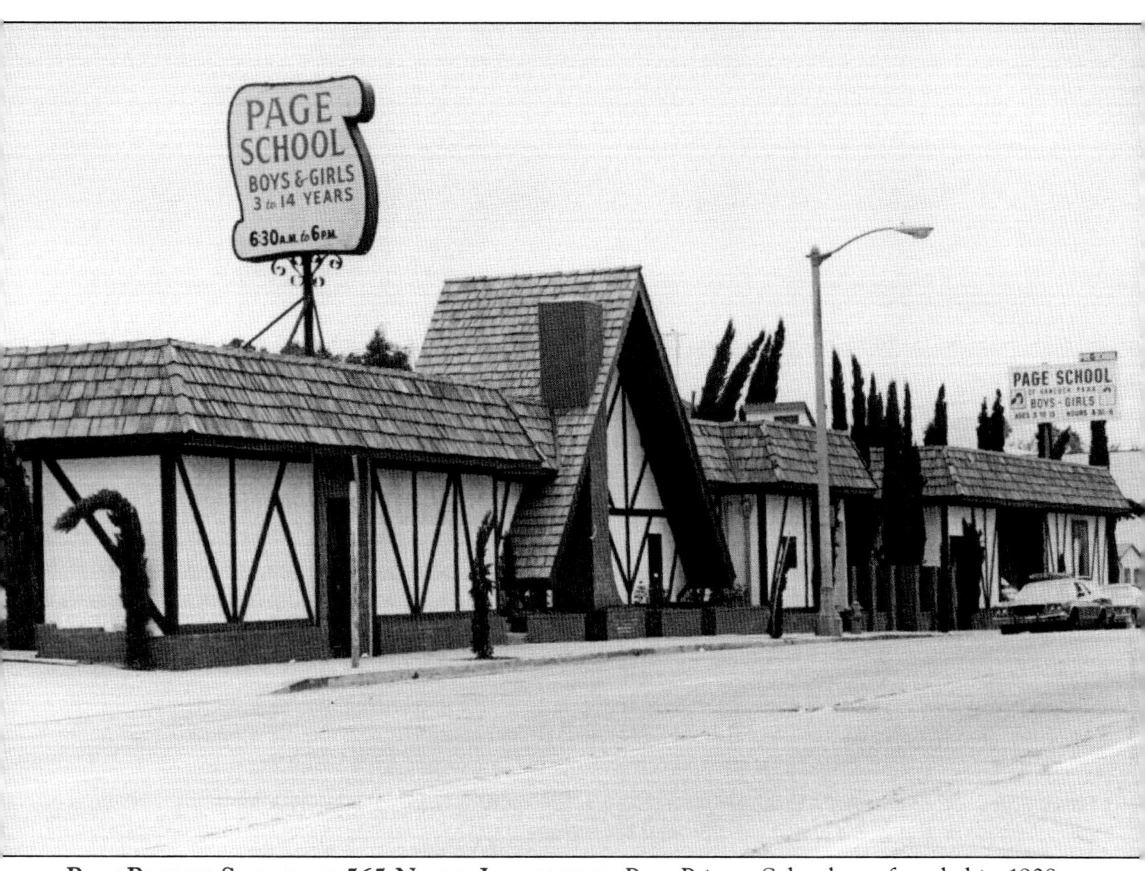

Page Private School at 565 North Larchmont. Page Private School was founded in 1908 by Robert and Della Page Gibbs and expanded by their daughter and son-in-law, Edith and Earle Russell Vaughan, who opened the Larchmont campus in the 1930s. The school is currently run by the third generation.

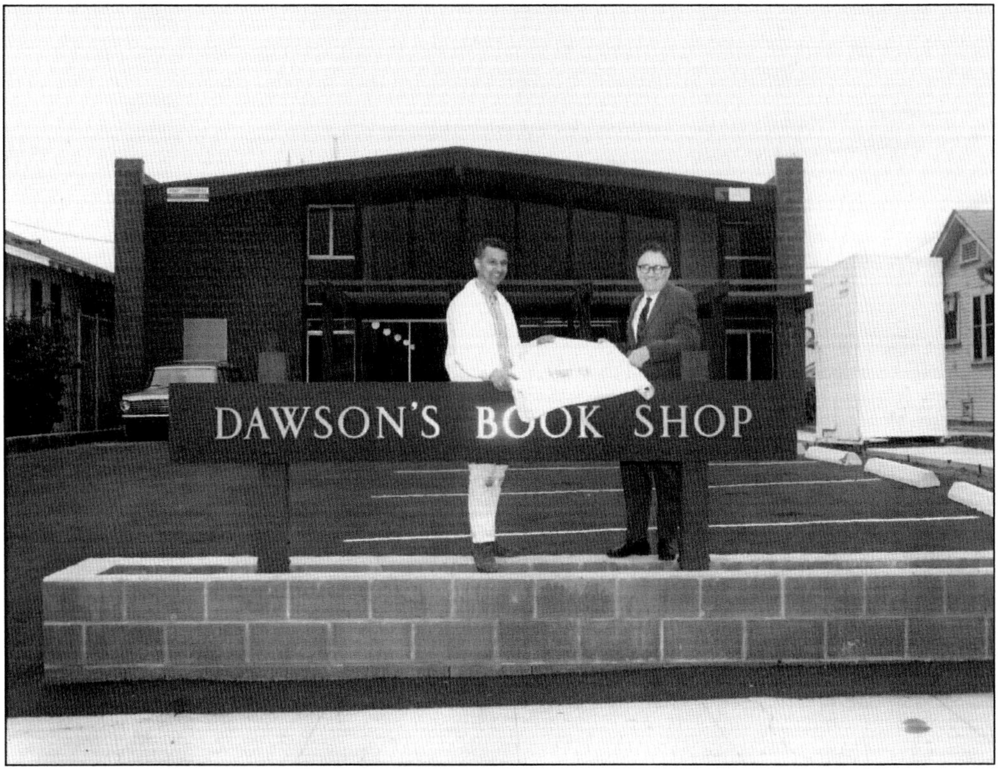

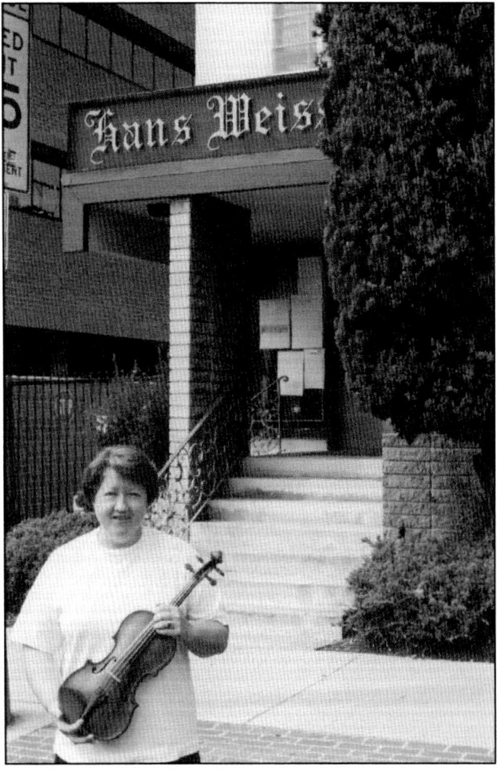

Dawson's Book Shop at 535 North Larchmont. Founded in 1905 by Ernest Dawson in downtown Los Angeles, Dawson's Book Shop moved to Larchmont in 1968, making it one of the oldest continuously operating book shops in the city of Los Angeles until it closed in 2010 after 42 years on Larchmont. Dawson's specialized in California history, Western Americana, and photography.

Hans Weisshaar Violin Shop at 627 North Larchmont. Master violin maker Hans Weisshaar first opened his business on Sunset Boulevard in 1947. In 1961, he constructed the two-story, Modern-style building at 627 Larchmont, remodeling a residence and garage built in 1921 to establish the first world-class violin making and restoration workshop in the western United States. Cellist Margaret Shipman, a graduate of University of Southern California, pictured here in 1994, went to work for Weisshaar in 1969. After 36 years, she transferred the business to Georg Eittinger. Of note is the wrought-iron guild sign Weisshaar commissioned in Germany.

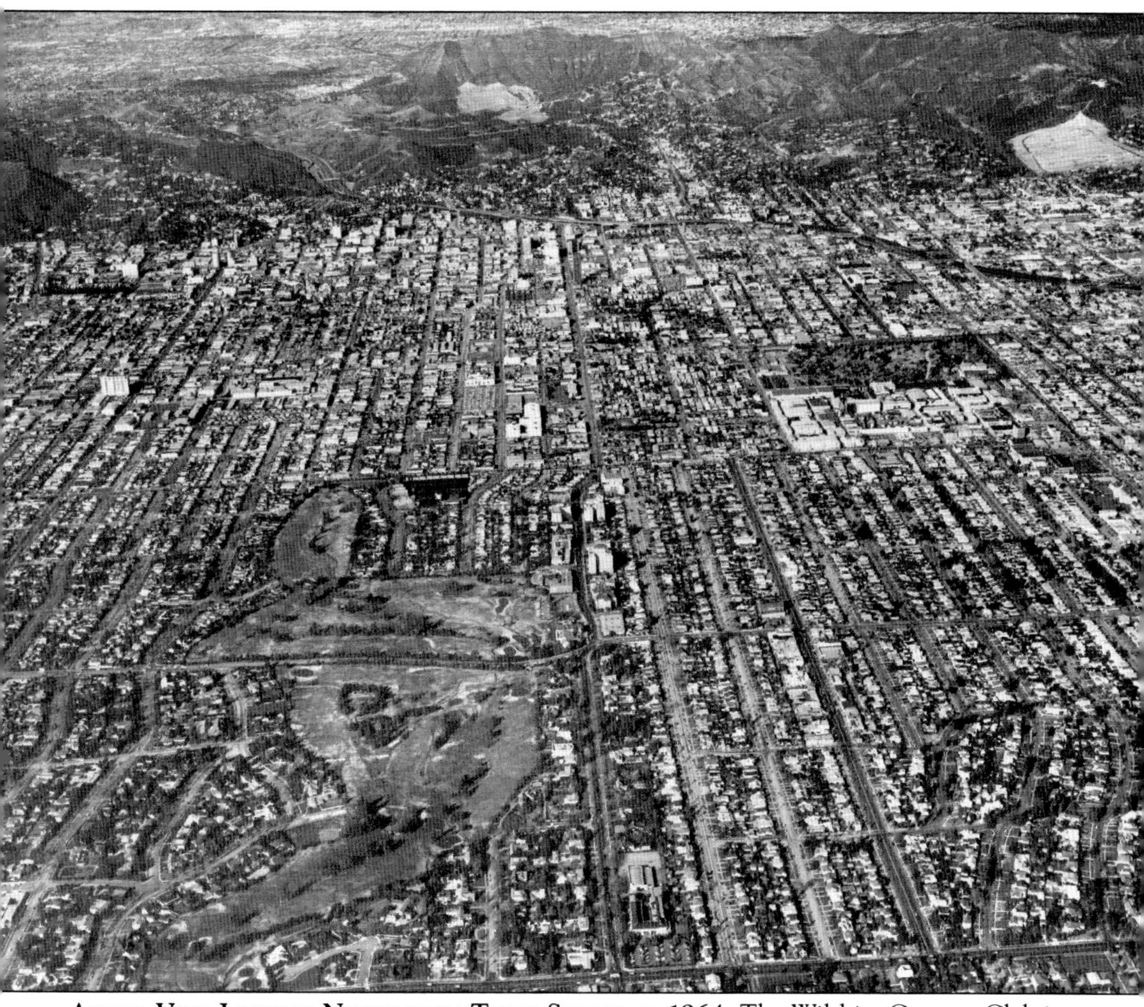

Aerial View Looking North from Third Street, c. 1964. The Wilshire Country Club is an island of green in the midst of the dense urban neighborhood that is Larchmont. A number of movie studios nearby provide jobs for residents and attract many more who support the local businesses on Larchmont.

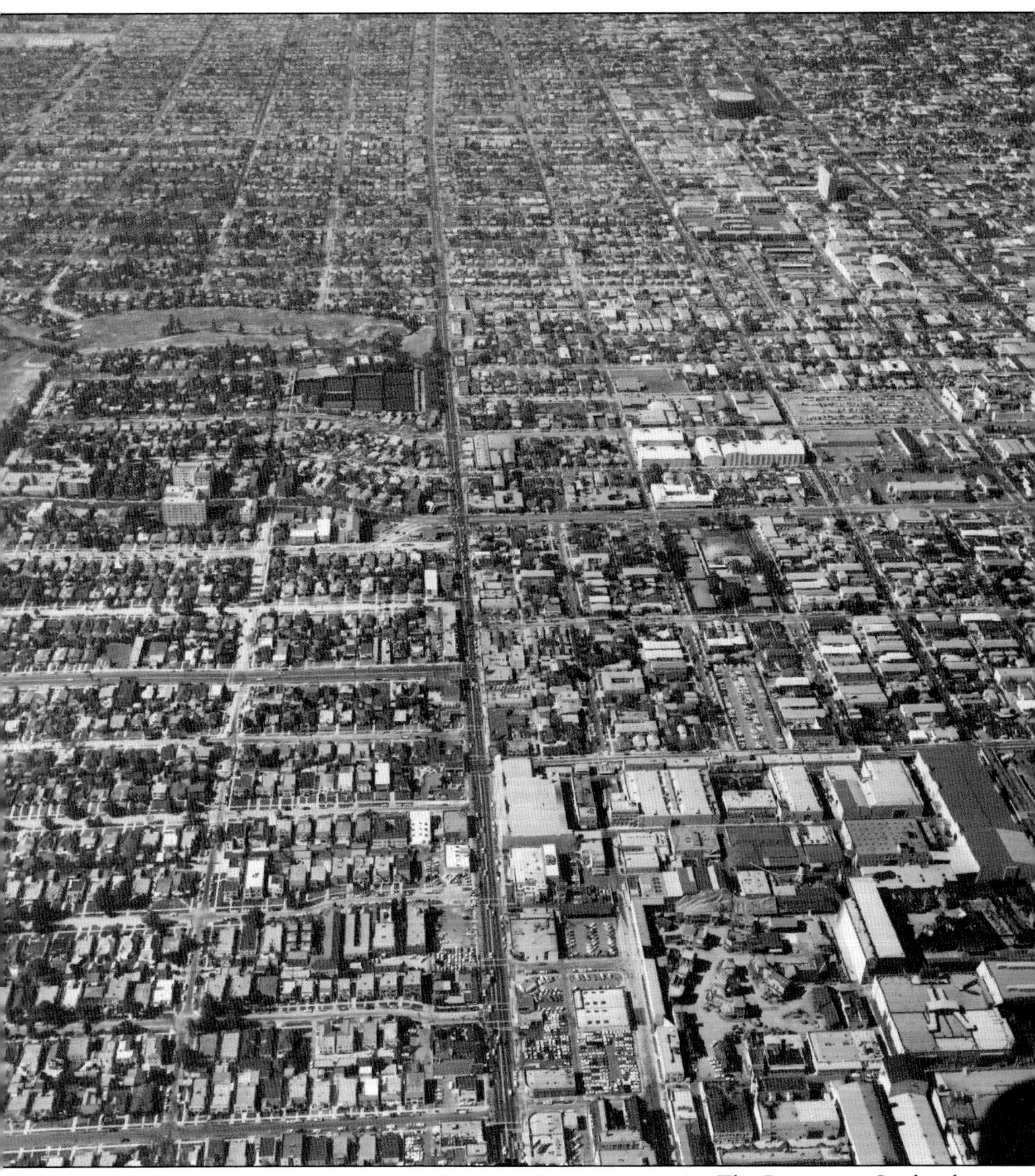

AERIAL VIEW LOOKING WEST ALONG MELROSE AVENUE, C. 1964. The Paramount Studios lot is visible in the lower right. Larchmont is the double-wide street ending at Melrose. Much of Larchmont was still residential, though more lots were being converted for commercial use.

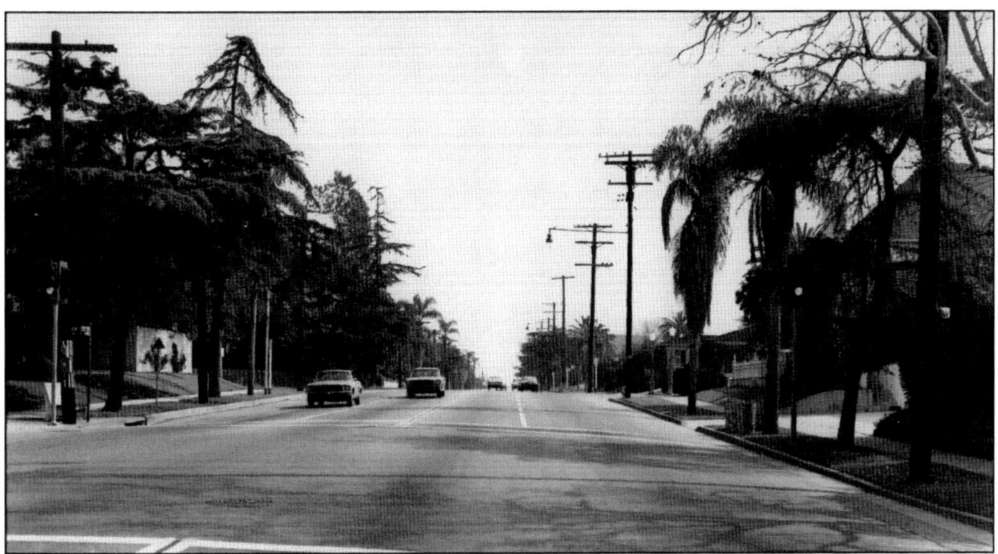

Third Street Looking East from Larchmont, 1968. Third Street has always been a major traffic artery that bisects the neighborhoods surrounding Larchmont, bringing traffic through a tree-lined streetscape. In early years, it offered easy access for prospective buyers to the neighborhoods and patrons for Larchmont businesses. In recent years, residents and city leaders seek ways to reduce the traffic and the negative impact it has on the neighborhood. Too bad there is not a trolley any longer! (Courtesy of Marc Wanamaker/Bison Archives.)

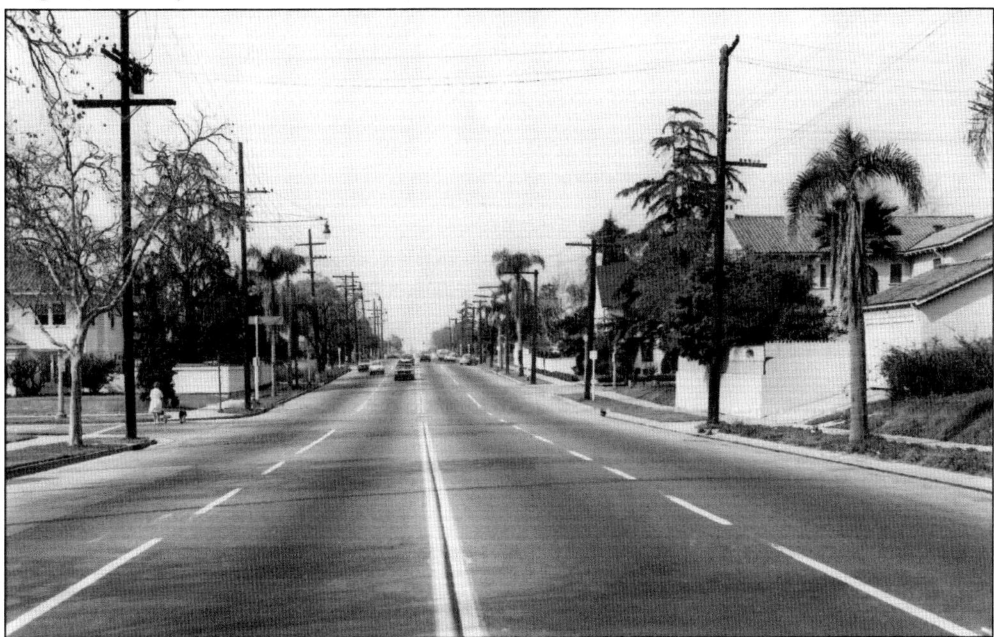

Third Street Heading West Approaching Larchmont, 1968. Windsor Square looks much like it did 60 years ago, but the street trees have matured, enhancing the value and beauty of the neighborhood. Civil unrest in Los Angeles would make these wonderful, old neighborhoods lose their value, but the trend would be reversed when things quieted down and people discovered their unique architectural character and the charm of nearby Larchmont. (Courtesy of Marc Wanamaker at Bison Archives.)

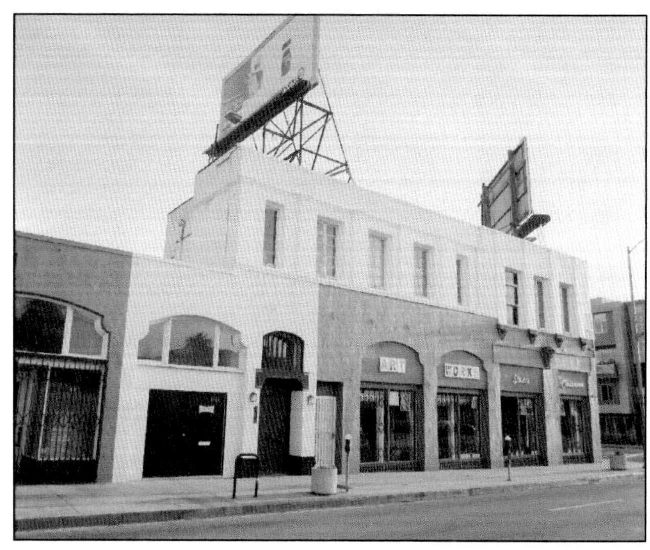

ART WORKS STUDIO AND CLASSROOM AT 660 NORTH LARCHMONT, 2012. 652-600 North Larchmont, at the southeast corner of Melrose Avenue, was built in 1925 for retail use and office space by Preston S. Wright & Company according to a listing in the 1921 edition of *Southwest Builder and Contractor* (the daily publication of the building industry in the West). Everett H. Merrill, a civil engineer, was the architect of the wood-frame, brick-exterior building. (Courtesy of Marc Wanamaker/Bison Archives.)

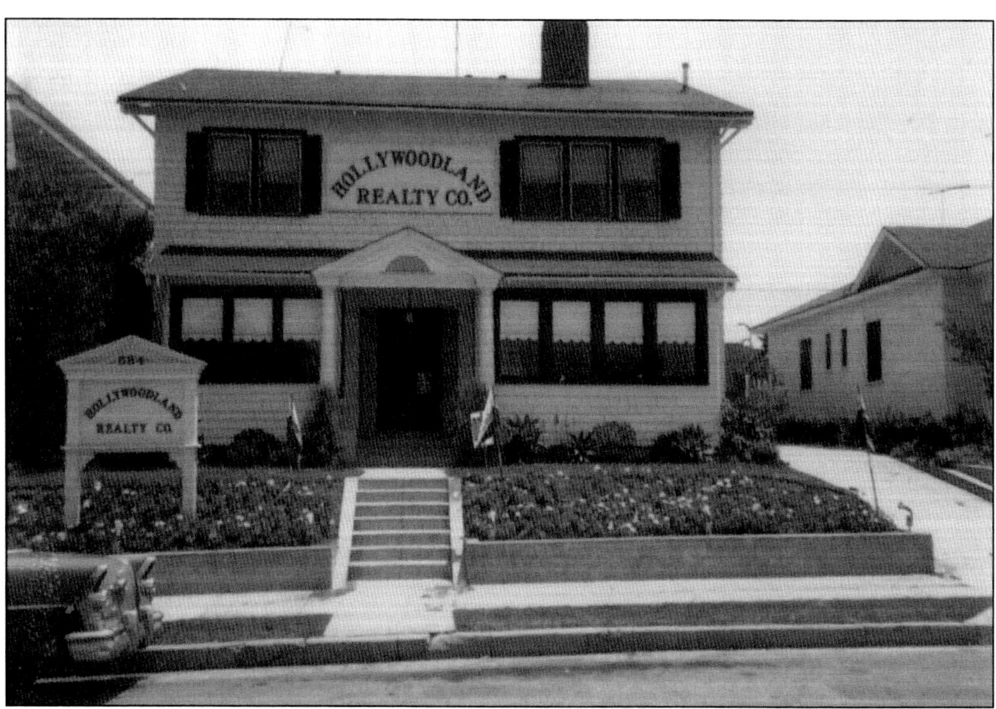

HOLLYWOODLAND REALTY CO. 584 NORTH LARCHMONT, 1950S. Hollywoodland Realty Co., operated by Edward T. Carroll through 2003, is now run by his daughter Patricia Carroll. Edward acquired the property, originally built as a residence, in the late 1950s. The wood-frame, Bungalow-style structure, built in 1913, was common on the street. In 1926, Mary (a teacher) and Minnie Allen (housing inspector for the Health Department according to the 1920 city phone directory) added a garage and enlarged the porch in 1935. (Courtesy of Patricia Carroll.)

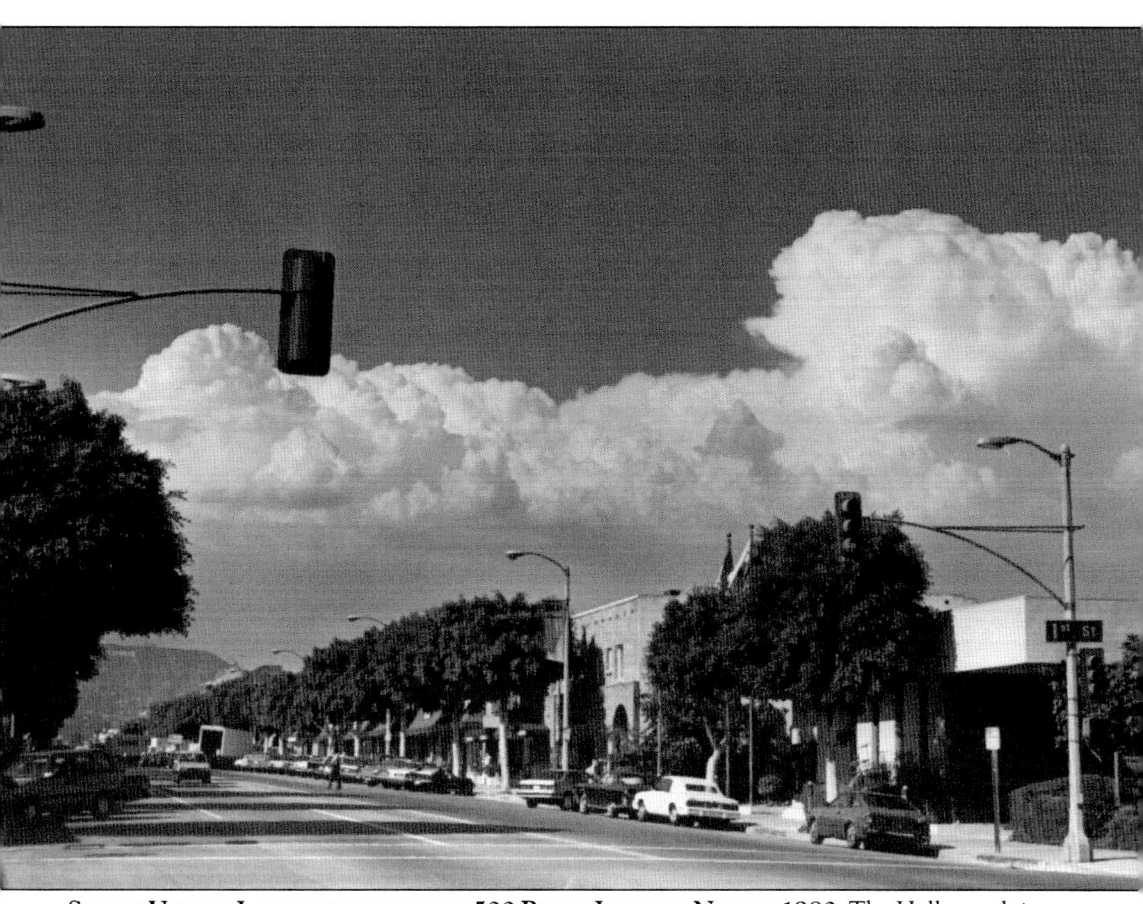

STREET VIEW OF LARCHMONT NEAR THE 500 BLOCK LOOKING NORTH, 1980. The Hollywood sign, now an icon of the entertainment industry and a symbol of Los Angeles's celebrity lifestyle, can be seen peeking through trees in the left center of the photograph. The sign adds to Larchmont's charm that attracts both celebrities and regular folk.

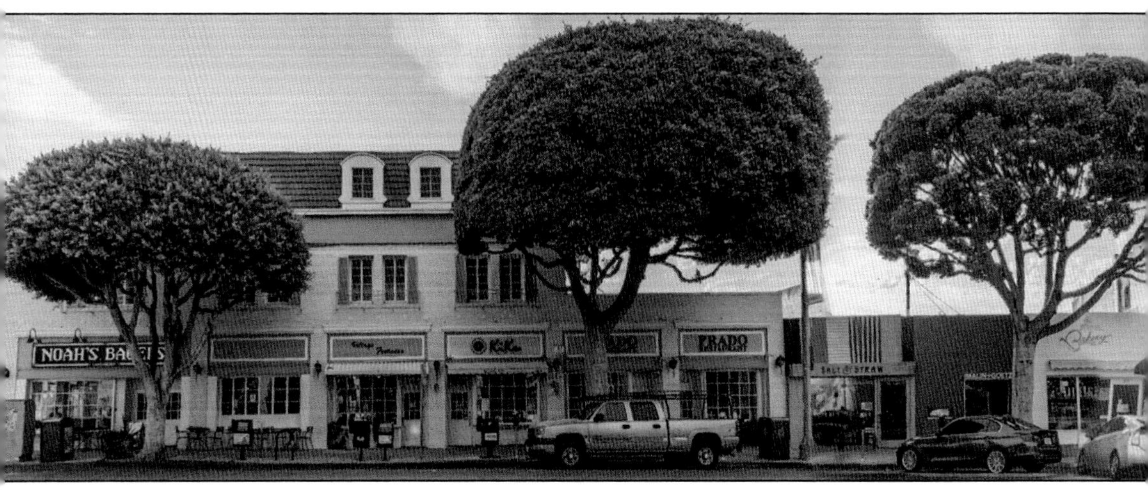

East Side of Larchmont Boulevard, South End. Pictured above at the southeast corner of 250 North Larchmont is a two-story brick structure built in 1925 as stores and an apartment, now offices and stores. Noah's Bagels has been at the corner since the early 1990s, and it is followed by Village Footwear; Kiku Sushi Restaurant; Prado Restaurant, serving Caribbean cuisine since 1991; newcomer Salt and Straw, a handmade ice cream store; MALIN+GOETZ apothecary and lab; Erin McKenna's vegan Bakery LA; and Louise's Trattoria, serving homemade Italian food since 1978. At 230 North Larchmont, a two-story brick building was constructed in 1925 as a Masonic lodge, with stores on the ground level. In 1967, Los Angeles's first yoga studio, now called Yogaworks, took up residence. Coffee bar Go Get Em Tiger is at street level. Next is Rite Aid, which formerly housed several grocery stores, and then there is Above the Fold Newsstand, which opened around 1990. The image below starts with Crumbs Bakery, at 216 North Larchmont, which is in one of the storefronts built in 1985 with underground parking. To the right is Pickett Fences, a clothing boutique opened in 1994 by Joane Hennenberger Pickett, who also served as

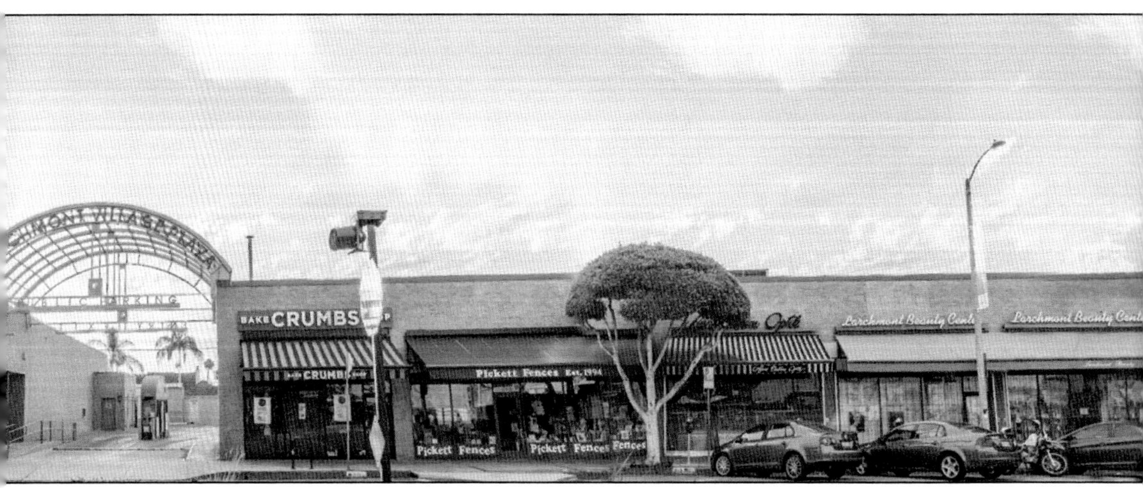

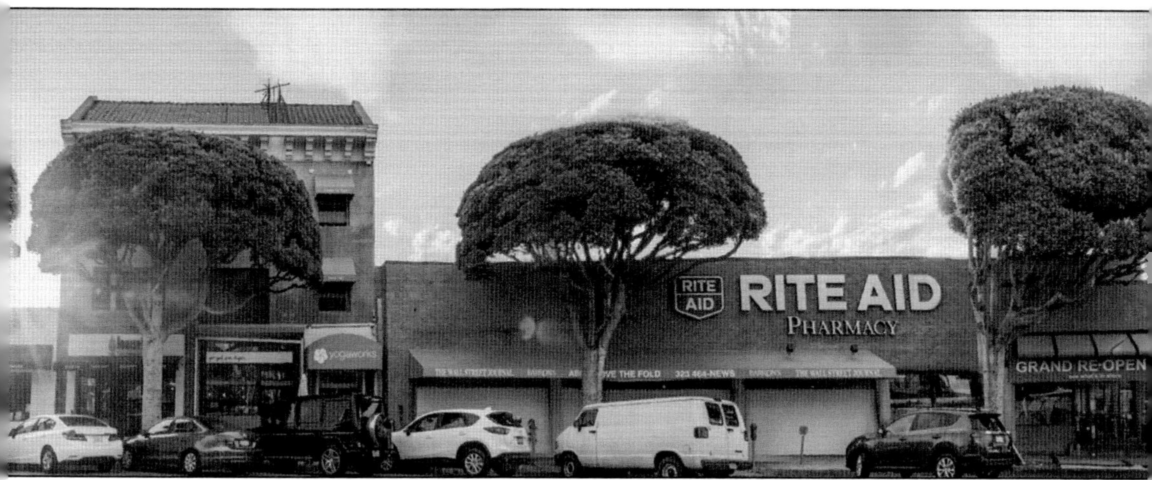

president of the Larchmont Boulevard Association; Hans Fiebig opened the next business, Hans Custom Optik, in the late 1970s; the Larchmont Beauty Center has been here since the 1980s; and Starbucks opened one of the first of many coffee shops around the same time. The 200 North Larchmont address was built up in 1925 with stores, offices, and apartments and was modified by owners LaBonte and Ramson a year later. The original facade is intact, making it one of the most charming buildings on the street. Flicka children's clothing was opened in 1992 by Liz Reilly and daughter Lisa, who now runs the shop with sister Kristen. Diptyque Paris, the company's first Los Angeles boutique that came to be in 2014, and Jamba Juice occupy the street level. The 150–154 North Larchmont address was constructed in 1925 as a two-story building with stores and apartments; it has been dramatically altered. Sam's Bagels, next to Jamba Juice, opened in 1980. Hardwear, at 152 North Larchmont, is named for Larchmont Hardware, which served the street for over 82 years until it closed in 2008. (Photograph by Joe F. Lombard.)

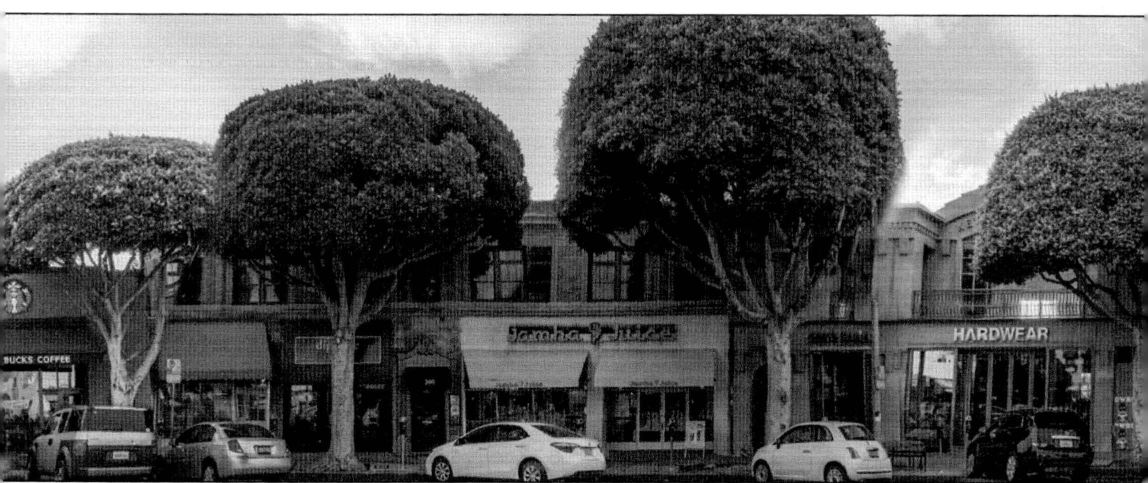

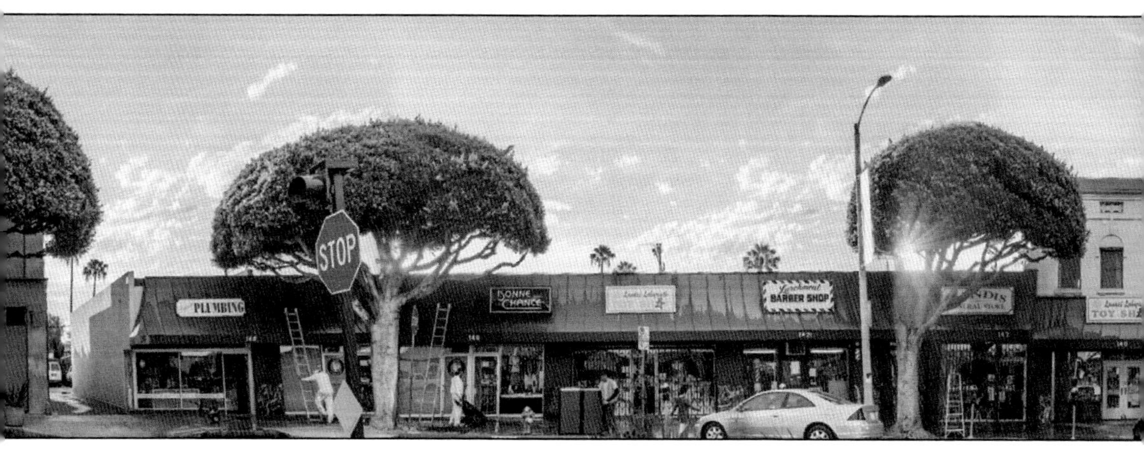

EAST SIDE OF LARCHMONT BOULEVARD, NORTH END. Above is Lipson Plumbing, which opened in the 1930s and occupies the first storefront in the last remaining LaBonte and Ramson building on Larchmont. The 148–124 ½ address has housed many different businesses over the last 90 years. At present, Bonne Chance women's clothing, Landis Labyrinth toy store, the Larchmont Barber Shop, Landis Gifts and Stationary, Haas & Company salon, State Farm insurance, CH Boutique and gift shop, Sage Lifestyle boutique, Chevalier's Books, and Jessica's From Sunset nail salon occupy the street-level shops. Judy M. Horton Garden Design is housed upstairs in one of

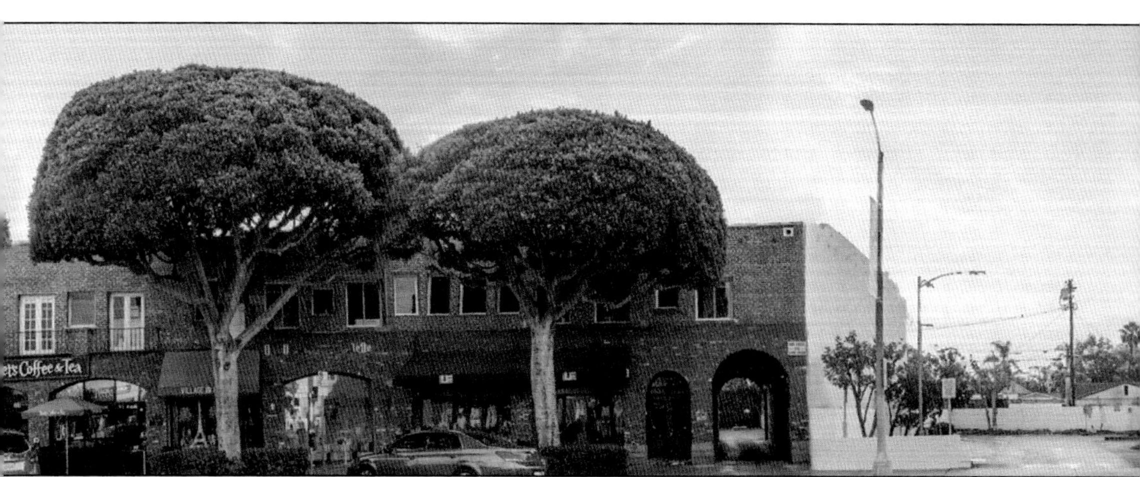

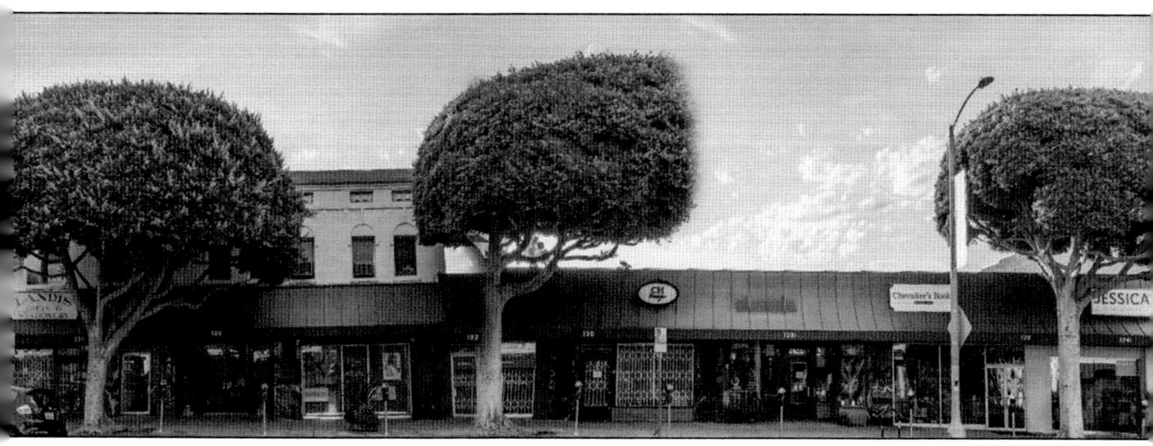

the former apartments. Pictured below, next to Peet's Coffee & Tea, is Village Heights gift shop (formerly Paul Thompson Jewelers), which opened in 1978. Next is Lette Bakery, which sells handmade French macaroons; and LF, a women's clothing store. Keller Williams Realty occupies the second-floor space (formerly Larchmont Hall). The two-story brick building was constructed in 1928 for $25,000. Bank of America is on the corner where the Larchmont Motor Service Station once stood. (Photograph by Joe F. Lombard.)

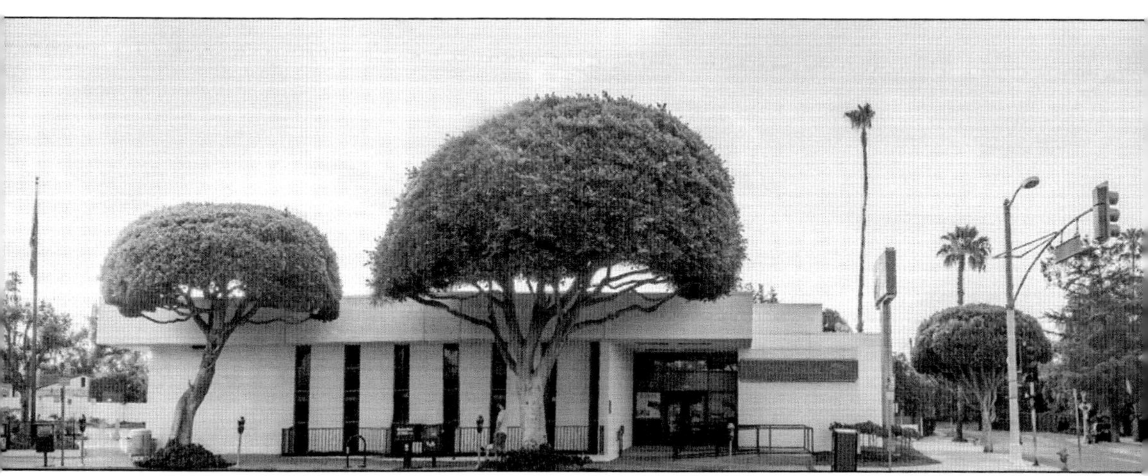

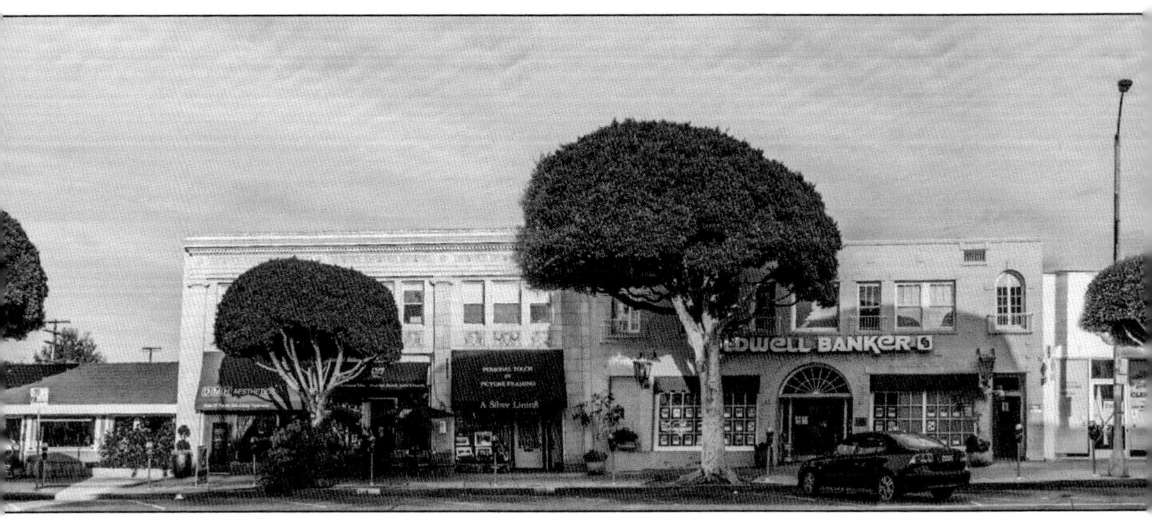

West Side of Larchmont Boulevard, South End. This image was constructed with photographs taken early in the morning when the angled parking spaces are empty so the facades of the buildings would be visible. There are several buildings with their original facades and architectural details, though most have been altered. At the corner is Chase Bank in a brick building constructed in 1924 as six storefronts at 101, 103, and 105 North Larchmont. In 1929, a real estate office was built at 107 North Larchmont. DMH Aesthetics, Le Pain Quotidien bakery and restaurant, and A Silver Lining frame shop occupy the ground floor of 111, 113, 115 & 115 ½, which was originally a two-story building constructed in 1925 as stores and apartments for two families. In 1926, a dry-cleaning plant was built at 113 North Larchmont. There are currently offices on the second floor. Coldwell Banker Real Estate occupies the ground floor of 119 North Larchmont, built in

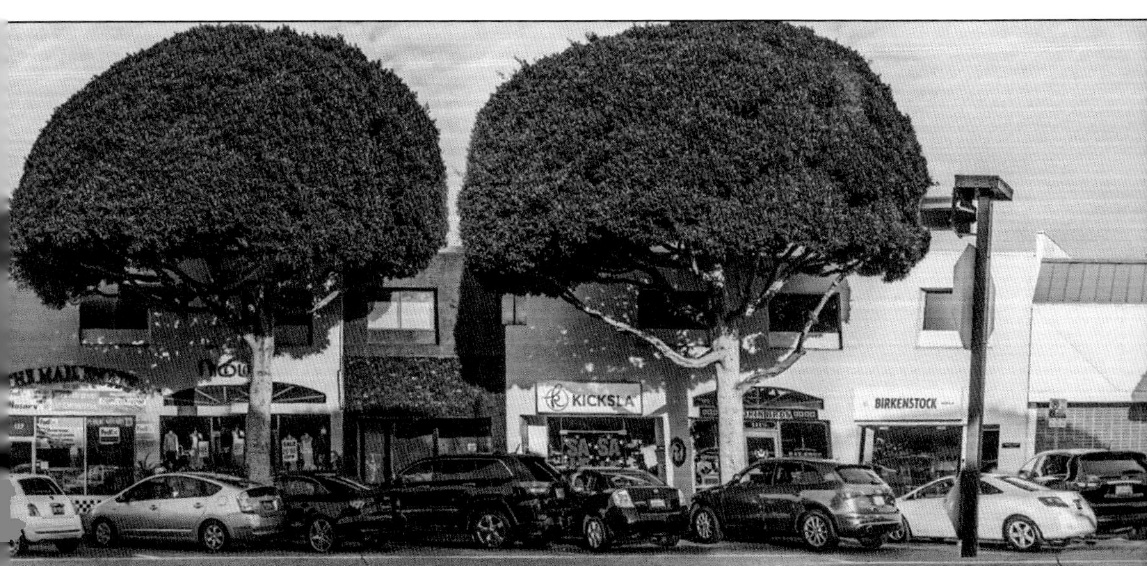

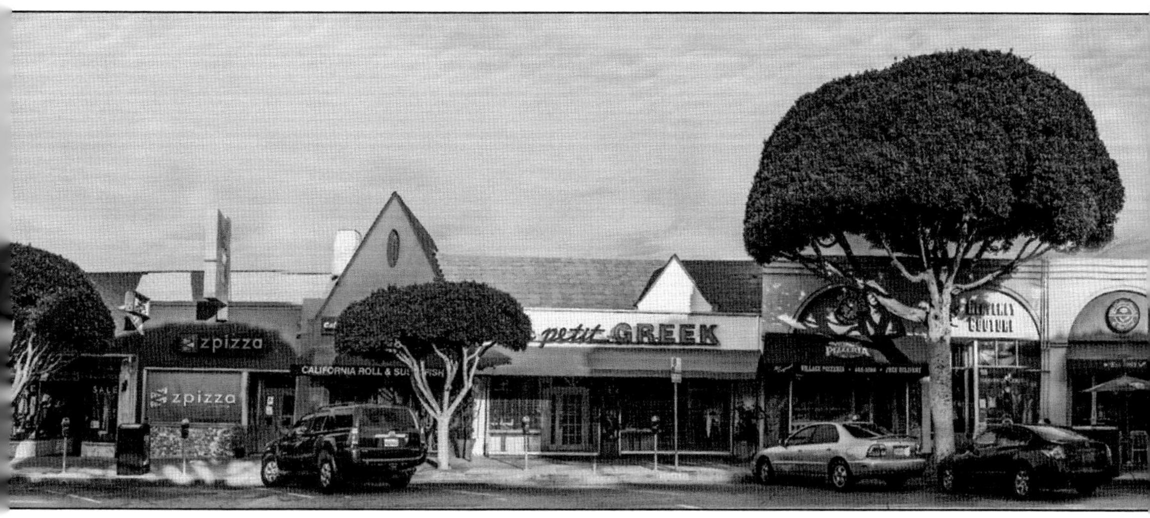

1924 as a five-unit apartment house. The Larchmont Juicery, Library clothing, Z Pizza, California Roll and Sushi, and Le Petit Greek restaurant (opened in 1988) are also seen. Village Pizzeria, Heavenly Couture, and Coffee Bean and Tea Leaf all occupy the former Albert T. Balzer gourmet grocery store, built in 1926. Much of the facade has been altered, but the three arched windows remain. The Mail Shoppe, Nicole, Groundworks Coffee, KicksLA shoes, Gorin Brothers Hats, and Birkenstock (a temporary pop-up store) are at street level with offices above. Records show building permits for stores and apartments issued in 1922. Flywheel occupies the site of the former movie theater constructed at 149 North Larchmont in 1921. The building was demolished, and the addresses have been renumbered. USBank, at 157 North Larchmont, occupies the original Landis Department store and has been renumbered. (Photograph by Joe F. Lombard.)

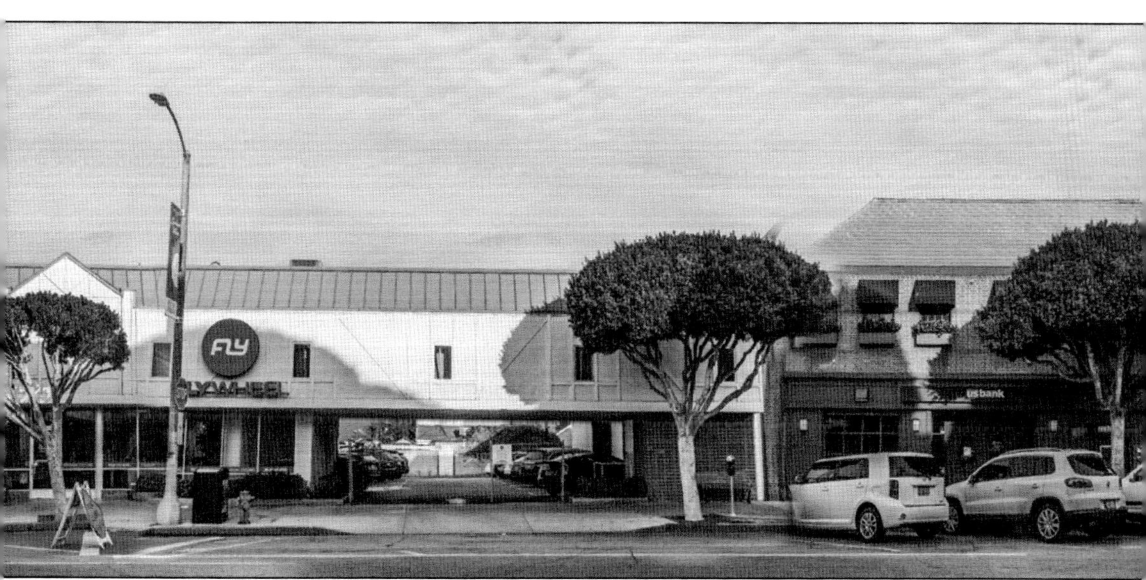

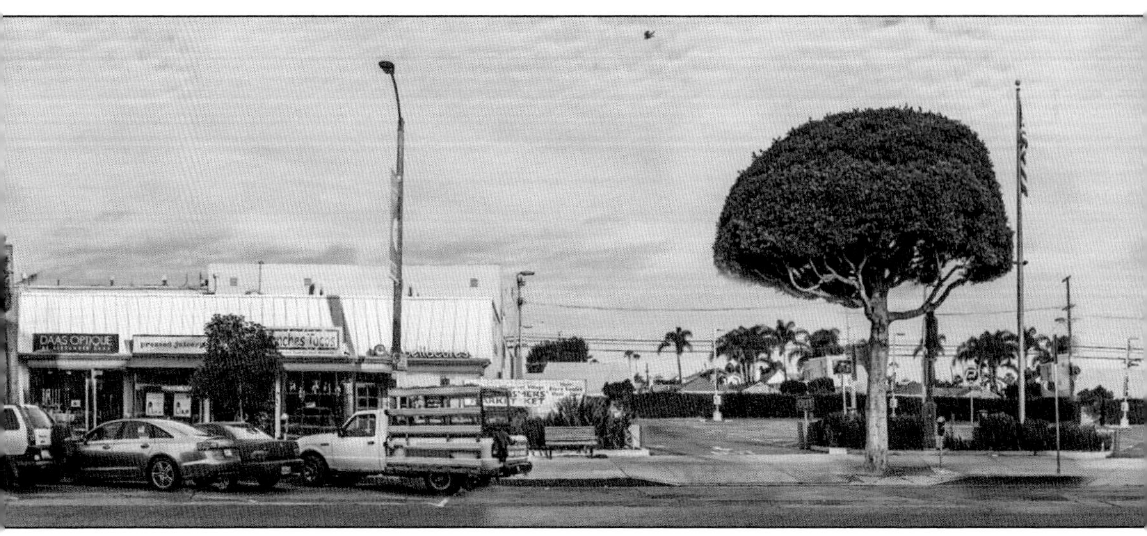

West Side of Larchmont Boulevard, North End. Above, Daas Optique, Press Juicery, Pinches Tacos, and Bellacures nail salon occupy the storefronts of one building that could have been moved onto the site in 1924. New buildings were then constructed in 1939, numbered 161 through 205 ½. The city parking lot at 209 North Larchmont was formerly a gasoline station and is currently the site of the Larchmont Family Fair, held every October around Halloween near the Sunday Farmers' Market. Radiance of Life skin care, Burger Lounge, and Alternative Apparel occupy the storefronts at 215, 217, and 219, respectively, of the 1924 two-story building. The brick building housing Larchmont Village Wine, Spirits and Cheese (223), and Vernetti Italian Restaurant (225) was constructed in 1926 and maybe had four storefronts initially. Below, 227 North Larchmont is vacant; the building was constructed in 1924 as stores. It was altered a great

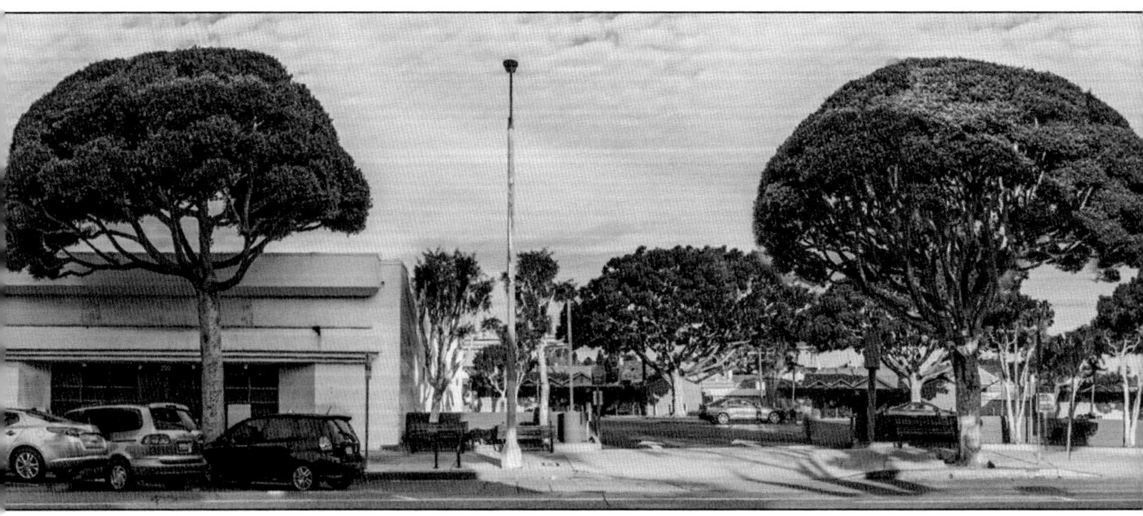

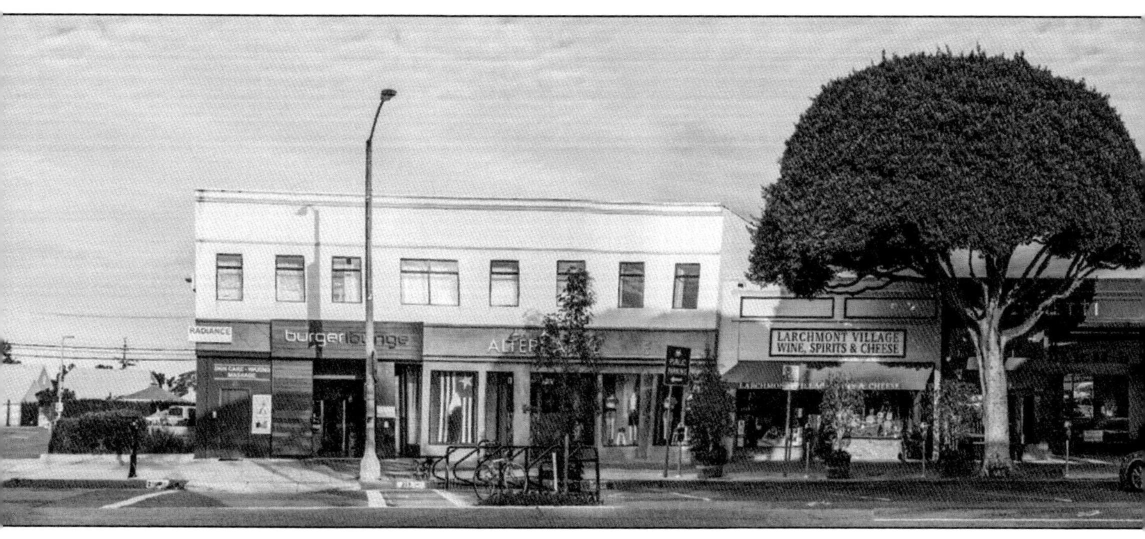

deal over the years. The parking lot for Wells Fargo (233–235) was built as stores in 1922 and torn down in 1974. The adjacent building, 237–239 North Larchmont, was constructed in 1923 as a three-unit apartment house and later changed to stores. The 239–241 address was torn down in 1974. The 245 North Larchmont site became a bank in 1953, and now it is a Wells Fargo. Several of these addresses were renumbered over the years. At the corner is 247–251 North Larchmont, which is now Coldwell Banker Real Estate on the ground level with offices on the second floor. Constructed in 1920 as stores with apartments above, the building has undergone many interior and exterior changes, with various signs coming and going; however, the facade remains much like it was when constructed. (Panorama photograph by Joe F. Lombard.)

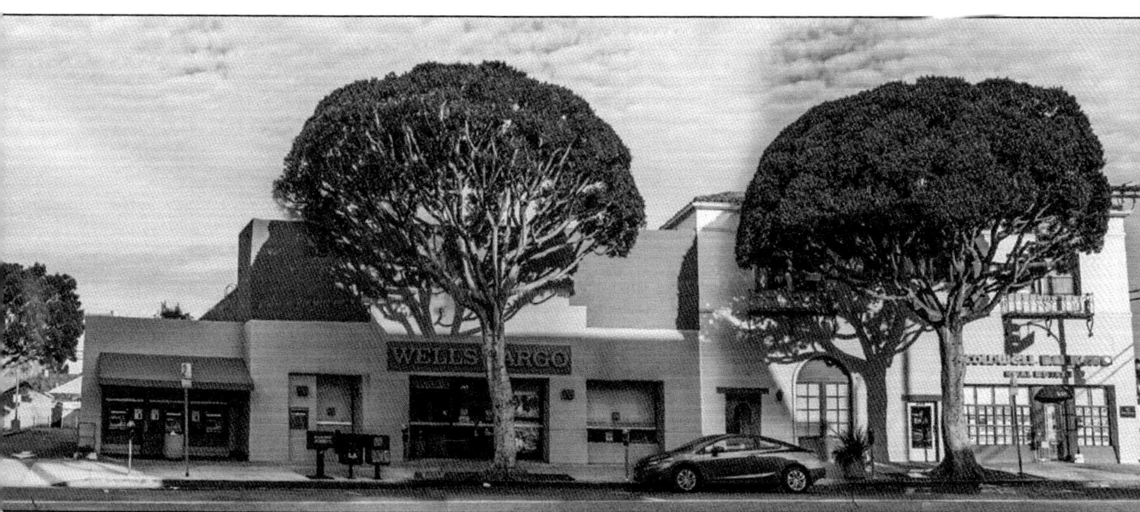

Consistent with our mission to preserve history on a local level, this book was printed in South Carolina on American-made paper and manufactured entirely in the United States. Products carrying the accredited Forest Stewardship Council (FSC) label are printed on 100 percent FSC-certified paper.

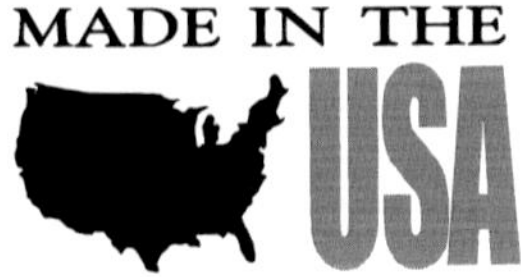